Jung and Christianity in Dialogue

Robert L. Moore
Daniel J. Meckel
editors

Jung and Christianity in Dialogue

FAITH, FEMINISM, AND HERMENEUTICS

Paulist Press
New York ◊ *Mahwah*

Acknowledgements: The Publisher gratefully acknowledges the use of the following materials, used with permission: Homans, Peter, "C.G. Jung: Christian or Post-Christian Psychologist?" in *Essays on Jung and the Study of Religion,* Luther H. Martin and James Goss, eds., University Press of America 1985, pp. 26–44; Bockus, Frank M., "The Archetypal Self: Theological Values in Jung's Psychology," in *The Dialogue Between Theology and Psychology,* Peter Homans, ed., University of Chicago Press, 1968:221–248; Dourley, John P., "Jung, Tillich, and Aspects of Western Christian Development" *Thought* III, March 1977, pp. 18–49; Goldenberg, Naomi R., "A Feminist Critique of Jung," *Signs: Journal of Women in Culture and Society* 2, No. 2, 1976, pp. 443–449; Wehr, Demaris S., "Religious and Social Dimensions of Jung's Concept of the Archetype: A Feminist Perspective," in *Feminist Archetypal Theory: Interdisciplinary Re-Visions of Jungian Thought,* Estella Lauter and Carol Rupprecht, eds., University of Tennessee Press, Knoxville, 1985, pp. 22–45; Homans, Peter, "Psychology and Hermeneutics: Jung's Contribution," *Zygon,* December 1969, Vol. 4, No. 4, pp. 333–372; Rollins, Wayne G., "Jung on Scripture and Hermeneutics: Retrospect and Prospect," in *Essays on Jung and the Study of Religion,* Luther H. Martin and James Goss, eds., University Press of America 1985, pp. 81–94; Loftus, Robert J., "Depth Psychology and Religious Vocations," *Chicago Studies,* Vol. 21, Summer 1982, No. 2, pp. 111–124; Hall, James A., "Jungian Concepts in Religious Counseling," *Perkins Journal,* Fall 1982, 36, pp. 23–29; Hunt, Swanee, "The Anthropology of Carl Jung: Implications for Pastoral Care," *Journal of Religion and Health,* Vol. 22, No. 3, Fall 1983, pp. 191–211.

Library of Congress Cataloging-in-Publication Data

Jung and Christianity in dialogue : faith, feminism, and hermeneutics/
    Robert L. Moore, Daniel J. Meckel, editors.
        p.   cm.
    Includes bibliographical references.
    ISBN 0-8091-3187-0
    1. Christianity—Psychology. 2. Jung, C. G. (Carl Gustav),
1875–1961—Religion. 3. Psychoanalysis and religion. 4. Feminist
theology. 5. Hermeneutics. 6. Pastoral counseling. I. Moore,
Robert L. II. Meckel, Daniel J.
BR110.J85   1990
261.5′15—dc20   90-36713
                                                                    CIP

Published by Paulist Press
997 Macarthur Blvd.
Mahwah, N.J. 07430

Printed and bound in the United States of America

Contents

JUNG AND HERMENEUTICS

JUNG AND PASTORAL CARE

DEDICATION

This book is dedicated to two important contributors to the study of Jung and spirituality. First we would like to honor the memory of Victor White, whose pioneering work with Jung framed many of the issues treated in this volume. We also recognize the ongoing contributions of Edward F. Edinger, M.D., which demonstrate the importance of Jung's psychology for human spirituality.

The work of these individuals has served as an important inspiration for this series.

R.L.M
D.J.M
Chicago, 1990

APPRECIATIONS

We are very grateful to all of those individuals who made this volume possible. Above all, thanks go to the authors, whose creative writings represent some of the most excellent work yet done on the topic of Jung and Christianity. These pieces will now be read by the large and diverse audience they deserve. We applaud you!

The staff at Paulist Press continues to provide us with the support and encouragement necessary to building the *Jung and Spirituality* series into a major forum for the Jung-Religion dialogue. Editors Kevin Lynch, Lawrence Boadt and Donald Brophy have offered valuable and much-needed guidance in the construction of this and other volumes. Georgia Christo has been a terrific help to us in editorial and technical matters, and a delight to work with. Thanks also to Bob Byrns and Hugh Lally for effectively marketing the books in this series, to Theresa Sparacio in the production department for her meticulous expertise, and to Tim McKeen for creatively executing the cover designs in this series.

In Chicago, we thank President Kenneth Smith and Dean Graydon Snyder of the Chicago Theological Seminary for their support of this project. Margaret Shanahan has creatively conceptualized the cover for this volume; Max Havlick continues to be an ever-present resource of help and technical information; and Patrick Nugent has contributed his valuable research efforts.

Thank you all!

R.L.M.
D.J.M.

JUNG AND SPIRITUALITY

The *Jung and Spirituality* series provides a forum for the critical interaction between Jungian psychology and living spiritual traditions. The series serves two important goals.

The first goal is: *To enhance a creative exploration of the contributions and criticisms which Jung's psychology can offer to religion.* Jungian thought has far-reaching implications for the understanding and practice of spirituality. Interest in these implications continues to expand in both Christian and non-Christian religious communities. People are increasingly aware of the depth and insight which a Jungian perspective adds to the human experiences of the sacred. And yet the use of Jungian psychoanalysis clearly does not eliminate the need for careful philosophical, theological and ethical reflection or for maintaining one's centeredness in a spiritual tradition.

Thus the second goal is: *To bring creative insights and critical tools of religious studies and practice to bear on Jungian thought.* Many volumes in the *Jung and Spirituality* series work to define the borders of the Jungian and spiritual traditions, to bring the spiritual dimensions of Jung's work into relief, and to deepen those dimensions. We believe that an important outcome of the Jung-Spirituality dialogue is greater cooperation of psychology and spirituality. Such cooperation will move us ahead in the formation of a postmodern spirituality, equal to the challenges of the twenty-first century.

Robert L. Moore
Series Editor

Daniel J. Meckel
Managing Editor

Preface

In a recent fundamentalist Christian publication Jung and his school of psychoanalysis were excoriated as being dangerous enemies of Christianity. The alarmed author of the essay had concluded that any use of Jungian perspectives in interpretation of religious texts, dogma, and practices would lead away from their "true" meaning. The conclusion, of course, was that Christians should not study and appropriate Jungian hermeneutical principles in their attempt to understand the meaning of their faith.

The author of this fundamentalist publication had obviously noticed the burgeoning interest in the dialogue between Christianity and Jungian psychoanalysis. Publications which apply Jungian insights to the understanding of Christian theology and spirituality are appearing in the literature of many different Christian communities, both Catholic and Protestant. Those who are aware of the increasing international interest in the spiritual significance of Jung's psychology have noted a significant increase in the number of conferences devoted to this topic around the world. With Jungian ideas continuing to grow in influence on both the theory and practice of human spirituality, Christian and non-Christian, it is inevitable that those who are committed to a premodern, tribal hermeneutics of culture and personality will feel increasingly threatened—and rightly so. If Jung is right, if the human spiritual birthright is imprinted in the depths of each human soul—if the human race finds its unity in the depths of the psyche in the soul's encounter with the human face of the God within, then all who have tried to turn God into a commodity controlled by their religious corporations have a right to be fearful. Jung's influence certainly fosters a greater impatience with religious narcissism—infantile grandiosity in religious garb. Clearly, if religious communities have a prosocial future, they must find ways to limit their contributions to human pseudospeciation and

1

religious tribalism—and Jung's psychology is a powerful impetus toward that end.

Yet there are legitimate reservations about Jung and Jung's ideas which are often articulated by representatives of specific spiritual and theological traditions. The tension which exists in the dialogue between these religious traditions and Jungian psychoanalysis is imaged clearly in the dedication of this volume to Edward Edinger and to the memory of Victor White. Edinger has done much to highlight the significance of Jung's work for a revisioning of human spirituality—going so far as to suggest that it is, in effect, a "new dispensation." Victor White, of course, was the important pioneer in exploring the significance of Jung's work for Christian spirituality. His appreciation of Jung's work, however, was a *critical* appreciation. He was clear that Jung was a psychiatrist and not a professional philosopher and/or theologian—and that there were important theological issues which Jung seemed, for whatever reason, not to understand or to value. Their friendship was a stormy one—but one which led to much valuable dialogue. Edinger and White, then, symbolize for us the stewardship of both ends of the dialogical spectrum which we see embodied in this volume of essays. We should be clear that this tension between a human spiritual tradition and Jung's powerful hermeneutics is not unique to this dialogue with Christianity. In subsequent volumes of this series we will see the dialogical tensions between Jung's thought and the other major traditions of human spirituality. What we are seeking to build through the medium of the series is *a vessel for fundamental conversation on human spirituality*—one founded upon the ethics of mutual respect and dialogue which must be honored by all of us if we are to find the taproot of our spiritual unity in religious diversity as a species. This unity will be necessary if we are to cooperate in leading the human race toward healing and away from global holocaust. The dialogue we are engaged in here is another step in the construction of that vessel.

The essays in this volume, then, are also critical appreciations —some much more critical than others. All, however, are serious and important contributions to this foundational inquiry into Jung's challenge to Christianity in areas of faith, feminism, and hermeneutics. We hope that you find them as informative, provocative, and stimulating as we have.

The Editors

Murray Stein

C.G. Jung, Psychologist and Theologian

Writing in 1973, James Heisig began his important article "Jung and Theology: A Bibliographical Essay" by remarking: "It would, I think, be fair to characterize the present state of scholarly relations between Jungian psychology and theology as chaotic" (p. 204). He listed 442 items in his bibliographical catalogue and may have been overcome by the mass of material that had grown up in this area to that date.

Since 1973, the quantity has increased by perhaps three or four fold, and it would now be superhuman to do what Heisig did then. The number of works is simply too large for a single person to master all of it and to stay abreast. Much of the material produced, however, is repetitious, owing to a lack of understanding and clarity on basic issues. While the dialogue between Jung's psychology and theology may still appear chaotic and disorderly, a few slivers of light have been shot through the darkness since Heisig performed his Herculean labors.

The least that one can say is that this large sum of books and essays does represent a considerable amount of interest and work on the relation between Jungian psychology and theology. A high level of interest has been sustained for several decades and shows no sign of falling off. On the contrary, it seems more lively than ever. Yet few serious attempts, other than Heisig's preliminary one in the aforementioned essay and his later book *Imago Dei*, as well as one by myself in *Jung's Treatment of Christianity*, have been made to sort out the patterns of engagement between Jungian psychology and theological approaches.

Heisig closed his essay by calling for a "painstaking re-examination of fundamental assumptions" (p. 232). The following essay is aimed at elucidating some of them.

At the outset it must be recognized that this considerable body of literature has its primary source in Jung's own life, work, and thought. For Jung, the relation between psychology and theology, between *logos* about *theos* (theology) and *logos* about psyche (psychology), was close and intertwined. This was the case for a number of personal and intellectual reasons. As his autobiography (1961) attests, the terms psyche and God were for all practical and existential purposes interchangeable in Jung's vocabulary. The experience of the psyche's wholeness was for Jung an experience of God (1961, p. 197). In his work as a psychoanalyst, too, Jung first observed and then assumed that analysis, if followed carefully and with the use of the correct attitude and methods, would extend beyond personal history into areas more properly characterized as mythical and religious.

To talk about this dimension of the psyche as it becomes manifest in analysis, to give it *logos*, requires an interpretive language more typical of traditional religious discourse about God (i.e., theology) than of the usual sort of psychological discourse about personal psychodynamics and development. Psychotherapy's very success as soul-healing was seen by Jung to depend on its being turned from reductive discourse and reflection into a religious and theological mode, where one no longer spoke only technically about complexes and analyzed them into their historical components but rather of daimons, of the will of God, of destiny, of synchronicity and larger meanings (cf. Stein, 1978). Here again the *logos* about psyche, within the context of Jung's work as a psychotherapist, became a *logos* about *theos:* words about ultimate concern and fitting to that theme.

The "words about psyche" and the "words about God" in Jung's published thought show a kind of interchangeability that has disturbed some professional theologians and alienated large portions of the professional psychological community. From theologians Jung heard the charge that he did not understand the meaning of transcendence, of evil, of the Trinity and other theological doctrines, while from some psychologists the word went out that Jung was "mystical." While many commentators on Jung, both casual and serious, have observed and reacted to this Hermetic play between psychological and religious-theological discourse—which occurs not only in Jung's works on more strictly religious and theological themes and materials but also in his works on more properly psychological ones—few seem to have understood the assumptions lying beneath this interplay. Criticism has therefore been oddly off the mark, and the main intellectual issues have not been engaged.

I hope to clear some ground for more accurately targeted discussion. Can Jungian psychology be used for theological purposes? If so, on what grounds?

With this query in mind, I would like to discuss two Jungs, one a psychologist, the other a theologian. What needs to be understood is the argument for the intimate connection between them. What is the basis for their cooperation? By what method do they arrive at a joint communiqué? What are the grounds for this joint communiqué?

JUNG, THE PSYCHOLOGIST

As a psychologist, Jung makes the basic assumption that all words, about anything at all, are *also* words about the psyche, because they are words *of* the psyche. Whether words occur in the form of descriptions, explanations, poetic expressions, abstract formulations, or whatever, they have at least a hidden, if not an explicit, subjective referent: they are always *also* statements about the psyche, no matter what their other, objective referent may be.

This is Jung's tenet #1.

By "words," I have in mind the very broad sense implied by *logos*, which lies embedded in the terms "psychology" and "theology." This includes actual words, but also thoughts, reasons and reasonings, intuitive speculations, images, feelings—any and all organized contents and products of consciousness.

Jung the psychologist is interested in the subjective referent of words, rather than the objective. What do they say about the psyche? The answer to this calls for psychological interpretation, and for this the psychologist employs terms whose explicit referent *is* to subjectivity, to the psyche: words like anima (soul) and animus (spirit), shadow, persona, self, ego, unconscious, complex, archetype, etc. These words refer explicitly to the psyche, and they are the vocabulary that makes up Jung's analytical psychology.

This prevailing interest in the subjective referent in all statements of human consciousness ignores, obviously, the distinction between concrete and abstract words, as well as that between emotional and cognitive functions. It allows psychology to glean material from all the other disciplines and domains of discourse. Without making claims one way or another for the objective validity of statements from other disciplines or claiming that the psyche is the only reality worth considering, this viewpoint releases the psychological thinker and interpreter from any limitations on the range of possible inquiry, since statements or notions about anything at all— the arts and sciences, the natural or the spiritual worlds, mathematics or everyday life—contain a reference to the psyche. To acquire the knack of finding the psyche in all words is what Jung would informally speak of as becoming "psychological." Psychological interpretation is the art of explicating the words about the psyche within the words about anything at all. It turns everything into psychology.

This is what happens, then, when the psychologist hears words about God. Whether these are spoken by patients, by professional theologians, or by church councils makes no difference to the psychologist, since they all have a subjective referent. Always these words about God are also words about the psyche. Moreover, the words about God that are spoken by the most untutored layperson, the most exalted theologian, and the most definitive church council have, for the psychologist, the *same* general subjective referent. Jung called this the "self."

In the domain of subjectivity, of the psyche, the self is an entity that is superordinate to the ego, or subjectively felt sense of "I." So in taking the stance of psychologist, one hears all words that refer to superordinate figures as words that are, at least partially or obliquely, words about the self.

This is an axiom of Jungian interpretation of religious or theological texts and utterances. But this same axiom applies equally to words that are explicitly about a fundamental theorem in mathematics, about kings and supreme rulers and ultimate institutions (e.g., the supreme court) in political science and sociology, about fathers and mothers in the utterances of children, as about God or the gods in religion and mythology. As far as psychology is concerned, all of these words about ultimate, superordinate, governing figures and powers refer to the same subjective factor, the self. And the words that persons speak about their relationship to such ultimate powers or values, or the dreams they have about such figures of authority, refer to the relationship within the domain of subjectivity between the ego and the self.

Some expressions of the self, however, are taken by the psychologist to be more complete than others. Figures that are superordinate to the ego but are not of ultimate status, but are rather somewhat relative to other such figures, are rendered in psychological language as archetypes. These are fragments of the self (Fordham) and partially express the self or an aspect of the self. Before they become integrated into human consciousness, the archetypes possess numinosity and an aura of power, and they make an impression on the ego of "the holy" (Otto). They are also usually taken to have teleological value and significance for ego-consciousness, in that they are required for fuller, more whole human living and functioning and by making their appearance are offering their availability for integration.

On the basis of this set of related views and assumptions, Jung the psychologist sets out in various of his writings to interpret religious and theological texts and utterances. His psychological interpretations are elucidations of the subjective elements expressed in these texts and statements. Words about God, whether they appear written down in texts, creeds, or scriptures, or are delivered orally by patients or preachers, or occur internally as thoughts, fantasies, images or dreams, tell the tale of structures and dynamics within the realm of subjectivity. By attending in this manner, the psychologist gains access to the subjective world of the individual (or, in the case of credal and traditional formulations, to the subjective world of a religious tradition) who is articulating the words about God. The psychological interpretation repeats these words as words about the psyche and seeks to address the question: What is the psychological meaning of these words?

To one extent or another, Jung uses this psychological approach in all of his published works on religious themes and texts. It is a fundamental assumption and rests on his understanding of the Kantian view that the human mind cannot know things as they are in themselves but is always limited by its own categories of understanding and perception. The psyche cannot leap outside of the psyche, as Jung was fond of asserting.

In his *Answer to Job,* for example, Jung interprets Jahweh as a representation of an archaic form of the self, Job as the ego, and

Satan as the *principium individuationis*. He interprets the Bible generally as a collectively experienced story of the process of individuation occurring within the collective psyche of the Hebrew people: the self (i.e., God) creates the ego (Adam and Eve, mankind); the ego falls into a state of inflation and is forced to become autonomous; it is thereby separated from the self (the fall from Paradise); the self remains archaic for a period of time and is finally forced into a process of development toward consciousness by the more conscious ego (Job); the self announces its approach to consciousness in dreams and prophesies and finally enters ego-consciousness (the incarnation of God in Jesus of Nazareth); the later coming of the Holy Spirit represents the emergence of the transcendent function. Thus the biblical text and the documented history of Judaism and Christianity are examined in this work (and elsewhere in Jung's writings) for their psychological meanings: what do these words, which refer ostensibly to objective persons, historical events, Deity, say about the psyche, about its origins, its development, its structure?

In the essay, "A Psychological Approach to the Dogma of the Trinity," Jung puts the same questions to the Trinitarian symbol. The Trinity is treated as a symbol of the self: the Father represents the self as a source of power and energy within the psyche, the prime mover; the Son represents an emergent structure (*logos*) of consciousness that supplants the previous, self-alienated ego (this is the theme of at-one-ment); the Holy Spirit represents the aspect or function of the self that becomes a mediating structure between the ego and the self. (In this essay, however, Jung does more than simply interpret the Trinitarian symbol; he also criticizes it and offers a reconstructed doctrine of God based on a Quaternitarian symbol. I will examine the assumption behind this critical and reconstructive move later.)

Among the secondary works on Jungian psychology and theology, there are many that reflect the application of this psychological interpretive approach to religious and theological materials. I will refer to this as genre #1, the psychological hermeneutic. It is one of the larger groups within the literature of dialogue between Jungian psychology and theology. This approach has appealed both to Jungian psychologists with an interest in religion and theology and to some religious and theological professionals who have found in Jungian psychology an attractive hermeneutic.

Perhaps the most sophisticated and expert practitioner of the psychological interpretation of biblical and theological materials has been Rivkah Schärf Kluger, who combined in her professional preparation a doctorate in Biblical Studies and the training of a Jungian analyst. *Satan in the Old Testament* and *Psyche and Bible* are her principal contributions. Both of these works are based on detailed scholarly studies of Old Testament materials and on the interpretive approach outlined above. Jung himself relied significantly on her interpretation of Satan for his *Answer to Job*.

Another important author in this genre is Edward Edinger, whose professional training is primarily in psychiatry and analytical psychology. He employs the psychological interpretive approach in his *Ego and Archetype*, where he discusses Christ as an image of the individuating ego, much along the lines of Jung in "A Psychological Approach to the Dogma of the Trinity" and *Aion*.

A more popular but still expert contribution to this genre is John Sanford's *The Kingdom Within*, a psychological interpretation of the parables of Jesus. Sanford, an Episcopal clergyman and Jungian analyst, employs a set of equations that derive from Jungian psychology but departs from Jung's own interpretations at significant points: He interprets Christ as a representation of the self, the Pharisees as representative of the persona and its concerns, Satan as the "inner adversary" or shadow, and the Kingdom of God as the inner world whose center is constituted by the self. For Sanford, the discoveries of depth psychology amount to a discovery of the reality of the inner world (p. 18), and this discovery and its practical applications make it possible for modern man to enter the same world of timeless spiritual truth to which the life and parables of Jesus point.

A second tenet of Jung the psychologist, which established also a second genre in the literature, gives the psychologist a powerful critical tool by which to make judgments concerning the adequacy of what claim to be complete and definitive statements about God (i.e., dogmas, doctrines, traditions of belief). It is actually a derivative, or corollary, of Tenet #1, and states that the psychologist has a privileged position that allows for evaluating the relative adequacy or incompleteness of theological statements about God.

Jung's argument runs as follows: the psychologist is in a position to discover the fundamental structures, dynamics, and development of the human psyche. This is, after all, the proper study of psychology. By using the critical-comparative method of investigation on materials that are primarily subjective in nature—dreams, fantasies, projections, fairy tales, myths—and on statements that have an intangible objective referent and are therefore highly prone to be filled with projections of subjective material, the psychologist can arrive at an increasingly complete and accurate approximation of the morphology and dynamics of the psyche. Among Jung's works, *Aion* is the most sustained and detailed statement on his understanding of the structure and dynamics of the self, arrived at by the critical-comparative method that he called empirical.

Secondly, on the basis of having worked out the structure and dynamics of subjectivity, the psychologist can measure the adequacy of any particular statements of or about the self. Since "words about God" (theology) are also "words about psyche" (psychology), because they are words of the psyche, the psychologist is in a position to judge the adequacy of what claim to be normative statements about God. Do they match up with what is known about the self?

As Jung pointed out repeatedly, the psychologist performs these operations not as a philosopher, a theologian, or a metaphysician, but as a psychologist. As psychologist, one speaks about subjectivity. The criterion for judging adequacy from this viewpoint is the completeness of expression that words, whatever their objective referent may be, give to subjectivity and its structure(s). Since the subjective referent of words about God is the self, those words can be judged as *psychologically* adequate or inadequate on the basis of the psychologist's understanding of the self.

It is possible, for example, that a statement about God would be adequate according to the criteria of a certain theological tradition, conforming to that tradition's theological and philosophical standards, but not be psychologically adequate because it fell short of the psychological criteria for a full and complete statement about the self. To be psychologically adequate, it must give the fullest possible expression to the self, and the psychologist is in a position to evaluate this.

Jung himself experienced a great deal of exasperation with theologians and religious figures because he could not get this point understood. From this gap in understanding there has arisen a sort of critical sub-genre in the literature. This is focused by criticism of Jung's statements based on philosophical, theological, and ethical arguments and considerations. Buber, for example, misconceived Jung as a Gnostic because Jung claimed to "know" and not believe. Victor White, another theologian, strenuously criticized Jung philosophically and theologically for his position on evil and his attacks on the doctrine of *privatio boni*. It is likely, in my view, that Jung often understood his critics better than they could understand him, because they failed to grasp his argument. Some of his last words to Victor White, with whom he tried to collaborate for some ten years, were that White could not follow a psychological argument (Jung 1973, pp. 539–41). White agreed, eventually, saying that they were trained in different philosophical schools (Jung 1975, p. 58, n. 1). The point was, though, that not philosophy but psychology was the mode of discourse, and the psyche's requirements are not those of philosophy. Neither philosophy, theology, nor ethics can arbitrate in matters of the psyche, though they may, as traditionally they have, at least in the short run, overrule the psyche by force.

What is most disturbing to theologians about Jung's positions on theological topics is his stubborn refusal to release some words about God from their rootedness in subjectivity, his refusal to allow for the possibility of subject-transcending words. (Again, I am using "words" in the broad sense of *logoi*, to include all contents and expression of human subjects, of any form or structure whatsoever, from metaphysical claims to "tongues.") The psychologist, who speaks about the psyche and is indeed the psyche's advocate, will not allow for a condition under which the spirit completely transcends the psyche.

This tenet and the debates swirling around it have produced a second genre in the literature of Jungian thought and theology. This we could name the genre of the psychological critique of theology, with a sub-group made up of constructive and reconstructive suggestions for theology, for Christian theology in particular. Jung's own work on such Christian doctrines as the Trinity and Christology lies at the base of this genre. In the secondary literature are works like my own *Jung's Treatment of Christianity* and "Jung's Green Christ." The works of Jungian analyst and Roman Catholic priest John Dourley also fall into this group.

Theological critics of this position have also appeared, among whom Robert Doran is perhaps the most insightful and articulate. Since Doran's work highlights the main issues, it is worthy of special attention. A student of Bernard Lonergan and Jung, Doran shows a keen sensitivity to the importance of subjectivity in theological method and in religious, moral, and intellectual life. Like Victor White, Doran has great sympathy for Jung's approach insofar as it reveals the foundations of subjectivity and makes possible a self-appropriation of what he calls "foundational subjectivity" (pp. 14–15). But like White, too, Doran parts company with Jung on moral, philosophical, and theological grounds. One of the reasons for his dissatisfaction with Jung's thought, ultimately, centers on the issue of transcendence and on Jung's refusal to allow for the spirit to leap completely clear of the psyche. The suspiciousness of the psychologist would suggest that Doran has designs on the psyche: the purpose of considering the psyche at all is, for him, to allow the spirit to gain mastery over it in its movement toward self-transcendence. Doran describes this inner drama in terms of the Orestes myth: the persecuted and finally redeemed matricide is a cipher for the ego struggling toward self-transcendence and for its flight from inauthenticity (p. 7).

Doran would agree with Jung that the movement of intellectual, moral, and religious life from inauthenticity through conversion toward self-transcendence can be interpreted psychologically and that these developments in the existential subject can be spoken of psychologically, but finally, at the "far reaches of the psyche" (p. 265), there is a kind of experience that must be spoken of with words that no longer have a subjective referent: "Intentionality and the psyche it has conscripted into its service must at this point surrender to the gift of God's love poured forth in our hearts by the Holy Spirit who has been given to us. The symbol of this surrender, the embodiment of the Self at these far reaches of the psyche, is the Crucified" (*ibid.*). Here the words "God" and "Holy Spirit" have, for Doran, no subjective referent; they are free of the psyche. For Jung, the psychologist, there can be no such privileged words.

Doran, the theologian, draws a clear line between the psychological self and God. The domain of subjectivity, the self, has upper and lower boundaries: at the upper end it is transcended by spirit ("the absolute limit of the process of going beyond that is God"—

p. 21) and at the lower end by matter (physiological processes in the body). While Jung would agree with this in theory (Jung 1954), he would not agree with Doran's further assertion that the human mind can have any knowledge of these psyche-transcending realities or speak words about them that have no subjective referent. Because of Doran's conviction that this kind of radical self-transcendence is possible through faith, he can argue that theology ultimately has the right to speak words about God that are not subject to psychological criteria of adequacy.

Beyond the "far reaches of the psyche," the psychologist must keep silence. Jung, the psychologist, would not go beyond this boundary of the psyche: *all* experience and *all* words about experience are and must always remain psychological.

JUNG, THE THEOLOGIAN

I turn now to the other Jung, the theological one. The two Jungs, psychologist and theologian, live side by side in relative harmony. I am not pointing here to an inner conflict in Jung's personality or in his vocation. As Jung worked it out, the theologian complements the psychologist in himself and carries out a further interpretive task, taking up where the first leaves off, without contradicting him or calling the psychological perspective into question.

Jung's movement from psychology (words about the psyche) to theology (words about God) is, unlike Doran's move, not based on establishing a privileged territory of image, experience, and discourse that lies beyond the reach of the psyche. Nor does he appeal to divine revelation. There is no gap. Theology for Jung is, rather, a transformation from psychology, a shift of language and understanding within the same territory and still within the realm of the psyche.

The question is: What was the principle, or tenet, by which this transformation was effected? How could Jung maintain that words about the psyche (psychology) can also be words about God (theology)?

Peter Homans has scrutinized the ways in which theologians tend to open gaps between experience and doctrine by appealing to the notion of transcendence, while depth psychology tends to resist such gaps and to interpret this leap to spirit as a manifestation of an unresolved father complex. In examining the method of Jung the theologian, one finds that he creates a possibility for theology, for words about God, without relying on a gap between psychology and theology. This possibility rests on an hypothesis, or an intuition, of correspondence between the structure(s) of subjectivity and the structure(s) of objectivity.

I will refer to this notion of correspondence as Tenet #3.

According to the two tenets discussed already, all words, in the sense of *logoi* (thoughts, words, fantasies, images, etc.), have a subjective referent, and a careful comparative-critical investigation of these words reveals the foundations of subjectivity. According to the tenet of correspondence between subjectivity and objectivity, however, the true *logoi* about subjectivity (psychology) possess an objective referent, and a close scrutiny of the structure(s) of subjectivity reveals structure(s) of objectivity. Subjectivity and objectivity are two sides of a single coin, as it were, and not radically separate and different. This tenet allows for a passage to theology *through* psychology. Rather than a procedure for increasing levels of self-transcendence to a place of the gap beyond which lies the possibility for theology proper, this method works by a principle of homology among structures of reality. A true psychology will lead to, or reflect, a true theology.

To counterpose the Jungian myth to Doran's myth of Orestes, the transformation of psychology into theology lies via a "return to the mothers" rather than via a "slaying of the mother" and "persuasion of the Furies" to join a spiritual culture (cf. Doran, p. 273). Through submersion in the depths of subjectivity (the Mother), one discovers structures, orders and powers, called archetypes by Jung, which correspond to the structures, orders and powers of objectivity. To speak about this area of his research into the ground of subjectivity and objectivity, Jung used the concept of synchronicity and the term *anima mundi*, a term appropriate to both psychology and ontology. The link between subjectivity and objectivity, he argued, is the archetype, which possesses the property of "transgressivity" (Jung 1952c, para. 964). The archetype is both subjective and objective.

Foregoing here a discussion of the examples and evidence cited by Jung to argue for the transgressivity of archetypes and for the correspondence between the structure(s) of subjectivity and objectivity, I would also prefer to refrain from commenting on assessments of Jung's thought as solipsistic. If one understands the basic premise, it is evident that he did genuinely intend to enter the domain of objectivity, albeit through the door of psychic structure(s). This should be examined as an interesting and potentially fruitful method for approaching objectivity itself, a method whose assumptions would of course have to stand up to serious critical scrutiny. If one does not understand Jung's intention here, however, his thought will often simply look bizarre.

Turning to what Jung did with this transformation of "words about psyche" into "words about God," we come to genre #3 in the literature, which could be called the interpretation of psychological experience as religious.

The formula yielded by the principle of correspondence is that words about the self are also words about God. This needs some clarification, since "words about the self" need not refer explicitly to the self as a psychological entity. As pointed out already, all words that refer ostensibly to superordinate structures and powers— whether in politics, in religion and theology, in economics, in family relations, in natural science and mathematics—may be identified as referring, within subjectivity, to the self. Once these words have been interpreted and referred back to their subjective ground in the self, it becomes possible to see that they also refer to God, since the self's objective referent is God. This is a rather roundabout way of agreeing with Tillich, for whom God and "ultimate concern" were equivalent terms. For Jung, the conscious subject's orientation to the self is the same as the orientation to God, and the experience of the self equals the experience of God. This orientation may be positive or negative, accepting or rejecting, obscure or relatively lucid, and the conscious ego's experience of the self may be negligible, partial, or relatively full.

On the basis of this formula, Jung the psychologist becomes a practical theologian when he claims that at bottom all neurotic problems are religious problems and that the individuation process, which involves gaining and establishing a vital and conscious relation between the ego and the self, is a religious process. The conscious individual's active involvement with the unconscious, through dream work and active imagination, is Jung's version of living the spiritual life.

The transformation of psychological into religious-theological language that comes about in this way has led, in the secondary Jungian literature, to the occasional use of the term "religious instinct" (cf. for example Meier, pp. 64ff.). The notion is that the individuation process, as described by analysts in their discussions of case materials, is equivalent to the search for a relationship with God. This view has also occasionally produced an equation between the analyst, who stands in the service of the individuation process for analysands, and the minister or priest, who serves to mediate relations between human subjects and God. Jungian analysis, whose fundamental goal is to foster a healthy and vital relation between the ego and the self, is, according to this viewpoint, a procedure for orienting broken persons to God. Psychotherapy is therefore a religious enterprise, striving to establish a positive relation between consciousness and the fundamental structures and powers of subjectivity, which ultimately transcend the subject and mirror the divine life within the Godhead.

A significant body of literature has grown up around the application of this formula. Central to this genre is the contribution made by Jung himself: *Psychology and Alchemy,* in which Jung comments on a long dream series that increasingly reveals symbols of the self; *Memories, Dreams, Reflections,* his autobiography, which employs the formula extensively in equating psychological and religious experience; his exhaustive comparisons between the individuation process and Kundalini Yoga and the Spiritual Exercises of Ignatius Loyola in still unpublished seminars. Many other individual essays and portions of larger works could be mentioned.

In the secondary literature, Ester Harding's *Journey into Self* is exemplary, as is Gerhard Adler's *The Living Symbol* (a case study). A more recent contribution is Lionel Corbett's paper, "Transformation of the Image of God Leading to Self-Initiation into Old Age." One of the most interesting, serious works in this genre is the recent book by Carrin Dunne, *Behold Woman,* an account of psychological process and reflection as feminist theology. In many ways, this genre looks like the most lively in recent times, promising many valuable future contributions.

Besides making possible this third genre in the literature, this same formula has enabled a discussion to emerge that is more formally theological and metaphysical in character. If the words about the self are also words about God, and if the psychologist is in a position to establish the fundamental structures of subjectivity, the psychologist is in a position to offer theologically substantive and constructive reflection. This is the basis in Jung's thought for a natural, or empirical, theology, a fourth genre, which could be called a psychologically based natural theology.

This has remained a relatively undeveloped genre in the literature. It is distinguishable from the third by its more explicit, self-consciously theological and metaphysical nature. It is different from genre #2 in that it is not reconstructive of an already established theology but begins from the ground up on its own foundations. This genre, like the others, has its roots in Jung's own work.

As a psychologist, Jung uses his critical-comparative method to establish the fundamental morphology and dynamics of the self. Using his transformational formula, he then argues that this corresponds to the morphology and dynamics of objectivity, i.e., to God. From this understanding of the self, he derives his interpretation of Judeo-Christian history and his doctrine of God as quaternitarian and as a *unio oppositorum* of good and evil. So far this is mostly reconstructive of Christian theology, but in certain passages of his works, especially in *Aion* and in the paper on synchronicity, Jung ventures further and speculates about such matters as "acausal orderedness" (1952, para. 965) and "creative acts" (para. 167).

This side of Jung's thought has received further treatment and extension by M.L. von Franz in her books, *Number and Time* and *Projection and Re-Collection in Jungian Psychology*. It has also been elaborated upon by ira Progoff in his *Jung, Synchronicity, and Human Destiny*. The comparisons drawn between the thought of Jung and Teilhard, as reported upon in the journal *Anima* (Fall 1976 and Spring 1977), belong to this literature. Morton Kelsey's *Myth, History and Faith*, with its emphasis on the "reality of the spiritual world," derives from and belongs to this genre as well.

In summary: I have presented two Jungs, the psychologist and the theologian, and have specified the three basic tenets that allowed him to engage in his own special kind of dialogue between psychology and theology. I have also presented four genres that have developed in the literature as a result of these tenets or of some combination of them.

The three tenets are: all words, whatever their objective referent, are also words about the psyche, hence words about God (theology) are also words about the psyche (psychology); the psychologist, knowing about the structures and dynamics of the psyche, is in a position to evaluate and to make critical-constructive observations about the completeness of doctrines about God; the words about the fullness of the psyche (self) are also words about God (theology), because of a correspondence that exists between the structures of subjectivity and those of objectivity.

The four genres that have descended from the use of these tenets are, first, the psychological interpretation of religious and theological texts; second, the psychological critique of theological ideas; third, a theological interpretation of psychological experience; and fourth, a natural theology based on the structures of subjectivity.

The first and third of these genres have been developed rather fully, while the second and fourth are still relatively undeveloped. Few, if any, authors (other than Jung himself) combine the full range of work possible if all three tenets cited were to be employed as a whole. This kind of systematic work remains to be done.

The critical literature is, with some exceptions such as James Heisig's *Imago Dei*, rather unsophisticated and off the mark because the major tenets have not been adequately grasped.

References

Adler, G. 1961. *The Living Symbol.* New York: Pantheon Books.

Buber, M. 1957. *Eclipse of God.* New York: Harper and Brothers.

Corbett, L. 1987. "Transformation of the Image of God Leading to Self-initiation into Old Age." In *Betwixt and Between,* ed. L. Mahdi, S. Foster, and M. Little, pp. 371–388. LaSalle, IL: Open Court.

Doran, R. 1977. *Subject and Psyche: Ricoeur, Jung, and the Search for Foundations.* Washington, D.C.: University Press of America.

Edinger, E. 1972. *Ego and Archetype.* New York: Putnam.

————. 1979. "Depth Psychology as the New Dispensation," *Quadrant* 12/2:4–25.

Dourley, J.P. 1984. *The Illness That We Are: A Jungian Critique of Christianity.* Toronto: Inner City Books.

Dunne, C. 1989. *Behold Woman: A Jungian Approach to Feminist Theology*. Wilmette, IL: Chiron Publications.

Fordham, M. 1985. "The Self in Jung's Works." In *Explorations into the Self*, pp. 5–33. London: Academic Press.

Franz, M.L. von. 1974. *Number and Time*. Evanston: Northwestern University Press.

———. 1980. *Projection and Re-collection in Jungian Psychology*. LaSalle, IL and London: Open Court.

Harding, E. 1956. *Journey into Self*. New York: Longmans, Green.

Heisig, J. 1973. "Jung and Theology: A Bibliographical Essay." *Spring* 1973: 204–55.

———. 1979. *Imago Dei: A Study of Jung's Psychology of Religion*. Lewisburg: Bucknell University Press.

Homans, P. 1970. *Theology after Freud*. New York: Bobbs-Merrill Co.

Jung, C.G. 1942. "Transformation Symbolism in the Mass." In *Collected Works*, 11:201–96. Princeton: Princeton University Press, 1969.

———. 1951. *Aion: Researches into the Phenomenology of the Self*. In *Collected Works*, vol. 9, part 2. Princeton: Princeton University Press, 1968.

———. 1952a. *Answer to Job*. In *Collected Works*, 11: 355–470. Princeton: Princeton University Press, 1958.

———. 1952b. "Psychology and Alchemy." In *Collected Works*, vol. 11. Princeton: Princeton University Press, 1968.

———. 1952c. *Synchronicity: An Acausal Connecting Principle*. In *Collected Works*, 8: 417–531. Princeton: Princeton University Press, 1960.

———. 1954. "On the Nature of the Psyche." In *Collected Works*, 8: 159–234. Princeton: Princeton University Press, 1969.

———. 1961. *Memories, Dreams, Reflections*. New York: Random House.

———. 1973. *Letters*, vol. 1. Princeton: Princeton University Press.

———. 1975. *Letters*, vol. 2. Princeton: Princeton University Press.

Kelsey, M. 1974. *Myth, History and Faith*. New York: Paulist Press.

Kluger, R. 1967. *Satan in the Old Testament*. Evanston: Northwestern University Press.

———. 1974. *Psyche and Bible*. New York: Spring Publications.

Meier, C.A. 1977. *Jung's Analytical Psychology and Religion*. Carbondale, IL: Southern Illinois University Press.

Otto, R. 1958. *The Idea of the Holy*. New York: Oxford University Press.

Progoff, I. 1973. *Jung, Synchronicity and Human Destiny*. New York: Julian Press.

Sanford, J. 1970. *The Kingdom Within: A Study of the Inner Meaning of Jesus' Sayings*. Philadelphia and New York: J.B. Lippincott Co.

Stein, M. 1978. "Psychological Interpretation: A Language of Images."
    Dragonflies, Fall: 91–105.
———. 1985. *Jung's Treatment of Christianity: The Psychotherapy of a
    Religious Tradition*. Wilmette, IL: Chiron Publications.
———. 1987. "Jung's Green Christ: A Healing Symbol for Christianity."
    In *Jung's Challenge to Contemporary Religion*, ed. M. Stein and R.
    Moore, pp. 1–13. Wilmette, IL: Chiron Publications.
White, V. 1960. *Soul and Psyche: An Enquiry into the Relationship of Psy-
    chology and Religion*. London: Collins.

Peter Homans

C.G. Jung: Christian or Post-Christian Psychologist?

I. INTRODUCTION: JUNG'S (TWO-FOLD) APPROACH TO CHRISTIANITY

To the reader even moderately familiar with Jung's writings, and for any reader guided by the secondary literature on Jung, it is clear that religion is a central theme in his mature work. In his mature years Jung writes about religion again and again, dealing with various aspects of it: primitive religions and archaic man; Eastern religions; the relation of psychotherapy to the work of the clergyman; but above all about Christianity and Christian dogma, in particular the dogma of the existence or transcendence of God.

This feature of Jung's mature thought finds a parallel in his personal life. The experience of religion pervaded his turbulent childhood and early adolescence. During his psychoanalytic years religious concerns colored his thinking about Freud's work and the writing of *Symbols of Transformation*. During the critical period described in his autobiography as the time of "Confrontation with the Unconscious" (1913–1918), he struggled with the tension between traditional Christianity on the one hand and modernity on the other hand. At the close of this period (1918–1921) Jung wrote the first versions of the *Two Essays on Analytical Psychology*,[1] which became a definitive statement of his major ideas, and which outlined the structure of the individuation process. The individuation process became the center of Jung's mature thought. Later (from 1921 onward) he turned his mind back upon the phenomenon of religion, which had vexed him throughout so much of his early life, and interpreted it—or, rather, as I will explain shortly, re-interpreted it—according to his unique system of psychological ideas, all of which explicated the individuation process.

21

So, the question regarding Jung's relation to religion in the mature years is not whether it was a bona fide theme. Rather, the question is, given the fact that religion was a central theme, what was Jung's view of it? This question contains a central issue in understanding Jung's thought as a whole, one which has created many of the polarizations among critics of Jung, and can be explicated as follows. Did Jung, like Freud, develop a set of interpretive categories by means of which he could "see through" and thereby explain away traditional Christianity? Or, did he, in devising his system of unique ideas, conceive of a way to translate traditional Christianity into terminology acceptable to the modern individual, without appreciably altering the traditional doctrines? In other words, was Jung a Christian or a post-Christian psychologist?

The correct response to this question is that both aspects of it must be answered in the affirmative, but that neither one in itself comprises the whole of his approach. Jung did not opt for either of these alternatives in an exclusive manner. Rather, his thought on religion is a complex attempt to synthesize both. By applying the individuation process to traditional Christianity, Jung in effect created a double movement of reduction and retrieval of meaning. In one sense he *was* reductive: he interpreted the totality of Christian faith in the light of analytical psychology. This psychology became for him the key for "seeing through" the otherwise opaque character of the Christian faith. All the major tenets of Christianity were interpreted as instances of archetypes in the collective unconscious. The individuation process was the lens through which Jung viewed the Christian faith. It was a new set of categories, derived from his researches and his contact with Freud, completely foreign to the Christian tradition. Without this psychology that faith simply did not make any sense. Jung's interpretation of Christianity was in this sense very different from Christianity's own self-interpretation of itself. In this sense his psychology embodied what Paul Ricoeur has called a "hermeneutics of suspicion."[2]

But Jung's psychology contained a second movement, built upon the first, in which he attempted to retrieve religious meaning from the Christian tradition and incorporate it into his psychological theory of the person. Once the reductive movement had been made —once the psychological meaning of doctrine had been disclosed— then Jung proceeded to clothe these constructs with positive meaning and value, arguing that they were in fact essential if modern man, uprooted and dissociated from his traditional roots, was ever to re-relate himself to Christian tradition. Hence he claimed that the archetypes and the individuation process, while not part of the vocabulary of the traditional Christian, nevertheless captured the hidden essence of that tradition. Thus Jung's psychology contained within it, alongside its hermeneutics of suspicion, a "hermeneutics of affirmation." In order to emphasize the presence of a double movement in Jung's psychology, in which both rejection and affirmation were present, I call his approach a re-interpretation rather than simply one more interpretation. In all this Jung gave expression to an important facet of his personal identity—which existed alongside that of originative psychologist and social critic—that of prophet or re-interpreter of traditional Christianity.

In proposing that a double movement was present in Jung's stance toward traditional Christianity, I am taking issue with existing discussions of Jung's view of religion. On the one hand there are the positively toned theological interpreters—such as Cox,[3] Schaer,[4] and V. White[5]—who have argued that his psychology is simply a re-statement in psychological terms of the principal tenets of the Christian faith. These writers have not given sufficient attention to the massive evidence which supports Jung's life-long struggle to repudiate Christianity—to free himself from its oppressive claims upon his life. Nor do they see the great extent to which Jung, in his mature writings, found traditional Christianity utterly incomprehensible. To say that a particular doctrine or tenet of faith is "really" an archetype of the collective unconscious is to assign to it a meaning quite different from that which the Christian tradition gives it.

On the other hand it is equally necessary—in order to achieve a correct and full sense of Jung's stance toward religion—to oppose the anti-Jungians such as Hostie,[6] Philip,[7] Rieff,[8] and Johnson,[9] who argue that Jung simply psychologized the Christian faith and in doing so completely secularized it. These critics have ignored the element of affirmation. They have not seen how classical Christian experience provided an absolutely essential matrix, or "field," or experiential context out of which the individuation process took its peculiar shape. Thus, for Jung, the traditional beliefs in God, Christ, the Trinity and the Church were all necessary background for the modern individual if he was to come to understand himself in a new way. Traditional Christianity was the indispensable context within which the individuation process could occur. Paradoxically, it was there in order to be put aside. In Jung's mind, analytical psychology evolved out of the Christian tradition, but the result was just as religious as was the context out of which it emerged.

It is helpful, in order to clarify this argument further, to point out that Jung's psychology was really comprised of three types of images of man. First, there was the good Christian, either Catholic or Protestant, who believed unquestioningly in the tenets of his faith and for this very reason was not needful of psychology. For such a person, traditional doctrine successfully organized unconscious processes and hence protected him from becoming neurotic. But Jung was primarily interested in a second type, the so-called modern man, who was fully self-conscious, rational and extraverted, who was oriented to science and the modern state, and who, because he was unconnected with the past, was vulnerable to the unconscious. And then there was the "Jungian man," who was modern in that he rejected the literalism and authoritarianism of traditional Christianity, but who also was in part traditional, in the sense that he was ready to re-interpret Christian symbols in the light of analytical psychology. Thus Jung's view of religion was complex: during his mature life he tried to weave his way through the tension between traditional religion and modernity and his psychology is an attempt —through its double movement of reduction and affirmation—to close the gap between what most people believe to be two un-bridgeable orientations to the world.

This estimate of Jung's view of religion is clearly confirmed by the delineation of the individuation process found in the *Two Essays*. In that statement he defined the final stage of individuation as an encounter with a god-image which had a distinctly Christian cast to it. The consolidation of the archetype of the anima created a new sense of inflation, a merger with the deity which produced the feeling that "I and the Father are One."[10] In order to come to terms with this merger, the patient could, Jung said, concretize or absolutize this image of God as "Father in Heaven."[11] This would be the traditional Christian solution. But he cautioned against such a move, for to do so would only produce a new sense of moral inferiority and oppression—a fundamental prerequisite of traditional faith. In so saying Jung repudiated the Christianity of tradition and took the side of modern man, suspicious of all commitment to theological dogma. But he did not stop here. He went on to introduce the concept of the collective unconscious and the archetypes, in particular the archetype of the self, and to apply these interpretively to the theological situation. He spoke of the self not only as a mid-point between conscious and unconscious, but also as "the god within us."[12] And he defined the emergence of the self as a natural and spontaneous process—which is to say it was not dependent on traditional theological dogma. Thus, by means of the categories of analytical psychology Jung was able first to repudiate traditional Christianity, and second to affirm the formation of the self as a genuine resultant of evolution out of the context of the initial theological situation.

Throughout his mature writings Jung never deviated from this approach to religion. True, he wrote a number of articles on Eastern religions, but his purpose in this was to emphasize what the West lacked. He did not share the interests of the historian of religion. Rather, he was predominantly concerned with the Christian faith. Through analytical psychology Jung reinterpreted traditional Christianity, first by repudiating its formulations, but then going on to show how the situation of classic faith provided the experiential matrix out of which the individuation process could evolve. Now, with this understanding of Jung's strategy firmly in hand, we briefly turn to his explicit writings on religion. While the basic strategy is present throughout all his many and varied analyses of religious questions, and provides the reader with a unified perspective upon their otherwise great diversity, it is particularly evident in his best-known work on the subject, *Psychology and Religion*.[13] This text focuses Jung's central preoccupation: the psychological nature of the Christian doctrine of God.

II. THE THEMES OF SUSPICION AND AFFIRMATION IN "PSYCHOLOGY AND RELIGION"

At the very beginning of the book Jung set the stage for his basic strategy with regard to religion by distinguishing between religion on the one hand and dogmas or creeds on the other. He defined religion as "a careful consideration of certain dynamic factors that are conceived as powers: spirits, demons, Gods, laws, ideas, ideals. . . ."[14] Religion, he wished to make clear, was an experience of a particular type—that is, it was immediate, subjective and therefore psychological. He equated it with what the Protestant theologian, Rudolph Otto, meant by "the numinous"—suggesting awe and reverence in relation to a supreme object. And later in the book he spoke of religious experience as "immediate experience"—by which he meant the experience of the irruption into an overly rational ego-consciousness of collective, archetypal material, an experience which in its own way inspires awe and dread or fear as well. In contrast to religious experience Jung juxtaposed dogmas and creeds. These were, he said, "codified and dogmatized forms of original religious experience."[15] A dogma is formed when the immediate religious experience is congealed into a rigid and elaborate structure of ideas.

Thus, at the very outset of his book, Jung prepared the reader for his unique approach to religion. For dogma was the language of traditional Christianity, whereas religious experience was the target of analytical psychology. Jung's task was to unearth the structures and processes of religious experience, which dogma had obscured and repressed. By exposing the hidden roots of dogma, Jung would reductively interpret Christianity; but, by then demonstrating the underground source of dogma in universal religious experience, he would affirm and re-interpret traditional Christianity. The key to this double movement was the new system of ideas known as analytical psychology, and, in particular, the individuation process.

In order to carry his argument forward, Jung presented his readers with details of a practical case, several dreams of one of his patients in his psychotherapeutic practice. The life-situation of this dreamer was an important piece of Jung's argument. For he embodied Jung's concept of modern man: a scientifically-minded intellectual who, because of his commitment to modernity, could no longer believe in creeds and dogmas and who, furthermore, like most moderns, identified religion entirely with creeds and dogmatic tenets. Jung then analyzed these dreams and demonstrated that they contained images of the archetype of the quaternity, what he called a mandala. Such dreams reflected, he argued, the presence of immediate experience, of the numinous, and were religious in nature. They were, in fact, when properly interpreted, "symbols of God." Jung gave two further reasons for this conclusion. First, the comparative method had shown that ancient thinkers had associated quaternities with God. But Jung also suggested that mandalas were expressions of a religious attitude because the people who dream them link this symbol to the highest value in their personality. "Religion," he said, "is a relation to the highest and most powerful value . . . that psychological fact which wields the greatest power in your system functions as a god."[16]

Having established that dreams and visions of quaternities and mandalas were evidence of the presence of God in the experiential life of the subject, Jung was forced to reflect upon traditional formulations of the nature of the deity. He rightly turned to the doctrine of the Trinity as the privileged form in which the character of deity had been expressed in Christian faith. And he concluded that the Trinity, with its exclusive emphasis upon three rather than four elements in the divine life, was excessively rational and one-sided. The doctrine of the Trinity had repressed the principle of evil and the principle of femininity from the nature of God, and hence also from the consciousness of man. The quaternity, on the other hand, made room for these elements and as such was a more complete and also fully natural symbol of the godhead. But Jung's major concern with the mandala was not simply with the Trinity per se—he discussed this at length in a separate essay on the subject—but also with what mandalas presaged for the fate of the image of God in the modern world.

In traditional Christianity the image of God existed external to the believer's psyche, and he submitted to and was reconciled with that image. But in the mandala dreams of modern man, Jung said, "the place of the deity seems to be taken by the wholeness of man."[17] Jung called this wholeness or totality of man the Self, the end result of the individuation process. The emergence on the modern scene of mandala dreams signified, it would seem, the disappearance of the traditional view of God and the appearance of the Self.

Once again Jung had brought into play what I have called the strategy of a double movement. By means of the categories of analytical psychology he was able to interpret psychologically the key Christian theological formulation of the nature of God. The image of God embodied in the Trinity was repressive, and it distorted psychological reality accordingly. Thus Jung reduced Christian theology to psychology in the spirit of a hermeneutics of suspicion. But then he went on to show how the reality of the deity, while no longer an object of traditional faith, continues to live in the form of a structure of the self, undergirding as it were "the wholeness of man." His point is reminiscent of his concept of the self as "the God within us" found in the *Two Essays*. By virtue of the interpretive power of analytical psychology, the self evolves out of the matrix of traditional faith. In such fashion did Jung attempt to retrieve meaning from the Christian tradition. Here is his hermeneutics of affirmation.

Toward the end of the book Jung introduced one of his most important concepts, "the withdrawal of projections," which illustrated with further clarity his strategy of a double attitude toward traditional Christianity.[18] Primitive man lived in a state of almost total projection: he projected inner emotions onto external objects and persons and consequently lived in a condition of relatively minimal self-consciousness and self-knowledge. But as Western history progressed, it produced circumstances which brought the gradual withdrawal of projections and a consequent increase in consciousness and knowledge of both self and world. Physical science caused the withdrawal of "the most distant projections." Echoing Max Weber's concept of disenchantment, Jung referred to this as the first stage in the despiritualization of the world. The early discoveries of modern science became the foundations of the modern outlook, shaping as they did an entire view of the world. According to Jung, it was the essence of modern man to examine all his projections. Modern man "cannot project the divine image any longer"[19]—that is, he is no longer able to believe in the existence of God, as described by the traditional dogmas of the church. While Jung did not mention Freud in this context, it is clear that the latter's psychology of religion epitomized this stance of modern man. Hence the impasse of modernity: modern man can no longer believe—he has withdrawn his projections—but when he does so, he becomes an isolated ego-consciousness. Jung resolved this conflict by adducing analytical psychology: "if we want to know what happens when the idea of God is no longer projected as an autonomous entity, this is the answer of the unconscious psyche."[20]

The "answer of the unconscious psyche" was of course the answer of the entire individuation process and it bore a double relation to the predicament of modernity. Analytical psychology focused its attention primarily on the affects and images (instincts and archetypes) which undergird the traditional theological doctrines and the attitudes of loyalty which believers bring to them. As such it in effect counseled the withdrawal of projections. While Jung continually insisted throughout his diverse writings on religion that he always returned, insofar as he could, the believing Catholic or Protestant to his traditional faith, this was largely a matter of practical therapeutic strategy. For it is just as clear that his analytical psychology "saw through" the projections of traditional believers. He in effect postulated an archetypal infrastructure—what I would call "the archetype beneath the doctrine"—to traditional belief. Thus, while the good Catholic or Protestant may not know it, his religious faith was motivated by the forces which analytical psychology described. The conceptualization of these forces constituted a system of ideas and a corresponding reality very different from traditional faith. For one to say, "I believe in God the Father," and for one to say, "I am at this moment stirred by an archetype," are two very different explanations of an inner state at a particular moment. In all of this, the thrust of analytical psychology is against traditional Christianity. It is a hermeneutics of suspicion, an unmasking process, a reductive approach, in which dogmas and creeds —the sole modes of conceptualization of traditional faith—are repudiated.

But the withdrawal of projections was only the first of a double movement. Jung believed that he had discovered a natural healing process which occurred when projections were withdrawn—a healing process which would replace, or rather carry forward, the projective process. In the dreams and visions of his patients, especially when they took the form of mandalas, Jung saw a process at work which was remarkably similar to the processes which he believed undergirded the most traditional belief systems. His theory and techniques simply brought this process to a higher level of self-consciousness than they had attained under the conditions of traditional faith. The withdrawal of projections activated new psychological forces, unknown to the traditional believer, which were then raised to a new level of awareness and integrated into self-consciousness. Jung thus ascribed to his own system of ideas a significance functionally equivalent to traditional belief systems. As he put it in an essay written several years earlier:

It is as though, at the climax of the illness, the destructive powers were converted into healing forces. This is brought about by the archetypes wakening to independent life ... as a religiously minded person would say: guidance has come from God. With most of my patients I have to avoid this formulation, apt though it is, for it reminds them too much of what they had to reject in the first place. I must express myself in more modest terms and say that the psyche has awakened to spontaneous activity: and indeed this formulation is better suited to the observable facts. ... To the patient it is nothing less than a revelation. . . .[21]

Here is Jung's attempt to retrieve meaning from the Christian tradition, his hermeneutics of affirmation.

SITUATING JUNG'S THEORY OF RELIGION IN ITS SOCIO-CULTURAL CONTEXT

The question of the extent to which Jung's psychology is Christian and the extent to which it is post-Christian can be further illuminated by situating it more precisely in its socio-cultural context, and, in particular, in the context of the phenomenon of modernity. For, at the heart of Jung's thought on religion was his conviction that traditional Christianity and modernity were radically at odds with one another, and he spent much of his life devising a conceptual system which could reconcile the two. In this case we approach Jung's psychology "from the outside" so to speak, whereas the preceding analysis focused on its internal characteristics. Two theories of modernity, those of Peter Berger and Victor Turner, provide appropriate schema for this task.

Berger's analysis of contemporary life centers upon the process of modernization but especially upon the modernization of consciousness.[22] It is the essence of modern consciousness to be irrevocably structured by the technological aspects of industrial production. The individual of today transfers the engineering ethos of modern technology and bureaucracy to his personal consciousness and emotional life. This ethos, characterized by mechanicity, reproducibility and measurability, produces in consciousness the traits of abstraction, functional rationality and instrumentality. Modern consciousness is therefore capable of a degree of self-analysis and self-abstraction never before achieved. As such it is separated from traditional sources of feeling and meaning—it is, in effect, "homeless."

This modernization of consciousness has produced two contrary movements in thought and society. First, it has created an intense nostalgia for the integrative symbols of the past, resulting in a traditionalism which defensively re-affirms ancient symbols of community. Berger calls this movement "counter-modernization." But the modernization of consciousness has also produced an attempt to oppose modernity's emphasis upon the anonymity and abstraction of rationalistic individuality through the creation of new values and a new sense of community which cannot be derived from a sense of tradition. Berger calls this trend "de-modernization," and finds it best expressed in contemporary youth culture, the counter-culture and the anti-repression psychologies of such writers as Norman O. Brown and R.D. Laing. The principal affirmation of demodernization is the conviction that modern people must re-discover a real and "naked" self which exists beyond institutions and roles—a meta-institutional self—and that the sources for this new self lie in the future creation of fresh and new values. Thus the trend in the direction of de-modernization is even more privatized than is the modernization process itself.

Jung's psychology articulates substantially with all three of the trends described by Berger, although in the final analysis I am inclined to place the accent upon the third, de-modernization, while nevertheless retaining the other two. Jung's system takes full cognizance of the modernization of consciousness by affirming that modern man must accept the fact that collective ideals and the collective consciousness form the persona, an essential ingredient of his personality. Jung's descriptions of modern man as mass man embody well the principle of functional rationality. The consciousness of modern man was for him truly "homeless." But this state of affairs was also the beginning of the process of individuation. The breakdown of the persona activated the archetypes of the collective unconscious, and called for their assimilation into the ego, thereby broadening the scope of modern man's consciousness and alleviating his condition of homelessness. The archetypes might well be called "structures of tradition." As such their existence and the need for their assimilation constituted the dimension of counter-modernization in Jung's psychology: they are symbols rooted in the ancient past which, when assimilated, unify modern consciousness and overcome its homeless condition.

Jung's psychology did not, however, stop here. He did indeed counsel a return to the past, but only in order that the past might be surpassed. The modern ego must, as it were, pass through the past, on its way to the future. If the individuation process is allowed to continue uninterrupted, the assimilation of the archetypes of the collective unconscious results in the formation of the self, a core of essential, personal uniqueness which exists beyond institutions and roles—in short, a truly "meta-institutional self." As such the self cannot be defined entirely in terms of conformity either to modernity or to tradition; rather, it constitutes a genuinely new structure, composed of more than simply an amalgam of the two. The Jungian self assimilates the past, by means of the archetypes, but it also repudiates the past, for it "sees through" the claims of tradition by penetrating to their archetypal infrastructure. Thus the emergence of the self, the final state of the individuation process, while it is built in part upon modernizing and counter-modernizing processes, also attempts to go beyond these in the direction of de-modernization, a view of the person which is entirely new, being neither simply modern nor simply traditional. Jung's psychology is, therefore, an attempt first to codify and then to synthesize all three of these trends as they exist in present-day social and intellectual life, into one unitary system of thought.

Berger's analysis of modernity illumines the question of the status of Jung's view of religion vis-à-vis Christianity, because it permits us to view the double movement of suspicion and affirmation in a sociological perspective. The thrust toward de-modernization appears in Jung's psychology in the suspicion and unmasking of traditional Christianity. This is the modern and post-modern facet of Jung's thought. In this sense he is a post-Christian psychologist. But there is also a thrust toward counter-modernization, a move in a backward direction, in order to recover and retrieve something essential from the past. This is Jung's hermeneutics of retrieval, his debt to his Christian heritage. Much of the appeal of Jung's psychology of religion lies in its synthesis of these trends.

There can be little doubt but that Jung's psychology belongs in the most general sense to that genre of thought the overall aim of which is to reflect critically and innovatively upon the problem of modernity and tradition, and that, in consequence of this, his system is best understood in terms of frameworks such as Berger's, addressed as it is precisely to this problem. But it is the purpose of these remarks to situate Jung's psychology in as broad a cultural context as possible, and since Berger's analysis focuses for the most part upon modernity and tradition in the West—although he does draw examples from primitive and non-Western cultures—it is appropriate to explore at least briefly an even broader perspective, that of cultural anthropology.

In point of fact, Jung's psychology submits quite readily to the categories of analysis provided by the anthropologist Victor Turner, in his well-known study, *The Ritual Process*.[23] Such an analysis suggests that Jungian psychology is an expression of massive cultural change, but that the conditions for such change, far from being restricted to the modern period in the West, can be found in other times and other places as well.

Turner's analysis of cultural change is set in the context of what he believes to be two fundamental modalities of human relatedness, which he designates as social structure on the one hand and liminality or communitas on the other hand, although he is almost entirely absorbed by the nature of the latter. Structure refers to the form of social relatedness characterized by heavily institutionalized norms, roles and status positions. These produce an ethos of differentiation and hierarchy, and people view themselves in ways assigned to them by law, custom, convention and ceremonial. From time to time, however, people withdraw from these normal modes of social interaction and enter a structureless or liminal phase in which the customary rules of social organization no longer apply.

This new type of social organization differs point for point from the old. First, the conditions of liminality produce intense comradeship and egalitarianism which involve the whole man in relation to other whole men, creating an overarching sentiment of humankindness. Second, whereas social structure is highly routinized and practical, liminality is charged with affect, immediacy and spontaneity. Third, such social relatedness generates myths, symbols, rituals and philosophical systems. These newly produced systems of imagery and thought serve as a means of re-classifying men's relation to nature, society and culture, as these were conceived under the more orderly conditions of social structure. Finally, the members of communitas together submit to the general authority of ritual elders.

Jung's psychology portrays a form of liminality or communitas. This becomes clear if it is viewed as in essence describing the individuation process, and if that process is considered to be continuous with cultural processes, which include the experiences and principles of psychotherapy, and not simply as a system of ideas. Individuation begins with a withdrawal from normal modes of social action, epitomized by the breakdown of the persona and all that it entails. Such a withdrawal activates the transference relationship, which is accompanied by an intense desire on the part of the patient to be encountered as a whole person. Jung repeatedly counseled a therapeutic attitude characterized by forthrightness and directness, advising his followers to treat their patients as whole persons—otherwise, how were they to become whole themselves? Such attitudes meant eschewing the conventional roles of doctor and physician. The individuation process produced intense spontaneity and affective immediacy, but central to the process as a whole was the creation, at the level of fantasy and mental imagery, of myths, rituals and philosophical systems. Again and again Jung emphasized the potential of the collective unconscious to create, in the form of archetypes, alternative views of reality, views which were necessarily at odds with the ethos of the conventional world from which the patient came. And of course the Jungian therapist serves the function of a ritual elder, a wise man who understands the process of passage from the conventional world, through the unconscious, to that of the new self. He is therefore capable of serving as a guide for those undertaking the experience of individuation. And, as in the case of liminality, much of the imagery of the individuation process consists of the themes of birth and re-birth. It would seem inevitable that such a motif would appear in the mental life of persons who experience themselves as "betwixt and between"—as in transition from one order of reality to another.

But Jung's psychology also departs from Turner's analysis of structure and liminality, and this departure illumines what is its most important and outstanding feature. According to Turner, all liminality must eventually dissolve. It is a state of intensity which cannot exist for very long without some sort of structure to stabilize it. This occurs in one of two ways: either the individual returns to the surrounding social structure—energized to be sure by his own new experiences—or else liminal communities develop their own internal social structure, a condition which Turner calls "normative communitas." However, neither of these alternatives applies to Jung's system nor do they adequately characterize the community of Jungian patients, therapists and teachers. The individuated self of the committed Jungian returns to the social order only in an extremely instrumental manner, and the social organization of the Jungian community is very loose and unstructured, although there is some hierarchy in the contrasting positions of, say, a lay Jungian as opposed to a supervising analyst. For these reasons it is more correct to say that Jung's psychology presents the student of cultural change with a form of "permanent liminality" in which there is no need to return to social structure, or to generate a social structure internal to the community. Instead, the individuated person simply continues to interpret himself and the world about him in terms of Jungian categories. In point of fact, for the Jungian—be he patient, therapist or teacher—the problem of social order ceases to exist at all: it has been replaced by the problem of inner, psychological order.

Turner's analysis of structure and liminality provides a broad, cultural perspective upon the nature of Jung's psychology as a whole, and especially his psychological theory of religion. Social structure, as Turner conceives it, appears in Jung's thought as an individual's conformity to the doctrines of traditional Christianity, which is accompanied by an uncritical and unreflective adaptation to the institutions of the social order—in this instance, the institution of the traditional church. Hence Jung's hermeneutic of suspicion, the first of his two-fold movement, is, from Turner's perspective, a critical move against social structure. On the other hand, the second phase of Jung's double movement consists of the emergence of the individuation process, in which the individual turns away from the dogmas of traditional Christianity, in other words, away from structure, and directs his attention to the inner workings of the self, which engages the images of genuine religious experience. These images lie beneath, so to speak, beliefs and dogma. This second move, which is Jung's attempt to retrieve meaning from traditional Christianity, can be understood as a move toward liminality and all that it suggests. Only under the conditions of liminality is genuine religion possible for Jung.

This shift of the locus of meaning and order from the social and traditional to the inner, personal, psychological sphere is the central conceptual leit-motif running throughout both Jung's psychology and his theory of religion. The fact that his psychology of religion so richly structures the inner diffuseness which accompanies suspicion of the social order and of traditional religion is his greatest achievement. But the fact that his thought eschews the social order and the possibility that religion might organize that order is also a major limitation. Jung did not see the pervasiveness—so convincingly emphasized by current social science—of the institutional organization of the private sector. Thus, the final assessment of Jung's work must remain a double one.

Notes

1. C.G. Jung, *Two Essays on Analytical Psychology*, trans. R.F.C. Hull, *Collected Works*, Vol. 7 (New York: Pantheon Books, Inc., 1966).
2. Paul Ricoeur, *Freud and Philosophy*, trans. Denis Savage (New Haven: Yale University Press, 1970).
3. D. Cox, *Jung and St. Paul* (New York: Association Press, 1959).
4. H. Schaer, *Religion and the Cure of Souls in Jung's Psychology* (New York: Pantheon Books, Inc., 1950).
5. V. White, *God and the Unconscious* (Cleveland: The World Publishing Company, 1952).
6. R. Hostie, *Religion and the Psychology of C.G. Jung* (New York: Sheed and Ward, 1957).
7. H.L. Philip, *Jung and the Problem of Evil* (London: Rockliff, 1958).
8. P. Rieff, *The Triumph of the Therapeutic* (New York: Harper and Row, 1966).
9. W.A. Johnson, *The Search for Transcendence* (New York: Harper and Row, 1974).
10. C.G. Jung, *Two Essays on Analytical Psychology*, p. 229.
11. *Ibid.*, p. 235.
12. *Ibid.*, p. 238.
13. C.G. Jung, *Psychology and Religion*, trans. R.F.C. Hull, *Collected Works*, Vol. 11 (New York: Pantheon Books, Inc., 1963), pp. 3–106.
14. *Ibid.*, p. 8.
15. *Ibid.*, p. 9.
16. *Ibid.*, p. 81.
17. *Ibid.*, p. 82.
18. *Ibid.*, pp. 83, 87.

19. *Ibid.*, p. 95.
20. *Ibid.*, p. 96.
21. C.G. Jung, "Psychotherapists or Clergy," *Collected Works*, Vol. 11, p. 345.
22. Peter Berger, *The Homeless Mind*, with B. Berger and H. Kellner (New York: Random House, 1973).
23. Victor Turner, *The Ritual Process* (Chicago: Aldine Publishing Company, 1969).

Frank M. Bockus

The Archetypal Self: Theological Values in Jung's Psychology

The modern search for self-knowledge has evolved to the point where we can appreciate, more fully than before, Carl Jung's psychology of the self. Today he deserves widespread interest, not only among students of human nature, such as behavioral scientists and theologians, but among thoughtful people generally.

Jung's psychology is centered on a conception of the *self*. By focusing on the self in its many aspects, we can best utilize his views for a contemporary understanding of humankind. But material on the self is dispersed throughout the many volumes of his collected works. In this paper I intend to explicate his theory of the self by abstracting from several writings, and to indicate briefly its present-day relevance for an interdisciplinary anthropology and theology.

Such studies are needed at this time for several reasons. First, with the publication in 1960 of *The Structure and Dynamics of the Psyche*, we gained access to Jung's own interpretation of the "system theory" philosophy underlying his work. Such philosophical data are crucial for a theological evaluation. The material in that volume clarifies the evolving methodology of much of his earlier work and illuminates the philosophical conflict he experienced with other psychologists early in his career. To them, he seemed to work on alien problems and to hold inadmissible assumptions, whereas to Jung the assumptions and theories of other scholars seemed too mechanical and reductionistic. Through his acquaintance with field theory in microphysics and through the application of this theory to psychology, Jung in his later writing clarified his philosophy in a more formal manner.

Second, self theory has come to the forefront of the modern study of the person, and Jung's exploration of this issue affords a rich resource. His direct inquiry into such topics as the self-realization tendency, the mind-body relation, genetic bases of memory, and the self in culture, all drawn together in a self theory, offers a way of synthesizing many current threads of scholarship. In addition, the assumptions of his system theory are to be found in contemporary anthropology, particularly in the *organismic* view. Hence, our own most pressing issues and presuppositions enable us better to utilize Jung's work.

Jung's quest for humankind's common humanity, culminating in his theory of the *archetype,* led him inevitably into other disciplines. It was a consistent movement, which took him from his own most normative concept, the self, to a consideration of Christology, the normative concept of Christian theology. Jung held that Christ represents a concrete embodiment of the God-person relation inherent in the nature of all people. In this conception he offers a most provocative resource for current theological construction, and, as we shall see, the lines of his implicit theology are now being developed by philosophers and theologians.

Our purpose, then, is to make Jung's self theory more readily available, and through this exposure to suggest its integrative relevance for anthropology in general and for theology in particular. We believe that a general discussion of his ideas is necessary before their implications can be developed, and we are therefore inclined to focus more on the former task than the latter. The discussion will proceed cumulatively, first elaborating the self under its several aspects, but leading toward its relation to God and toward a methodological analysis, in which Jung's theological implications are extended.

THE ORIGINS OF THE SELF:
THE SELF-REALIZATION TENDENCY

Individuals begin their pilgrimage toward selfhood, according to Jung, millions of years before their birth. This statement is not as ridiculous as it may at first appear. Today it is commonly accepted that the newborn infant possesses inherited potentials of physical development. The child, subject to certain environmental factors of health or diet, possesses genetic predispositions of size, height, and contour. Jung sought to explore the inherited tendencies of psychological development as well. For some reason, many people find the idea of intrinsic systems of psychic functioning more difficult to accept. For Jung, human beings are born with inherited possibilities of psychic functioning, which characterize them as human. Such common characteristics predispose us to decidedly human mental states, as contrasted with other creatures. The child is endowed with inherent and collective potentials to be actualized anew during the course of his or her development, subject to certain environmental factors of human interaction and of social and cultural influence. Certain possibilities are realized more than others during the course of the individual's unique personal history. Jung writes:

> In view of the structure of the body, it would be astonishing if the psyche were the only biological phenomenon not to show clear traces of its evolutionary history, and it is altogether probable that these marks are closely connected with the instinctual base.[1]

The child's mind is a teeming reservoir of potential structures and dynamics of human functioning. Jung called this reality a collective unconscious—collective, because this base of the human mind is common to all, unconscious, because the potentials have not been brought into conscious realization. The collective unconscious presupposes that the psyche, everywhere, at all times and in all places, functions as a human mental process. In some respects it is an archaic and primitive reality, bearing the entire ancestral heritage of humanity over the course of human evolution.[2] As such, it is a creative reservoir. Speaking of this primitive mentality, Jung says:

> Man's unconscious contains all the patterns of life and behavior inherited from his ancestors. . . . It contains . . . the accumulated deposits from the lives of our ancestors, who by their very existence have contributed to the differentiation of the species.[3]

The collective unconscious in the newborn exists in a state of diffusion, a grown-togetherness of indistinct and undeveloped structures and processes.[4] In the course of human development, these potentials of the self become differentiated into separate functions and structures, grouping into systems and becoming increasingly more complex, as the personality takes on the richness of its singular traits of individuality. But at this collective stage, the various systems of thought and rationality have not begun to reach levels of abstraction where some aspect of the self's experience can be isolated from its context. Systems of feeling are incapable of shades of valuing. Systems of perceiving are too diffused with surrounding objects and persons in the external world. In short, psychic functioning, both internal and external, lies in a state of concrescence.

In his studies, Jung found similarities between the dreams of children and the child folklore of various cultures and historical periods. Further comparison, as we shall see more fully later, revealed similarities with the cultural forms of our ancestral history, including the folklore and mythology of primitive peoples. He also observed that such primitive states are characteristic of certain mental states in the dissociations of the mentally disturbed. These various, yet related, correlations prompted Jung to posit a collective base to the mind. Such a base is grounded in and emerges out of the psychological evolution of people, a state prior to an individual's personal history. Yet this common base links the individual to humankind in general. Every child begins with the psychic potential last attained by the human race.[5]

Since the newborn inherits both physical and psychological potentials of development, Jung held that the mind and the body are two aspects of one reality in a reciprocal and continuous relation to itself.[6] Neither should be subsumed into the other, as if one were secondary to the other. He rejected any suggestion of psychophysical parallelism, as if there were no interstitial connection between mind and body, but he also held that mind and body cannot simply be identified with each other.

Jung drew from physical concepts of light to illustrate his view of the connection between mind and body. Light is unified, but it contains infrared and ultraviolet aspects. So, too, it is with mind and body.[7] The collective unconscious, although ultimately a single reality, bears both an infrared or *ecto* psychic aspect in its relation to the body and an ultraviolet or *endo* psychic aspect, in which mental processes are separate from physical control. The physiological and biochemical aspect of this reality passes over in its most basic level into the body. At this level, mind is virtually analogous to the autonomous systems of the body. Mind is materialized, subject to biochemical and neurological processes. Likewise, the more physical the mind at this level, the more primitive, archaic, and instinctive it is.

For purposes of analysis, however, a "cut-off" line is required between mind and body, so that one can properly speak of the mind as a distinct system. At this point we find an important philosophical assumption of Jung, one having to do with the correlation between causality and indeterminism. We shall have more to say later about his thinking on this point, but we need to note here that, for Jung, the mind is free from causal control of the autonomous systems of the body to which it bears an "ultraviolet" relation. Instinct is transformed into psychic patterns of functioning. The collective unconscious in this phase bears the potential of producing images which operate as mental processes. Such images, arising from the depths of the mind, are represented in the cultural forms of mankind everywhere. They reflect humankind's universal and collective depths.

Basic to Jung's concept is the view that this collective base of psychological functioning conforms to laws and predispositions in essentially the same way that the body conforms to tendencies of physical development. Jung's concept of the *archetype* refers to the primordial images and mental patterns which originate in and remain partially governed by the collective base of the mind. Since these images recapitulate the evolution of humankind and the common human situations of all people everywhere, they reflect innate potentials of human development. Furthermore, when such images become operative in the mind, they provide the means by which the collective potentials can cease to be merely latent and can become effectively realized by the individual.

We can now speak more clearly of the self-realization tendency. "The meaning and purpose of the process [of self-realization]," Jung writes, "is the realization, in all its aspects, of the personality originally hidden away in the embryonic germ-plasm, the production and unfolding of the original, potential wholeness."[8] Self-realization is a natural and spontaneous process, through which the potentials of the self are made available to the individual through the depths of his or her own mind. It is as if the innumerable and ever-recurrent experiences and situations of humankind are indelibly fixed in the mind as a ready-made predisposition of human functioning. For example, the newborn child seems predisposed toward some form of response in relation to the mother. This is a prototypal situation, which, through constant repetition, has made a permanent impression on the collective base of the human psyche.[9]

Jung never analyzed the stages of human development as extensively as have contemporary thinkers. He did, however, attempt to identify the various aspects of self-development and the critical issues in the life history, and there is considerable similarity between Jung's understanding of the dynamics of the self-realization tendency and some of the prevalent contemporary theories of human development. Such current theory seems to hold that maturing human beings have infixed within their organisms a sequential series of physical, psychic, and social potentials. These potentials gradually emerge, and interact with, and are codetermined by significant persons and experiences within our social and cultural environment.[10] Emerging potentials are reciprocally regulated, completed, and invested with meaning through interaction with the concrete setting of one's personal history.

Jung held a similar view, although, as we said, he did not elaborate it in such detail. He referred to the interaction between the developing child and the environment as a process of unconscious identification. Furthermore, the dynamics of this process relate individuals throughout their lifetime to their environment and to the social patterns and cultural assumptions of the community around them. Basically, it reflects an indiscriminate projection or introjection between internal states and external objects. The child of few years, particularly, is a reflection of collective and environmental influences, owing to this identification. The really significant point in Jung's view is that human relations and cultural forms are not merely secondary to the depths of the mind and its tendencies. Instead, culture expresses the depths of the self and is an avenue to those depths.

It is plausible, Jung believed, to hold that the collective depth of the mind itself has been modified through the course of human evolution. Our potentials are themselves changing. Each generation "adds an infinitesimally small amount of variation and differentiation" to the accumulated, ancestral deposit of human experience.[11] Collective potentials are lived out in concrete embodiment in the real world, and this transaction between the self and the world probably alters the self.

THE STRUCTURES AND DYNAMICS OF THE SELF: SYSTEMS IN MOVEMENT

We turn now from the origins of the self to the development of distinct structures and dynamics. This is, above all, a differentiating process, the realization of original, collective potentials. Our purpose here will be not to present a series of steps toward selfhood, but to offer an exposition of the interpretive framework by which Jung viewed the dynamic processes of the self.

Of course, we do not experience our daily life in the technical categories that follow, and no claim is made that we do. The events of everyday living are transacted in the folk idioms of ordinary human conversation. What Jung offers us is a conceptual way of viewing the processes implied in the normal course of living, providing us with a perspective for deeper self-knowledge.

We said earlier that Jung's work coincides with certain recent developments in the life sciences. To show more fully this correspondence, we need a concept that affords explanatory power to Jung's thought in particular and to the life sciences in general. Such a uniting concept is the *open system.*

The open system is a view of reality increasingly employed in the life sciences. Over against that biological view which reduces the organism to isolated organs or systems, the open system conceives of highly interacting, complex, and overlapping elements, related to each other contextually.[12] A system is itself composed of extensive subsystems to which it is the wider context, and all are in a state of perpetual transformation. Thus a system is something more than the sum of its components, and any system's functioning within its superordinate system is different from its functioning in isolation. Only by considering a system's constituent subsystems and its larger context can it be understood.

A system is both centered and segregated. It is capable of extensive differentiation and greater complexity. At the same time the system bears characteristics of unity and integration. It tends to be centered either on some point or on some function within its overlapping context. Being centered, it possesses degrees of autonomy and uniqueness.

Every organic system maintains itself by a process of perpetual change of components. In fact, its very existence depends on its capacity to receive materials into itself and thus to change. For such change to take place, there has to be an inflow and an outflow between the system and its field. A system is *open* when materials or influences enter or leave it. It is closed when such interaction or change does not occur. Though the open system may attain a stationary state, in which it seems to exhibit a noncontextual and time-independent persistence, closer examination reveals even here a process of perpetual change through the building up and tearing down of subsystems.[13] Since an open system receives materials from other sources, it is not dependent entirely upon its own components. Nor is it bound by a never-changing set of conditions. Hence, a system can reach the same state or function by several different routes.

We can also view the self as an open system. This self system, however, like any other organic system, must be regarded from several angles. From one point of view, the self is the *total system* of the psyche. It is the superordinate system in relation to which the various structures and subsystems of the mind stand. From a second viewpoint, the self is the *centralizing tendency* of the psyche as a whole. It is the central point and function around which are clustered and integrated all the structures and dynamics. As one moves toward selfhood, one moves toward greater integrity and individuality. One becomes a unique center of one's personal history. From yet another standpoint, the self is the whole within which and in relation to which progressive differentiation and complexity proceed. The distinct structures of the self must be viewed in relation to the larger ground to which all are related. From a fourth vantage point, the self can be understood as the *goal* of human development. But this goal, grounded in a collective base, can be reached from a wide variety of developmental histories. Finally, the self, in yet another aspect, is an *archetypal tendency* which predisposes us toward human development.

The self system is comprised of these various aspects concurrently. Selfhood presupposes the development of each aspect and the mutual regulation of each in relation to the others. While the content of any individual life is the singular embodiment of its time and place in history and in the world, the structures of its self system partake of these various aspects.

The concept of the self system, however, reflects movement, interaction, and process. In fact, it is preeminently a dynamic conception; the open system is a process. An image from music provides an illustrative analogy. The movement of the processes of selfhood is like the flow of musical process in Igor Stravinsky's *The Rite of Spring*. In that work, various elements and movements, expressed and given musical form by the various instruments, all participate in one flowing process. New elements emerge out of the process. Flowing out of the whole but having an autonomy of their own, they stand opposed to one another at one point, merge into each other at another, harmonize at yet a third place, and flow into new concrescences of tone and form later. At no one moment is the work reducible to its antecedents. The work affords a sense of wholeness, of differentiated elements and developments, and of synthesis. There is throughout a sense of continuity and direction, even at moments of apparent discontinuity.

This understanding of process can clarify the meaning of some of Jung's more popular concepts. No two of his constructs were more misunderstood in popular psychology than those of extraversion and introversion. Recalling our definition of the steady state, we are prepared to grasp the way Jung employed these two concepts. Basically, they refer to relatively enduring attitudes or orientations of personality. A multitude of traits and processes become constellated so as to form a fairly constant tendency in the personality. Extraversion refers to the general propensity of the person to respond positively toward the environment. Introversion reflects a relatively enduring tendency to withdraw from the external world into one's internality.

While the given person's attitude may be slightly more developed on one side or the other, daily living for everyone entails adaptation to both external and internal reality. Everyone must function consistently in the world of work, of social systems, of family, and of cultural forms. At the same time, everyone must listen to internal states, to feelings, and to undeveloped resources within the self. Progression is the "daily advance of psychological adaptation" into creative interaction with the world.[14] Regression reflects adaptation to internal needs. Mental health requires adaptation on both inner and outer fronts.

Any moment in the self's development can be viewed from both a causal and a purposive standpoint. In this latter assumption, Jung parted company with many of his contemporaries. Any moment in the life history, to be sure, can be traced to its origins and initial conditions, to a sequential series of connections and antecedent causes. Fundamentally, however, this causal view of a psychic occasion is a closed system. Such an occasion is reducible to initial conditions which follow a causal sequence with no exchange of incoming influences.

The purposive or final perspective, on the other hand, considers the uniqueness of a psychic moment. Such a moment is a novel and unique configuration of the self, reflecting something other than the sum of a series of causal sequences. It is prospective and purposive, insofar as it possesses future intentions and directions. The self, from this purposive standpoint, arrives at any moment by way of paths that elude sequential analysis. Expressing this dual perspective, Jung says:

> It is customary to effect a theoretically inadmissible compromise by regarding a process as partly causal, partly final—a compromise which gives rise to all sorts of theoretical hybrids but which yields, it cannot be denied, a relatively faithful picture of reality.[15]

One consequence of this apparently contradictory view is that the self and its subsystems may both "run down" in a causal sense and "increase in energy" through progressive differentiation and openness. Also implied in this view is the compensatory and self-regulating tendency of psychic systems in relation to one another. Therefore, the differentiating, integrating, and self-regulating processes contain within themselves the risk of disintegration, dissociation, and self-alienation. Thus, in the process of self-realization—the progressive differentiation into complex psychic systems and into relatively stable orientations—certain functions and attitudes inevitably become more developed than others, resulting in a degree of one-sidedness.[16] Whatever is excluded from consciousness remains in an infantile, archaic, or unconscious state, but retains its potency for the tasks of daily existence. Conscious adaptation inhibits and counteracts these unconscious complexes.

In this state of imbalance, the self is alienated from its total self. A mild form of such imbalance arises when the directions and orientations of normal living are opposed and compromised by equally potent moods, feelings, and needs of the unconscious. Such an imbalance can be viewed both causally, in terms of the elements and stages leading to conflict, and purposively, in terms of the potential transformations inherent in it. In one sense such imbalance reflects a moral problem, inasmuch as it offers the individual an opportunity to assume responsibility for his or her total selfhood.

But even greater degrees of imbalance can occur, producing dissociation and disintegration. In this state, consciousness and the requirements of daily living are overthrown or even controlled by partial systems of the self, especially by the more archaic complexes of the unconscious. The self is alienated from itself both inwardly and outwardly.

With the promise of differentiation and self-realization comes the risk of fragmentation and self-alienation. But in both degrees of imbalance, the forces that have clustered in conflict contain within themselves the possibility of their own transformation. They reflect not only where the personality has been but also where it is tending. Even the most chaotic crises contain the potential of radical conversion.

ARCHETYPE: BRIDGING THE SELF AND ITS WORLD

We have seen how the structures and dynamics of the self develop out of an original wholeness common to all. Now we turn to yet another aspect of the self, to those processes by which individuals' responsibility for their own potential is sustained over their lifetime. The self continues to transcend itself in a self-surpassing realization of new potentials arising out of its archetypal depths. In some respects, this is a humanizing process, as individuals become identified with their common humanity. Each person bears responsibility for identifying with and incorporating the deeply human sensibilities inherent in common humanity.

The goal of the early years of life, including young adulthood, is the development of a highly individuated self. This is the time for the differentiation of a highly conscious, directed, and outwardly adapted self. Establishing one's place in the world of work, and taking responsibility for marriage and parenthood, require successful adaptation to the external world. The processes of abstraction, rationality, and direction are at a premium. At the center of consciousness stands a subsystem, the *ego*, the "I," which directs, abstracts, and adapts. The ego is predisposed in the larger self and is differentiated out of it. The realization of consciousness and its functioning is a basic task of these early years.

In this new phase of selfhood now under discussion, self-realization takes on a new aspect. From this new vantage point, consciousness and the ego are partial systems related to the archetypal ground common to all. The archetypal self, like an underground stream, continually inclines the self toward its common humanity, its intrinsic potential. Of this process, Jung says, "The inevitable one-sidedness of our conscious life is constantly being corrected and compensated by the universal human being in us, whose goal is the ultimate integration . . . the assimilation of the ego to a wider personality."[17]

The ego, while still the center of consciousness, ceases to be the center of the personality. Consciousness, confronted by its own limits, enters into a reciprocal regulation with the larger, unconscious self system. It is a centering and integrating process. The individual begins to realize that the values of rationality and technical competence are insufficient for the full life. Yet this transaction between consciousness and one's common humanity is in reality two sides of the same personality.

> If we picture the conscious mind, with the ego as the center, as being opposed to the unconscious, and if we now add to our mental picture the process of assimilating the unconscious, we can think of this assimilation as a kind of approximation of consciousness and unconscious, where the center of the total personality no longer coincides with the ego, but with a point midway between the conscious and the unconscious. This would be the point of a new equilibrium, a new centering of the total personality, a virtual center, which, on account of its focal position between consciousness and unconscious, ensures for the personality a new and more solid foundation.[18]

Never, however, should consciousness be overthrown. This is alienation from one's self as much as over-directedness and extreme rationality. One cannot live in the everyday world and be driven by some partial or irrational system of the unconscious. Assimilating the archetypal depths of the self, instead, involves fundamental shifts in the psychic economy, but without annihilating the values of conscious life.

How do we experience these deepest levels of the mind, and how do we make them an effective part of ourselves? As we saw earlier, Jung believed that *the archetypal depths of the mind are represented in images and symbols*. His intense study of culture, ethnology, and anthropology reflected his effort to explore the meaning of human symbols as expressions of common bases of human nature. In this side of his work he was badly misinterpreted. To anyone reading fragments of his writing, without regard for his overarching purpose, his investigations of folklore, mythology, dreams, and cultural and religious forms seem archaic, occult, and mystical. His method, basically a *comparative* approach, offered a procedure for going behind historical and cultural material to the common bases of the self.

Jung held that the symbols expressing the universal and critical situations of human experience were not merely accidental. Such symbols appear in diverse cultures and in different historical periods. In short, comparative cultural material affords a rich analogy with the determinative moments in the life history. Furthermore, humankind's most profound sensibilities are represented in the humanistic forms of culture and religion. Such forms tend to cluster around basic motifs indicative of the deepest levels of the mind.

If the archetypal depths of the mind are expressed in cultural forms and images, then these same forms afford a bridge to these same depths. The aim of self-realization, seen from this point of view, is to incorporate the archetypal realities contained in the primordial images. In this process the collective self and its potentials move from unconscious, archetypal tendencies to assimilation and embodiment within the personality. The individual partakes of his or her common humanity. The self is expressed in culture, and culture is an avenue to the self. Culture shapes personality, and personality, culture. Jung's views on the transforming power of culture are valuable for scholars of social psychology.

Briefly, two illustrations of these archetypal motifs can be given. One is rebirth, the transition from some moment or state in life to another. The self-transcending tendency of change and renewal is common to humankind everywhere, but the symbols expressing this process are infinite. Sometimes the theme is one of initiation from one state to another, or the death of one state and change into another. Usually, the agents of change are water or fire in these motifs. Sometimes the self is enlarged and sometimes diminished. Most often, rebirth reflects change in the internal state of the self or the self's transformation of its own structure.[19]

Centering of the self is a common motif. Jung called the motifs expressing this process *mandala symbols*. Here, too, the tendency toward integration characterizes a person as human, but the symbols are rich in their variation. In such symbols the center is represented by an innermost point, surrounded by peripheral elements. The cross, for instance, is a preeminent symbol of the centered self. The following dream is illustrative:

> On board ship. The dreamer is busied with a new method of taking his bearings. Sometimes he is too far away and sometimes too near: the right spot is in the middle. There is a chart on which is drawn a circle with its center.[20]

In this brief dream a moment in the life history is depicted. There is a definite sense of movement from past to future. There is direction and purpose. Self-regulation and balance are implied, as well as the peripheral points around the center. But the overwhelming value is centering and self-regulation. In filling in the content of the individual's life, the meaning of these symbols for him or her can be approached.

THE SELF AND CHRIST

Inevitably, Jung's inquiries into the archetype of the self and into its manifestation in religious symbolism led to an interest in Christology. While he never wrote systematically or at length on the relation between the self and Christ, he did approach the problem indirectly on several occasions, for example, in his Terry Lectures at Yale University[21] and in his research into the symbolism of the self in *Aion*.[22] He did have some well-defined views, and here, drawing from several of his works, we shall abstract three principles for understanding his thought.

THE GOD-HUMAN ARCHETYPE:
ORIGINS OF EVERYMAN

The original fact of human nature is the God-human archetype. In view of everything that has been said thus far, should we not say that the archetype of the self is the original fact in human nature? The introduction of the archetype of the God-human here is not an inconsistency, but the elaboration of a new aspect of selfhood, its transpersonal extension. The archetype of the self presupposes an indefinite extension beyond the single personality.

Theoretically, no limits can be assigned to the self. In its collective aspects, in its emergence through evolution and its open relation to the world around it, the self is grounded in reality itself. Jung calls this correlation the cosmic correspondence,[23] a correspondence between the individual as microcosm and the world as macrocosm. The collective base of the self binds one to one's world, yet at the same time it tears one apart from the world as a distinct and unique person. One participates in tendencies toward both a common humanity and an individuality.

The joint inherence of self and world is experienced as the life process, the chief symbol of which is "God." Symbols of God represent an intuition of the union of the self and its grounding in the processes of life, and are most powerful in the personality, centering the self-world correspondence and the self-realization tendency. Self-realization, in relation to God, is represented by such a symbol as the *Imago Dei*. This traditional formula affirms our creation in God's own image, implying an intrinsic relation between the two. *Imago Dei* represents the self-world correspondence, binding us to a common ground and thrusting us toward individuation.

Both *God* and *Imago Dei*, therefore, symbolically point *within* the self and *beyond* it. They express those aspects of the self which are transpersonal and illimitable. At the same time they reflect those aspects of the self which are most immediate and personal. These symbols are found in all cultures and historical periods, even if they represent nothing more than an assumption of the unity and ordering of life. Jung felt strongly that psychology should explore so universal and powerful a symbol and its role in the personality.

Jung never restricted "God" to the unconscious, although he did make other theological speculations. For example, he was convinced that, since the archetype of the God-human relates us to God, theology ought to construct a concept of divine relativity.

> "Absolute" means "cut off," "detached." To assert that God is absolute amounts to placing him outside all connections with mankind. Man cannot affect him or he man. Such a God would be of no consequence at all. We can in fairness only speak of a God who is relative to man, as man is to God . . . That kind of God could reach man.[24]

Self-realization, in one sense, is given from beyond the self, and at the same time it is an inherent tendency. Self-realization, viewed as Jung saw it, becomes a moral problem, insofar as we are responsible for the original potential with which we are endowed.

JESUS CHRIST: THE ARCHETYPE EMBODIED

The life of Jesus Christ can be understood as the personal and historical realization of the God-human archetype. Jesus Christ lived a concrete and unique life, which had, at the same time, an archetypal character.[25] Ultimately, every human life is archetypal in its collective bases. Hence, the clue to understanding Jung's thought is found in a bipolar movement, from microcosm to macrocosm, from the "other" prior to the self to the "other" common with the self, from potential to actual.

In Jesus Christ, we find that the archetype as potential became actual in his life. The archetype as indefinite and illimitable became definite and concretely embodied in him. The archetype as universal became unique. As eternal, in the sense of an ever-present reality, it became unitemporal. The archetype as collective became individuated. We can speak of the self-transcending side of the archetype in Jesus Christ as the "Son of God." We can speak of the personal aspects of his selfhood as the "Son of man."

We are justified, however, in a reverse understanding. On the basis of the archetype of the God-human, we can say that Christ's divine nature refers to his actuality, definiteness, uniqueness, individuality, and unitemporality. Incarnation is, from this point of view, the movement of God into human nature, into embodiment.

To enter history is to become actual and particular, conditioned by time and place in human experience. To understand fully the historical Jesus, we must consider the God-human relation to which Jesus constantly referred and which he sought to make transparent in his life. Anything less is poor history, if we seek to understand Jesus as he understood himself.

The archetype of the God-human requires, according to Jung, the doctrine of homoousia.[26] The movement from microcosm to macrocosm is a transition from two sides of the same reality or "substance." Jung says, "it makes a great deal of difference whether the self is 'of the same nature' as the father or only 'of similar nature'."[27]

THE TASK OF MODERN MAN: WITHDRAWING PROJECTION AND DISCOVERING THE SELF

The archetype of the God-man must be withdrawn from projection onto the historical Christ and must be regarded as the original fact inherent in the nature of the modern person. Projection is the transferring of a subjective content onto an external object. It represents a form of dissociation, since people fail to recognize the content as a part of themselves and to assimilate it into their selfhood. To the extent that the content remains unassimilated, the self is unrealized.

When an archetype is transferred onto an external person, the archetype becomes identified with the other and is dissociated from the self. When this happens, the other person is invested with values originating within the self. The process of projection is intensified if the other possesses qualities which stand as a lure for unconscious identification.

This, to Jung, is exactly the meaning of christological doctrines. The archetype embodied in Christ is also the archetype inherent in everyone. When projection occurs, as it did in the early Christian era, the concrete and historical Jesus virtually vanishes behind the archetypal projections onto him.[28] He is absorbed into the surrounding religious systems of this time and becomes their archetypal exponent.

As early as 1937, Jung identified one of the crucial problems of New Testament scholarship:

> This character [the archetypal character of the life of Christ] can be recognized from the numerous connections of the biographical details with worldwide myth-motifs. These undeniable connections are the main reason why it is so difficult for researchers into the life of Jesus to construct from the gospel reports an individual life divested of myth. In the gospels themselves the factual reports, legends, and myths are woven into a whole.[29]

If modern persons are to assume responsibility for themselves, they must withdraw their projections from the historical Christ. Under the condition of projection, they cannot become responsible for their own relationship with God, since God remains outside any connection with himself, and one's archetypal depths are not experienced as part of one's own selfhood. When the archetypal symbols are withdrawn from projections, however, they can be dealt with as disclosures of the original nature of modern humanity. Now the symbols can manifest the primordial reality of a common humanity. One can argue, in fact, that it was precisely these archetypal realities that Jesus sought to reveal to others.

When Jung calls on modern persons to assume responsibility for their own depths by withdrawing their projections, he is *not* doing away with the archetypal symbols. One continues to experience one's original reality by means of symbols, the representatives of archetypal realities. The depths of the self are expressed in the symbols and images of religion, culture, and mythology. They possess a mediating character, mediating the original self to the immediate self. They are vehicles of psychic transformation. "Experience of the Mass," Jung says, illustrating the transforming power of religious symbols, "is therefore a participation in a transcendence of life overcoming all limitations of time and space. It is a moment of eternity within time."[30]

In this dramatic Christian liturgy, the eternal aspect of the God-human archetype is experienced in unitemporality, and a moment in present individual and communal history shares in the ongoing depths of a common, timeless humanity. Such symbolic quality in religion demands preservation. Returning to the gospels, Jung says that "they would immediately lose their character of wholeness if one tried to separate the individual from the archetypal with a critical scalpel."[31]

God from Jung's point of view, seeks to become embodied in one's experience, to be incarnated in the world. When we know our own depths, our inherent grounding in the divine reality, God becomes effectually and concretely present in human affairs and human experience. Modern individuals must take their potential for self-realization with absolute moral seriousness. Alienated from their own depths, they are alienated from God. And alienated from God, they are estranged from themselves.

DISCOVERING THE SELF: AN APPROACH TO KNOWING

It is possible for us now to look backward at Jung's psychology of the self, to examine the methodology implied in his work. Methodology, as used here, refers to the presuppositions, delineations of problems, and methods of inquiry in Jung's work. Since Jung refused "to play favorites" with various philosophical categories, his methodology appears, at first, to be filled with contradictions, which, when viewed as part of a whole system, are actually correlations of categories taken from different sources. Furthermore, his strenuous effort to preserve these correlations opened up avenues of inquiry which were to be recognized by others only later. To recall, we have observed his syntheses of mind and body, of causality and indeterminism, of the individual and the collective, of process and effect, and of the transpersonal and personal.

Basic to his work was a bipolar approach, which sought both *understanding* of the individual in particular and *knowledge* of humankind in general. The former concern left him throughout his career an avowed clinician, interested in the uniqueness of persons. The latter concern moved him toward a persistent investigation of common features of human nature, toward cultural anthropology, ethnology, and religion. In *The Undiscovered Self*, one of his last works and one where his methodology was fully explicated, Jung wrote:

> There is and can be no self-knowledge based on theoretical assumptions, for the object of self-knowledge is an individual—a relative exception and an irregular phenomenon. Hence, it is not the universal and the regular which characterize the individual, but rather the unique. He is not to be understood as a recurrent unit but as something unique and singular which in the last analysis can neither be known nor compared with anything else.[32]

Failure to give complete recognition to the concrete individual renders a distorted picture of human uniqueness.[33]

Taken by itself, this viewpoint left Jung open to a one-sided criticism. Jung took the ideas and images of people seriously. Hence, some critics found him too relativistic. The fact that an idea or image exists in the mind, they argued, is no ground for its validity. Mental images must be subjected to criteria of verification, especially in the realm of religion.[34]

Curiously, the other side of Jung's method was concerned precisely with establishing an objective basis for mental ideas and images and for cultural and religious symbols. In fact, because Jung kept an open mind consistent with his phenomenal method, he refused to dismiss cultural and religious symbols, to be indifferent to them, or to assume that enlightenment would somehow eliminate them. Such universal symbols were, to him, the avenue for exploring humankind's common characteristics. Employing the comparative method, then, he sought the inherent tendencies, structures, and dynamics of the mind. His studies here led to the concept of the archetype. Interestingly, later in his career Jung often referred to the collective unconscious as the objective psyche, the common base of the self. Again, in *The Undiscovered Self*, Jung wrote:

> At the same time man, as a member of a species, can and must be described as a statistical unit; otherwise nothing general could be said about him. For this purpose he has to be regarded as a comparative unit. This results in a universally valid anthropology or psychology ... with an abstract picture of man as an average unit from which all individual features have been removed. ...

> Knowledge of man, or insight into human character, presupposes
> all sorts of knowledge about mankind in general.[35]

Unavoidably perhaps, such views left Jung subject to criticisms from another side. He was too withdrawn, too introspective, and too occult, some scholars claimed. He was not interested in the ordinary events of everyday human affairs. Indeed, it must be acknowledged that Jung's writings in comparative religion and ethnology, read out of context, seem strange to the modern mind. But by now it should be clear that this was but one side of Jung's method, making use of the tools available to him at the time for investigating aspects of human experience which he deemed important.

Jung constantly disclaimed any formal "expertise" in philosophy and theology. In fact, he rejected philosophy as he understood it formally. But the case can be made that he worked with an implicit process conception of reality and with a theology of divine relativity. Movement and direction pervade his thought. We must conclude that he held to his assumptions about the holistic, dynamic, and purposive nature of life in the midst of opposing presuppositions held by the thinkers of his day. To stress effect as well as cause, future as well as past, mind and body as unified, collided, in Jung's time, with the then widely-held presuppositions of mechanism, reductionism, and reactivism. The lines of disagreement can now be recognized more distinctly.

Jung did understand science differently from many of his contemporaries. Once more, we find that in this theory of scientific objectivity he refused to play favorites. The inquiring subject and investigated object, to him, existed in a strict relation to each other. No doubt his understanding of scientific method was influenced by his personal acquaintance with the microphysicist Wilhelm Pauli. He became increasingly interested in the complementarity principle in physics, and applied its implications to psychology. This principle seeks to recognize and to allow for the effect of the observer on the observed. Reality, in this conception of scientific method, forfeits some of its objectivity. Personal and tacit aspects of the experimental situation are recognized as part of the scientific process.

In accordance with this principle, Jung viewed the researching psychologist as standing in a strict relation to the mind, his object of inquiry. In effect, this meant that the inquirer must study the human mind within the medium of the mind. The conscious mind may be able to make the remainder of the self an object, but so, too, can consciousness receive images from the depths of the mind, as in dreams. At best, a psychological conception is limited to gradations of probability within the multidimensional field of the mind.

This system-theory methodology is firmly established in the current life sciences. We are still in a time of transition in the philosophy of science, however, as indicated by this criticism of Jung written in 1962:

> For most of us scientifically trained Occidentals who worship objectivity and stress causality . . . this basically oriental approach to reality . . . stresses the *configuration* rather than the *sequence* of events. . . . Despite strenuous effort at understanding, much of Jung's writings simply do not "make sense" to us.[36]

Jung, we have said, held an implicit theology of divine relativity. God is related to man in his archetypal depths and is always seeking embodiment in human experience and human history. The archetype of the God-man consists, we saw, of transpersonal and illimitable depths, which are nevertheless personal and immediate. Divine reality seeks concrete realization in man. One Protestant theologian writes of Jung's theology:

> The changes to which man is subject, his whole evolution, are in the last resort nothing less than a reflection of the becoming of God—the pattern of emergent Deity. . . . We can say with some truth, then, that this places Jung in a spiritual current whose representatives in philosophy are generally reckoned among the so-called "life-philosophers" . . . their theme is the changing and emerging God. . . . This doctrine is closely connected with the doctrine of the relativity of God; indeed, it is its necessary counterpart.[37]

We should not attempt to push Jung's conception of God beyond the point where he was content to leave it. But his view of God as both absolute and relative has parallel development, for example, in the contemporary theistic philosophy of Charles Hartshorne. Hartshorne's theory, elaborating and extending the process views of Alfred North Whitehead, has, in turn, greatly informed the work of several modern Christian theologians.[38]

In Hartshorne's thought, reality is a social system of interdependent and interpenetrating creatures, who exist and endure through the presence and influence of a dominant member. God is the supreme social creature who coordinates all creatures into a complex society.[39] God influences his world in a supremely relative and social manner. As such, he is both absolute and relative. If God were only absolute, he could in no way increase in value, would be self-sufficient, and could be entirely independent of his creation.[40] If he were only relative, he would be perfect and supreme in no way and would in every way be subject to change.

But although God is perfect and complete in some respects, he is not so in all. God's enduring character, in this conception, is his infallibility of knowing, his perfection of loving and valuing, and his adequacy with respect to his eternal purpose.[41] At the same time, he genuinely lives and shares in the actual world of each creature, taking its concreteness into himself. He is supremely related to all creatures at all times and in every aspect of their being.[42]

It has been our claim that Jung's self theory offers a rich resource for integrating many developments in contemporary anthropology, including its theological aspect. No attempt has been made here to utilize Jung for a broader interdisciplinary theory, although an interpretive framework has been present throughout in attempting to show his relevance. In making this material available and showing its relevance, a necessary preliminary step has been taken.

Notes

1. Carl Gustav Jung, *The Structure and Dynamics of the Psyche,* vol. 8 of *The Collected Works,* ed. Herbert Read, Michael Fordham, and Gerhard Adler, trans. R.F.C. Hull, Bollingen Series 20 (New York: Pantheon Books, 1960), p. 200.
2. *Ibid.,* p. 51.
3. *Ibid.,* p. 349.
4. Jung, *Psychological Types,* trans. H. Godwin Baynes (New York: Harcourt, Brace & Company, 1924), p. 533.
5. Jung, *The Structure and Dynamics . . . ,* p. 51ff.
6. *Ibid.,* p. 17.
7. *Ibid.,* p. 215.

8. Jung, *Two Essays on Analytical Psychology,* vol. 7 of *The Collected Works* (1953), p. 108.
9. Jung, *The Archetypes and the Collective Unconscious,* pt. 1, vol. 9 of *The Collected Works* (1959), p. 48.
10. Erik H. Erikson, *Childhood and Society* (New York: W.W. Norton & Company, 1950), p. 33.
11. Jung, *The Structure and Dynamics . . .* , p. 376.
12. Ludwig von Bertalanffy, "An Outline of General System Theory," *The British Journal for the Philosophy of Science,* 1, no. 2 (1950), pp. 143ff.
13. *Ibid.,* p. 155.
14. Jung, *The Structure and Dynamics . . .* , p. 32.
15. *Ibid.,* p. 6.
16. Jung, *Psychogenesis in Mental Disease,* vol. 3 of *The Collected Works* (1960), pp. 234ff.
17. *The Structure and Dynamics . . .* , p. 292.
18. Jung, *Two Essays . . .* , p. 219.
19. Jung, *The Archetypes and the Collective Unconscious,* p. 119.
20. Jung, *Psychology and Alchemy,* vol. 12 of *The Collected Works* (1953), p. 100.
21. Jung, *Psychology and Religion* (New Haven: Yale University Press, 1938).
22. Jung, *Aion: Researches into the Phenomenology of the Self,* vol. 9 of *The Collected Works* (1953).
23. Jung, *The Undiscovered Self,* trans. R.F.C. Hull (Boston: Little, Brown and Company, 1957), p. 60.
24. Jung, *Two Essays . . .* , p. 233.
25. Jung, *Psychology and Religion: West and East,* vol. 11 of *The Collected Works* (1958), p. 88.
26. This classical doctrine held that God and Christ were of the *same* "substance" instead of *similar* substance. Also see Jung, *Psychology and Religion,* p. 193.
27. Jung, *Symbols of Transformation,* vol. 5 of *The Collected Works* (1956), p. 391.
28. *Psychology and Religion,* p. 154.
29. *Ibid.,* p. 88.
30. *Psychological Reflections: An Anthology of the Writings of C.G. Jung,* ed. Jolande Jacobi, Bollingen Series 31 (New York: Pantheon Books, 1953), p. 324.
31. *Psychology and Religion,* p. 88.
32. *The Undiscovered Self,* p. 9.
33. This concept of *understanding* can be compared with Gordon Allport's

theory of the *idiographic* method in psychology. See his *Becoming* (New Haven: Yale University Press, 1955), p. 19.

34. Erich Fromm, *Psychoanalysis and Religion* (New Haven: Yale University Press, 1950), p. 15.

35. *The Undiscovered Self*, p. 9. Again, compare this concept of *knowledge* with Allport's theory of the *nomothetic* method in *Becoming*, p. 27.

36. William Douglas, "The Influence of Jung's Work: A Critical Comment," *Journal of Religion and Health*, 6, no. 3 (1962), p. 261.

37. Hans Schaer, *Religion and the Cure of Souls in Jung's Psychology*, trans. R.F.C. Hull, Bollingen Series 21 (New York: American Book-Stratford Press, 1950), pp. 214ff.

38. See for example: Norman Pittinger, *The World Incarnate* (New York: Harper and Brothers, 1959); Schubert Ogden, *Christ without Myth* (New York: Harper and Brothers, 1961); Daniel D. Williams, *God's Grace and Man's Hope* (New York: Harper and Brothers, 1949); and John Cobb, *A Christian Natural Theology* (Philadelphia: The Westminster Press, 1965).

39. Charles Hartshorne, *Reality As Social Process* (Glencoe, Ill.: The Free Press, 1953), p. 135.

40. *Ibid.*, p. 155ff.

41. *Ibid.*, p. 202.

42. *Ibid.*, p. 135.

John P. Dourley

Jung, Tillich, and Aspects of Western Christian Development*

I. THE STATEMENT OF THE QUESTION

Through the work of Jung and Tillich there runs as a constant and urgent refrain: the disturbing contention that Westerners have lost their capacity for religious experience because of their progressive loss of an understanding of the nature of religion itself.[1] By religious experience both men mean the human capacity to experience immediately the presence of God within human life and consciousness. Both share the conviction that the reality of God is imbedded in the fabric of life itself as the ultimate source of its integration, creativity, growth and enhancement. Since, then, the religious dimension of life is for them more than an optional super-addition to life from beyond, its loss is greatly to be mourned. For both the attenuation or total atrophy of our religious capacity and sensitivity means the loss of our vital relation to the source of our fullest humanization within ourselves and so cripples our personal and social realization wherever such loss occurs. Since both men, from their own perspectives, locate the reality of God as that immanent power within life which offers to life its fulfillment, the diminution of the religious sense means for them that people have lost touch with the deeper divine and life-giving source of their own being.[2] Human beings thus divested of their sense of their intrinsic holiness and worth look upon nature and others as equally destitute and so as susceptible to being formed and ordered in accord with the demands of shallow and technical rationality. Such an impoverished world view has forced upon people a truncated vision of their own humanity which has severed them from the divine in their depths

* The research for this article was done in part at the C.G. Jung Institute in Zurich on research grants from the Canada Council.

and so from their most creative source of energy. Understood in this sense the loss of the religious sensitivity necessarily impoverishes the resultant human situation, since by divesting people of their divine interior resources and energies it approaches an attack on the will to life itself.

Both Jung and Tillich carry their indictment of the current moribund state of human religious sensitivity further. Each in his own way contends that the Western religious and theological development itself is in large part responsible for religion's current demise at the heart of which lies the loss of a vital sense of divine immanence by the major religious traditions themselves. In short certain identifiable options taken by major theological, philosophical, and ecclesiastical authorities and events have paradoxically contributed to the death of religion in our day. By progressively locating the reality of God beyond life these traditions, authored and shaped by Christian minds, have distracted us from consideration of the possibility of experiencing God within life as its core, depth or ground. Thus Jung and Tillich argue, with very little variation, that the Christian theological development in certain of its major thrusts has, by a peculiar enantiodromia, made it difficult if not impossible to experience the power of the very symbols whose experiential meaning theology attempts to mediate to each age. Rather than lead us into the inaugural and life-giving revelatory experience out of which the symbols were born, theology has rendered them an unintelligible burden for the believer by locating the God of whom these symbols speak outside of life rather than in its depths from which both the experience of God and the symbols used to capture it are generated.[3]

To understand this point, more must be said about the general understanding of the nature of religion which both men share. For both religion is a constitutive (and perhaps the deepest) level of human awareness. For Jung the unconscious would seem to be the universal generator of the religious experience and so of the positive religions.[4] Tillich understands reason in its ground as so participating in the divine that reason in vital touch with its depth is for him religious reason or reason in revelatory ecstasy.[5] For both men, then, revelation and the process of symbol formation are closely related and are more than a process of reception of information about God given from beyond and to be read in a spirit of rational literalism.

Rather, revelation with its consequent constellation of symbols occurs when reason or ego consciousness comes into powerful intersection with its own depths and receives from its own depth perception of reality the symbols that give transforming meaning to life. Hence both men see as hostile to the human condition that understanding of humanity which would deny the reality of such depths of life. For both it would be a denial of the possibility of religion by a denial of the life-giving depth of life within life, the experience of which gives rise to the reality of religion.

Such a denial would be based on a misinterpretation of the direction from which religion happens. It would reduce revelation to simple information or to access to a certain previously inaccessible facticity. It would reduce the symbolic to the literal. It would function to prevent us from entering fully into the experience out of which our religious symbols arise and into which they and their theological elaboration are meant to lead their possessors. All of these defects derive from the loss of the sense of divine immanence in life as the possibility of the religious or revelatory experience. With this loss religion has lost its sense of mystery and mysticism and so has ceased in many instances to be a positive force in the lives of those who are "religious." The revelation has become a foreign imposition which serves to divide human beings in their self-understanding between the areas of faith and reason rather than to integrate and heal such divisions. It is to this alien nature of revelation and to its wholly other God that Tillich points when he notes that such a God is not the God from whom we are estranged but to whom we belong and in whose being we continue to participate even in our estrangement. Such a God is a simple stranger whose entry into human life further shatters its already tenuous unities.[6] For Tillich such an intrusion demonizes God and dehumanizes humanity.[7]

This analysis of the current religious situation reveals further problems. Because Christian religious and philosophical speculation has led to a widespread misinterpretation of the meaning and dynamic of religious experience in seeing it originating from without in the overture of a wholly transcendent God to humanity, this does not mean that the powers which generate religion within life have become inoperative. On the contrary, Tillich and Jung argue that these powers cannot be stilled because they are endemic to the

human psyche and being and so neither ontologically nor psychologically can they be extirpated from the human condition. Thus when
the conscious awareness of divine immanence as the basis of our
sense of ultimacy and so of the religious is lost it by no means
follows that our religion-making capacity is rendered inoperative.
Rather human beings, even when they have misunderstood the nature of religion, are forced by their nature to exercise their religion-
making capacity but under a host of disguises which are all the more
insidious and perverse precisely because they are no longer recognized as religious.[8]

In general the perversion of religion through the misconception
of its nature takes on the form of idolatry or the attribution of
ultimacy to the less than ultimate.[9] Jung and Tillich would seem to
agree that religion itself can become a form of life-constricting
idolatry when it reduces its totality to a part of itself. Tillich, in
particular, points to a religion which is only a moralism, only an
intellectualism, only a willfulness or only an affection as instances of
serious distortions of the meaning of religion with fragmenting and
repressive consequences in the life of the believer because so much
of the believer's humanity is denied in his or her belief.[10] In each of
these instances a part becomes the whole and the wholeness which
the true religious experience should offer is denied in the name of
religion itself.

The loss of the conscious awareness that the religious experience arises out of life itself has even more serious consequences
when hidden ultimates are associated with political ideologies which
then take on the function of religions often combined with a denial
of religion and nearly always combined with the denial that they
themselves are religious.[11] In such cases the absolute placed beyond
criticism is free to run riot usually with destructive consequences to
the society possessed by it.[12] Thus the effort to exorcise our sense of
the immanental genesis of religion or of our awareness of the absolute has had disastrous effects for both religious and political beings.
In the religious sphere it has placed God totally beyond humanity
and has in effect turned religion into an alienating and frequently
fragmenting force in life. In the political sphere, because the exor-
cism is bound to fail, its attempt has been the occasion of the usher-
ing in of a host of political gods whose demand for human sacrifice

has far outstripped that of the traditional deities. The history of the ideological struggles of the last two centuries bear stark witness to this process and problem.

Yet neither thinker is ultimately pessimistic about the human and religious situation. Both offer correctives to the religious plight they document. Tillich called for a return to an older theology based upon a strong sense of divine immanence as the basis for an understanding of both God's integrating presence to life and of his transcendence beyond it. He was convinced that this religious sensibility was most powerfully expressed in the Platonic-Augustinian tradition and in its historical recurrences.[13] The sense of the point of coincidence of the infinite and the finite in all that is lies at the heart of his understanding of God as the ground or power of being.[14] By it he meant that the being of every existent, human and sub-human, participated dialectically in the being of God wherein its truest reality was located from which it had fallen in existence yet from which it was never severed and to which it was driven to return.[15]

Jung, too, admitted a certain indebtedness to this side of Plato and Augustine[16] and called upon humanity to look inward to a power in the depths of each individual working there for the wholeness of the individual yet in some sense "supraordinate" to the individual and to the totality of individuals while remaining the deepest possibility of their interconnectedness.[17] Moreover he suggested the possibility of a most powerful and innovative natural theology by suggesting to the Christian that his or her symbols, so explicit and sophisticated in their current state, are somehow the possession of humankind itself and the fruit of the collective human experience.[18] Jung's spirit in here suggesting that the psyche is *naturaliter Christiana* is not imperial. Rather his remarks would seem to lay the ground for a more fruitful dialogue between Christian and non-Christian religions by showing that they all arise from a common matrix, share many symbols in common, and, through dialogue, could complement and complete the revelatory experience which gave birth to each. Such a conception of religion would remove claims to the exclusive possession of absolute truth from each positive religion while preserving the relative validity of the revelatory founding experience of each. The benefits to individual and political man of such a conception of religion are too obvious to be drawn out. Let it simply be said that an ecumenism based on a consensus of the unconscious is a distinct possibility in a Jungian framework and may yet prove fruitful in the religious arena.

After this brief statement of their similar evaluation of the modern religious mind, its difficulties, and regenerative possibilities, it seems appropriate to turn to their respective historical analyses of the major theological and ecclesial options which contributed to the current demise of the possibility of a lively and life-giving experience of religion. Following this account of similarities in their analysis of history a conclusion will show the common principles and norms which both thinkers seem to share and which control both their reading of history and their response to the present. At the heart of this response is their recommendation to modern people of the attitude they must adopt toward their being religious if this aspect of their life is to enhance and not destroy it.

II. JUNG AND THE WESTERN RELIGIOUS DEVELOPMENT

1) The Gnostic-Alchemical-Mystical Traditions

Jung, unlike Tillich, did not systematically address the development of Western Christian thought. However, an examination of those aspects of this development with which he does deal reveals a consistent reading of history from a discernibly normative perspective which affirms certain positions, traditions and ways of thinking, and criticizes and offers correctives to others.

A certain ambivalence characterizes much of Jung's thought about the Western Christian development. On the one hand he holds its symbols in high esteem as adequate and even powerful expressions of the psyche.[19] On the other he can accuse orthodoxy of forbidding to the believer the immediate experience of that to which the symbols point and out of which they arise.[20] What seems to ground this ambivalence is Jung's presupposition about the internal genesis of religion in human beings. Thus both his criticism and his admiration of Christianity and of other Western movements which touch the spirit take on consistency when it is posited that Jung, in principle, endorses those aspects of religious thought which internalize the divine and so intensify our awareness of the divine within, and opposes those trends which externalize God and relate him to us in terms of a radical transcendent discontinuity.

Thus Jung understands the origin and continued history of such movements as the gnostics and their continuators, the alchemists, as compensating the loss by orthodox theologies and spiritualities of the immediate experience of the divine reality and so of the unconscious as the source of the numinous.[21] Jung sees the gnostics as the first depth psychologists in vital touch with the unconscious and suggests that their insights could enliven contemporary Christian spirituality.[22] Jung strongly implies that it was their capacity to lead their adherents into the experience of the unconscious which explains both their power and their threat to an orthodoxy in which this ability had been diminished or lost.

Jung understands the significance of the alchemists in much the same way. Their deepest intent was to produce the gold of a consciousness in ever-increasing interplay with the unconscious.[23] Jung sees at the basis of this effort the search for the divine and even Christic presence in matter but more directly in the matter of the psyche itself. Speaking figuratively, they sought to extract the divine from matter and so to liberate God from matter by making him conscious in their own self-consciousness. This awakened and enhanced consciousness could be understood as both a liberation of God from unconsciousness or matter and as an incarnation of the divine in the ego-consciousness.[24] Jung himself seems to judge the position of the alchemists and, by implication, his own as heretical on two counts. In the first instance it seems to presuppose a residual presence of God in matter itself, here to be understood as the matter of the unconscious, and so would seem irreconcilable both with the idea of God as "wholly other" and with the idea of the reality of Christ as extraneous to humanity and to be introduced into history wholly from beyond.[25] In the second instance the alchemical position seems to endow human beings with the capacity for self-redemption and so to deny the priority of God in the redemptive process and the gratuity of grace. Moreover it would seem to extend access to grace well beyond ecclesial boundaries.[26] Here a serious problem must be faced in not only Jung's but the Christian's understanding of where the lines of heresy are to be drawn in the matter of God's presence to us, the nature of this presence, its gratuity and our response to it. Jung seems to imply that in any serious affirmation of God's immanence or ontological participation in creation, humanity and matter is heretical. Similarly he would seem to brand as heretical any serious cooperation of human beings with grace or the education of the experience of the divine although he does admit that the alchemists were very much aware that the success of their venture depended upon the activity of God or "Deo concedente."[27] If these remarks accurately describe Jung's understanding of heresy, one could ask, "If Jung had been fully aware of the orthodox tradition of Christian Platonism wherein God is encountered within life as its deepest residual reality and in which human beings are encouraged to assist in this encounter by turning inward, would he have been so fast in branding this aspect of gnostic and alchemical religiosity as heretical?" It would seem that this side of the tradition would be much more open to dialogue with his insight than that side of Christianity which apparently led him to assume so readily that he and the alchemists were heretical in this matter without further ado. Whatever the answer to this question may be, Jung obviously saw the enduring power of the gnostic and alchemical tradition to lie in their effort and ability to mediate an immediate experience of God or the unconscious. It is this same valuation that underlies Jung's consistent appreciation of the Christian mystical tradition based on his presupposition that such mystical experience constitutes the genesis and substance of religious experience itself and so of the religions and is always closely related to the operation of the unconscious.

2) *The Debate over Universals and the Ontological Argument*

Jung's endorsement of immanental positions is again evident but in a muted and indirect manner in his discussion of the debate over universals and, in particular, in his evaluation of Anselm's formulation of the ontological argument. Jung contends that the debate between the nominalist and realist related closely to the psychology of each. The former are psychologically predisposed to the particular and individual and much less to the communalities shared by individuals. In general Jung classifies them as extravertive. The realist is more impressed by similarities of individuals which then serve as the basis of the formation of universals and which, in turn, can be given an independent existence. Jung types the realist as introvertive.[28]

In his evaluation of this debate Jung takes the balanced position that both sides possess complementary aspects of the truth. An overstatement of nominalism's emphasis on individuality breeds its opposite in the creation of a fictive unity which undergirds all things. On the other hand, unmitigated realism absorbs the individual in the universal and produces an equally untenable imbalance toward diminished individuality.[29] Thus Jung emphasizes the need for complementarity and mutuality in this debate and even grants to Abelard a successful reconciliation of the opposites at the intellectual level.[30]

Yet in his treatment of Anselm's position in the debate Jung would seem to betray his own allegiance and to endorse the realist or Platonic position at least in the appreciation he shows for its capacity to withstand the attacks of some of history's finest minds. Here he argues in a manner almost identical to Tillich that the ontological argument is not an argument but rather a psychological conviction, proper to a certain cast of mind or spirit, that the ideal or absolute must exist.[31] Thus the ontological argument is based on an ineradicable psychological fact which has survived the attacks of Guanilo in Anselm's time and of no less a mind than Kant's at the beginning of the modern period of philosophy. Jung might also have added that it survived its dismissal by Thomas Aquinas in the thirteenth century. The phenomenon of the ontological argument's endurance and sophisticated reaffirmation by Hegel following and contradicting Kant is due, in Jung's opinion, not to its inherent logic but to its being grounded in the universal *consensus gentium*.[32] Jung's position here could be read to mean that the ontological argument grounds its staying power on an immediate psychological experience and hence is psychologically self-evident and as such precedes all rational discourse as a psychic *a priori*.

It is in this context that Jung introduces his concept of *esse in anima* as the mediating unity of the realist's *esse in intellectu* and the nominalist's *intellectu in re*.[33] There are some ambiguities in precisely what Jung means by *esse in anima* but certain of its functions he clearly states. *Esse in anima*, which he closely relates both to the psyche or soul itself and to its power of fantasy, is that in the soul which gives life to the idea and intensifies sensation.[34] Thus it enlivens our psyche with the ideal without being the ideal's puppet-like executor and relates us also to the empirical extramental without being a purely passive recipient of the external. In this sense it mediates between the extremes of an impersonal realism which would make the soul submissive to transpersonal powers and a sense bound empiricism which would make the soul a passive reflector of extramentality. Further *esse in anima* is always experienced as a supreme psychic value. In discussing this aspect of its reality Jung moves into God-language and would seem to attribute to *esse in anima* our constitutional tendency to conceive of the idea of God and usually to locate the reality of this idea of God in some external reality or aspect thereof. Thus Jung's concept of *esse in anima* would seem to account for both the capacity of the psyche to generate the idea of God and to project the idea of God beyond the soul in which it is generated.[35]

Jung, again like Tillich,[36] sees this process operative in Kant's second critique. It would seem, therefore, not unfair to Jung's thought so to interpret it as to mean that he understands Kant's second critique, based upon the human universal experience of the moral demand, to be a form of the ontological argument cast into moral categories. In this he would have the support of certain Kantian scholars and of Tillich himself.[37]

Furthermore Jung argues that the *esse in anima* explains the many different ideas of God which pour in such profusion from the human mind and soul. Rather than being scandalized by the seemingly contradictory multiplication of conceptions of God, Jung is more attracted to the significance of the universality and apparent inevitability of their appearance in the human psyche.[38] In a similar manner, Tillich also argues that faith understood as ultimate concern is universal though that upon which it confers ultimacy and how it conceives of the ultimate may vary greatly.[39] Both thinkers thus ground the particular or positive variants of our experience of God, i.e., the positive religions, on the universal and inescapable fact of this experience itself and both seem to locate the indestructibility of the ontological argument in this experience.[40]

When Jung proceeds to relate *esse in anima* to fantasy and to creative imagination he would seem to imply further that this aspect of the human psyche, which gives rise to our sense of God, is also the source or wellspring of all of our creative productivity in whatever field it may become operative.[41] Furthermore he describes *esse in anima* as the ultimate force for the unifying of those opposites which can sunder and so diminish a healthy life process.[42] This unifying and healing quality would also make of it the ultimate life-giving resource within humanity itself. Thus in his treatment of the ontological argument it is difficult to escape the conclusion that Jung seems well disposed to it and understands it as a statement of the human experience of the immanence, if not of the divine itself, then at least of a power which leads human beings to posit such a reality with an inevitability that is recurrent and universal.

3) Eckhart

It is this same appreciation of the experience of God as arising from within that explains Jung's attraction to the mystical tradition especially as it takes form in Eckhart's thought. Jung would seem to see in Eckhart a classical instance of his own understanding of the psychogenesis of religious experience. In particular he seems to see in some of Eckhart's formulations his own dialectical understanding of how religion can function both as the most positive force in life as well as a negative and destructive force. Early in his fullest treatment of Eckhart's thought, Jung contends that a connection exists between gnosis and German mysticism based upon their shared experience of the interiority of God.[43] Jung argues here explicitly that the ultimate worth of the soul is to be found in its dialectical inherence in the being of God. In dealing with this theme in relation to Eckhart, Jung attributes to him a very modern idea. Under the rubric of God's relativity Jung claims that Eckhart affirms that God and human beings are functions of each other in that we in some real sense contribute to the fullness or realization of God just as God is the source and author of our being. What Jung here attributes to Eckhart is very close to the thought of such moderns as Hegel and Teilhard de Chardin. Hegel's knowledge of and indebtedness to Eckhart are well known.[44] However interpreted, his complex system does affirm that the evolution of human consciousness is at heart a process of divine becoming which culminates in the fulfillment in mutual unity of divine and human self-consciousness. Teilhard's conception of the divine pleroma or fullness to be realized in the eschatological unity of created consciousness with God is

an explicit effort to validate creation and the human effort by showing how it contributes to the being of God and how, therefore, God
must create in order to fulfill himself.[45]

Consistent with his understanding of religion in general, Jung
argues that Eckhart's religious experience originates in the activation of an inner archetypal dynamism which is always accompanied
by a heightened sense of vitality and being.[46] It is at precisely this
point that Jung shows clearly how the activation of this archetype, at
the basis of all religious experience, can act creatively or less creatively. The activation of the dynamism that gives rise to the religious
experience usually leads to a projection of that which is experienced
onto something external to oneself. Thus, by an almost inevitable
trick of our psyche, our experience of God and of ourselves as God's
image leads us to project the reality of God onto something external
to ourselves. In so doing we place the holy entirely beyond ourselves
and so alienate it from ourselves in a process whereby we become its
servant as it becomes our idol. In Jung's view Eckhart's greatness,
and by implication the greatness of all the true mystics, lies in his
withdrawing the projection. In so doing Eckhart became capable of
experiencing both himself and the world as invested with supreme
worth because of his participation in the being of the divine within
himself and within all things.[47] In this sense, quoted with evident
approval by Jung, Eckhart can say God is man and man is God in a
way which strongly affirms God's immanence without denying his
transcendence. The reality of God is experienced within human
beings as the source of their energy and power but always as more
than them. The Godhead is never exhausted in its creative incarna-
tions just as the unconscious is never wholly exhausted in its conscious concretions.[48] In this process of withdrawing the projection
of God which accompanies the experience of God the energies
which we had previously invested in his projection become now
more truly our own. We come to realize that the divine is being
brought to birth in our own depths and the experience of this inner
birth is both the basis of our truest humanity, of our most invigorat-
ing energies, and of our self-understanding as image of God.[49]

Conscious life thus related to the unconscious would become an
ongoing process of the intensifying incarnation of the divine as such
consciousness would be continually nourished by the unconscious
whose power it would ever more concretize without ever exhaust-

ing. The life of the psyche would become an ever more fruitful interplay between consciousness and its life-giving unconscious source.

Thus evidence from his evaluation of these medieval debates and mystical traditions points to Jung's personal endorsement of an immanental point of departure in his understanding of the psychogenesis of religious experience and symbol formation. In this context it is interesting to point out that though he dialogued with Thomistic theologians he never evaluated Aquinas' theology on the specific question of divine immanence. Many of Jung's references to Aquinas relate to the latter's possible authorship of certain alchemical texts, an attribution which Jung came to realize was false. His few references to his reading of genuine works of Aquinas show him to have been unimpressed. He mentions that he failed to find refreshment in Aquinas.[50] He further refers to the lifeless, desert quality of his thought.[51] In a strange seeming inconsistency, Jung admits the harm done to the religious psyche by the introduction of Aristotelianism into thirteenth century scholasticism but speaks of Aquinas in such a way as to minimize his role in this innovation when, in fact, it is commonly recognized as one of Aquinas' major achievements if not his greatest.[52] It is precisely in this juncture of the development of Christian thought that Tillich identifies a major step taken toward the demise of human religious and symbolic sensitivities. Tillich is explicit in arguing that Aquinas' use of Aristotle cut the very quick of the ontological argument and made possible a conception of mind cut off from its depths which Tillich feels led eventually to such rationalist developments as secularism, rational atheism and the double truth theory.[53] More will be said of this when Tillich is treated at greater length. Jung too acknowledges the damage that so disturbs Tillich but strangely exculpates Aquinas or gives to him a mitigating role in the process of the Aristotelianization and so impoverishment of the religious consciousness.

However, certain streams of Jung's thought expressed in other contexts would appear to show Jung's ultimate incompatibility with certain central positions in Aquinas' ontology and epistemology. Jung's appreciation of the ontological argument and Aquinas' rejection of it have already been pointed out.[54] But Aquinas' reason for his rejection is significant and worthy of elaboration. Aquinas rejects the ontological argument on the basis of his acceptance of an Aristotelian principle which Jung more than once explicitly rejects as hostile to the basic model of the psyche on which his psychology rests. The principle states, "Nothing in the intellect which was not previously in the senses."[55] To Aquinas this principle means that all knowledge originates in the senses as the windows through which everything that comes into the mind must pass. Since God is not an object of the senses he is, therefore, not immediately knowable to human beings. With Jung, however, the human psyche itself would seem to possess an *a priori* structure and dynamism, the archetypes, which no doubt are activated in the interplay between psyche and sensible extramental reality but which have an autonomous existence and even life of their own prior to human experience. Thus Jung and Aquinas seem to hold irreconcilable views on the nature and origin of human experience and especially as regards our knowledge of God. At the basis of this difference is the question of possible human *a priori* knowledge of God. Such knowledge of God would seem to be affirmed by Jung through the *a priori* structure of the psyche. Such knowledge of God is clearly denied by Aquinas. This difference implies that both thinkers work with different ontologies and epistemologies and so with different models of the nature of God's presence to and activity within life. For Jung the experience of God is latent as an abiding possibility in our experience of our psyche. For Aquinas it is not. Human beings may reason to God by applying various principles of reason (usually variants of the principle of causality) to empirical reality and also receive further revelation from God beyond the natural capacities of their reason.[56] But Aquinas denied any pre-possession by human beings of facilities which when activated in intercourse with the world of sense would lead to immediate experience of God. Frank admission of these radical differences would serve to clarify dialogue between the Thomistic and Jungian mind by eliminating false hopes of an easy compatibility which only betray the mind and spirit of each.

4) The Reformation

Moving from the Middle Ages to the Reformation, Jung's views on the underlying meaning of Protestantism and Catholicism are appreciative and critical of each and seem to proceed from the same principles that control his reading of the religious history of the West. Jung speaks highly of Protestantism and its immediate predecessors in various spirit movements with the emphasis they placed upon people's immediate experience of God.[57] But this unmediated unity with God was fraught with its own difficulties. When this unity was achieved, Protestants had to withstand through their own resources the impact with the living God unaided by sacrament or cult.[58] So also they were thrown on their own resources in the face of their guilt divested as they were of recourse to sacramental forgiveness.[59] Such a robust spirituality demanded by Protestantism could thus lead to an intensely creative experience of God but also to the possibility of a barbaric self-destruction.[60] On the other hand, Catholicism had the advantages of a sophisticated sacramental system which could mediate, when working properly, a more controlled and even access to the divine but which constantly faced the temptation of substituting itself for the experience it was meant to mediate.

While Jung bestows high praise on certain aspects of Reformed thought, and especially the power of its initial insights, yet he is very critical of its historical development on the grounds that it has become increasingly rational.[61] He speaks with disfavor of the loss of the sense of mystery following upon the abandonment of dogmas and rite which he understands to be expressions of and vehicles into the unconscious.[62] Further he argues that the sense of the symbolic has ceded in Reformed thought to a rationalism and historicism whose understanding of the nature of religion and its expression in religious literature and the scriptures is sterile.[63] In this context he admires the Catholic retention of sacrament and rite as more adequate to the religious nature of humanity possessed of an unconscious.

In the foregoing analysis Jung aligns himself on many points with Tillich's understanding of the root meaning of Catholicism and Protestantism. Tillich himself was of the opinion that the rationalism characterizing later Protestantism had denied people's religious depths which then broke through on their own dynamic, pointed us back to our depths now perceived in secular modalities, and, in so doing, gave birth to the tradition of depth psychology.[64] He further felt that in every theology the sense of human depths must be retained since it is from these depths the religious experience arises and it is to these depths it always points. In particular, Tillich felt that some form of sacramental thinking must be retained if the holy was seriously to be conceived as within creation. Tillich thus spoke of Catholic substance, meaning the religious substance in being and life itself as participating in the divine, and of the Protestant principle, meaning human critical and rational reflection on this substance in the interests of preventing idolatry, as two indispensable and complementary aspects of the religious spirit which would have to be reintegrated if Christianity was to escape imbalance through the denial of either.[65] Jung, too, in calling for a reviviscence of the true sense of religion would seem to share Tillich's appreciation of both sides of the Christian tradition. He appreciates both the Protestant search for the immediate experience of God and the Catholic retention of the symbolic and sacramental possibility. In particular regarding modern Catholicism, Jung shows great appreciation of its continued devotion to Mary and its proclamation of the dogma of the Assumption.[66] He saw these factors as complementing the implicit male deity and accompanying rationalism that so characterized his experience of Protestantism. The Assumption he understood to be a symbolic affirmation of the presence of the feminine in the divinity. Perhaps it is not surprising that Tillich too expresses appreciation of the Catholic retention of a feminine element in its devotion and sought himself to locate a feminine aspect in the Trinitarian Godhead itself.[67]

In his evaluation of Protestantism and Catholicism Jung seems consistently to affirm that which affirms the experienceable presence of God in the fabric of psyche and life and to criticize that which locates God beyond life, addressing it from without with an informational revelation to be appropriated exclusively by the powers of conscious reason and followed by the conscious will. These same values are again in evidence in his response to modern philosophical and religious thought.

5) The Modern Period

In delineating his own intellectual heritage Jung frequently states his indebtedness to Kant. He would seem to understand the archetypes as the dynamic and structural preconditions of psychic life much in the same sense that Kant understood the forms and categories of the mind as the precondition of its operation as well as the determinants of the boundaries of its responsible use.[68] Though there is this admitted likeness in their respective epistemologies, certain differences in the two thinkers should be noted. Kant performed his critique of reason in the name of establishing its own limits within which it could operate effectively and show its products to be in keeping with its capacities. Consequently Kant denied the possibility of scientific knowledge of the noumenal in which category he included the soul, the cosmos and God as well as the disciplines related to their study, namely, rational psychology, cosmology and natural theology.[69] Thus one of the major thrusts of Kant's first critique was to establish a well defined restraint on the mind from acting *ultra vires* in the above mentioned arenas especially when claims to the doing of science were attached to such operation. Soul, cosmos and God, it is true, were regulative principles of the mind without which the mind could not operate but these realities were of such a nature that scientific purchase upon them by the finite mind was constitutionally impossible. In describing the perimeters with which the mind can function validly Jung shows less of Kant's restraint. Through his theory of the archetypes, Jung does retain something of Kant's insight into the existence of pre-existing structures which make possible and limit human awareness. But Jung greatly extends the limits of human possibilities of awareness by granting to human experience through its archetypal basis a valid knowledge not only of the phenomenal world but of that world which Kant would probably call noumenal and rule out of the court of licit human and certainly scientific experience.[70] As previously implied Jung may argue that Kant himself, in his second critique and possibly in some of his later writings, reintroduces the noumenal in the shape of human moral experience and its absolute demand.[71] Nevertheless, Jung would, as he claims, be a successor of Kant and of the turn Kant gave to human self-understanding in so much as Jung follows Kant into human interiority and subjectivity to find there the preconditions of human knowledge and the boundaries of its extent. It would appear also true that Jung found a much richer interiority than did Kant and in doing so pushed forward the borders of human perception in every direction.

Jung also shows an acute appreciation of the historical efforts made by significant members of the philosophical community to transcend the limitations placed upon human experience by Kant.[72]

In general Jung does not look favorably on the greatest of these efforts, that of Hegel. He pays him the tribute of being a "psychologist manqué."[73] However, he more consistently attributes to him an inflated use of language in the service of an inflated ideational system which vastly overstated the boundaries of competence of the mind.[74] Thus Jung describes the excesses of Hegel's response to Kant as partaking of a certain Nietzschean inflation.[75] In short he seems to think that Hegel's efforts to escape the constrictions of Kant's understanding of the limits of reason led to a use of mind and language which was unwittingly possessed by the unconscious, and which may have equated reason with the unconscious and so attained the heights of inflation.[76] In this evaluation of Hegel's response to Kant, Jung again shares much with Tillich, who more than once refers to Hegel's hubris even though admitting that he learned much from him.[77]

In his analysis of the crucial period of philosophical development in the wake of Kant and Hegel, Jung shows considerable empathy for Schelling, with whom Hegel was an early collaborator but who became one of Hegel's first major contradictors. He names Schelling and Carus as establishing a more realistic and satisfying dialectic in their models of God's presence to humanity and in the relationship between the unconscious and the conscious.[78] Schelling was to declare in his attack on Hegel's philosophy after the latter's death that it had no place for a "positive philosophy" by which he meant that it was insensitive to the negativities of actual concrete existence. Hegel's unqualified essentialism thus needed an existentialist corrective to counter its inflation and hubris.[79]

In aligning himself with the later Schelling, Jung would seem to be endorsing a certain existential position at least in response to Hegel's inflated essentialism. Here Jung is addressing a problem that has been at the heart of much of the philosophical endeavor since the time of classical German romanticism and idealism and which has an immediate correlation to the psychological. If Hegel overstates the case for unity between the human and divine or between the conscious and the unconscious and so authors a psychologically inflating and hence destructive philosophy, care must be taken lest the response to Hegel so sunder these polarities that the type of community of being and so of fruitful interchange between them, elsewhere endorsed by Jung in his central conception of the individuation process, be rendered impossible. The result of such sundering and the consequent unrelatedness of the sundered polarities takes historically the form of a sterile rationalism on one hand or an unqualified acceptance of the irrational and absurd on the other. In both of these extremes the human psyche suffers from the absence of its complement—to be gained from unity with its opposite. The rationalist needs the life of unreason. The irrationalist needs the support of form.

The existential reaction to Hegel as it took forceful shape in the thought of Kierkegaard seems to deny the reality of a communion in being of the conscious and unconscious or of God and humanity. Kierkegaard so distances the realities of God and human beings that they could only be united in the wholly gratuitous and seemingly arbitrary revelation of Jesus Christ for which there was no archetypal basis as the principle of expectation, demand and reception.[80] Such a model of God's presence to man from without not only underlies Kierkegaard's nineteenth century thought and what Jung calls the "Kierkegaardian neurosis"[81] but has a discernible twentieth century heir in the theology of Karl Barth.[82]

Thus, while he rejects Hegel, Jung is also keenly aware of the problems consequent upon such a rejection when it becomes extreme. This explains his reference to the neurotic potential of Kierkegaard's understanding of unqualified divine transcendence and his negative remarks about Barthian theology.[83] With regard to Kierkegaard Jung is explicit in stating that his thinking stands in need of a corrective to be supplied by the understanding of an immanent presence of God whose voice is heard within.[84]

Thus Jung writing from a psychological perspective shows an acute appreciation of one of the most critical philosophical and theological problems of the last two centuries, namely, the relationship between divine immanence and transcendence. From what he writes, sometimes in passing, about the thought of the principals in this discussion Jung seems to reject both Hegel's over-identification of the realities of God and humanity and Kierkegaard's absolute dichotomy between them. Perhaps he most clearly states his own balanced position in answer to Buber.[85] Here he implies that our experience of the immanental religious powers or archetypes convinces us of their reality and numinosity and that our experience, though invariably immanent in its origin, inevitably gives rise to our sense of an autonomous power other than our ego operative in this encounter.

The foregoing is written in full cognizance of Jung's own claims that his findings were of the phenomenal and empirical order and as such had no metaphysical consequences.[86] By this disclaimer Jung clearly means that his psychological analysis of the human experience of God as rooted in the psyche does not "prove" the existence of a God beyond the psyche. Yet it is difficult to escape the suspicion that in these utterances he was protecting himself against both scientist and philosopher-theologian, lest they both, from their different disciplinary perspectives and for different reasons, accuse him of over-stepping the limits of his science. Certain of his formulations can be read to indicate that he thought the archetypal basis of the human experience of God related us to the only reality of God that we could experience, namely, the God mediated through the psyche. Moreover, he claims at times that it is in this experience that mythology, theology and metaphysics have their common origin.[87] Perhaps this is the licit intent of the ontological argument which would also account for its peculiar staying power.

While it would be unjust to turn Jung into a philosopher or theologian against his expressed will, nevertheless his psychology does lend itself to the construction of a metaphysical model of the nature of God's presence to humanity and of humanity's experience of God. Moreover, his psychology seems to align itself more easily and consistently with certain discernible philosophical and theological traditions and to distance itself from others. From the preceding exposition of Jung's response to major areas and events in the development of Western Christian thought the following conclusions emerge. Jung's psychology of religion is suffused with a strong sense of the immanence of God from which the experience of God's transcendence derives.[88] The enabling possibility, then, of our religious experience is grounded within and not beyond ourselves. The beyond becomes a function of human interior experience. To the extent that Platonic, in contradistinction to Aristotelian, philosophy has been more sensitive to this interiority both in itself and in its historical recurrences at the service of theological reflection, it would seem that Jung's psychology has a greater natural affinity with Platonic rather than Aristotelian expressions of the Christian consciousness.[89] Thus in his evaluation of Western Christianity the appreciation of the sense of divine immanence aligns Jung, in his own estimation, with Augustine, the medieval realists, Anselm's ontological argument, the mystical tradition including gnosticism and alchemy, with the Reformed emphasis on the immediate experience of God and with sacramentalism and its ritual re-enactment to the extent that they serve their proper function of mediating the depths from which they arise to the minds exposed to them. Consistent with this position Jung's thought opposes that extrinsicism which would deny an ontological continuity between human beings and God and so would affirm an absolute God wholly beyond the structures and powers within life and able to enter it only from without. Let us now turn to Paul Tillich and his analysis of many of these same problems.

III. PAUL TILLICH AND THE WESTERN CHRISTIAN DEVELOPMENT

Tillich's lectures on the history of the development of the Christian West are contained in two major works, *A History of Christian Thought*[90] and *Perspectives on 19th and 20th Century Protestant Theology*.[91] Some of this material is taken up more concisely in one of his major essays, "Two Types of Philosophy of Religion."[92] In this essay he briefly reviews the history of theological anthropology in Christianity. Here he contends that Augustine's model of religious humanity controlled Christian thought on the subject from the time of Augustine up to the high Middle Ages when it was displaced by its only serious alternative, the Aristotelian conception of human beings introduced by Thomas Aquinas. Tillich is firm in his contention that Aquinas, in his effort to integrate Aristotle with Christianity, denied a dialectical unity between God and humanity, and so bequeathed to the Western religious mind a split between the divine and the human which remains its problem to the present day. Tillich's reading of history, like Jung's, is done in virtue of a value or norm which adopts an immanental point of departure as the basis of his understanding of human beings as religious. He, too, is less open to theologies whose point of departure is an unqualified assertion of the transcendent. This will emerge through a more detailed examination of his treatment of many of the same issues already seen through Jung's eyes and will lay the basis for conclusions about the nature of religious reality to which both thinkers might give assent.

1) The Early Church up to Augustine

Tillich's tendencies toward both immanental and universalist positions are evident in his appreciation of the early development within Christianity of *Logos* Christologies. These Christologies conceive of the Christ figure as no doubt particular and concrete but also as the incarnation of the *logos* or life-giving meaning of reality, the pursuit of which has empowered the philosophical spirit from the human acquisition of consciousness.[93] Thus Tillich, like Jung, would base his Christological thinking on the interplay between the reality of the historical event of Christ and those forces in life which both demanded and received it in its happening. Moreover, both imply that the concreteness of this event in some sense has a universal meaning and expectation as the actualization of a permanent latency in the human psyche. Jung comes closest to this in his relating of Christ as *Logos* to Mercurius in such a way as to show the basis and so ineradicability of both in the psyche.[94]

Like Jung, Tillich is also aware of the power of the attraction on the mind exercised by early extra-Christian gnosis. He is, perhaps, less enthusiastic about it than Jung but identifies it explicitly as one of the greatest dangers faced by the early Church.[95] It should also be pointed out that in both his historical evaluation and in his systematic work Tillich takes the position that there is a licit and inescapable sense in which all religious knowing including Christian experience is a "gnosis."[96] By this he means that characteristically religious knowledge always combines a noetic with a powerfully affective element so that religious knowledge is always infused with love and a commitment to the level of being from which it arises.

Jung's indebtedness to Augustine has been referred to previously. It is clearly with the spirit of Augustine that Tillich aligns his theology and especially his philosophy of religion or his conception of the nature of God's presence to human beings.[97] The major thesis giving form to Tillich's analysis of the history of Western

Christian speculation is his contention that from Augustine to its demise in the thirteenth century at the hands of Aquinas Western Christianity endorsed a theological anthropology which understood human beings as religious because of the ontological presence of God within them in virtue of their created humanity itself. Tillich will trace this anthropology in its substantial continuity from Augustine through pseudo-Dionysius, the Victorines, Anselm to Francis of Assisi and the great early Franciscan theologians, of whom he names Alexander of Hales, Bonaventure and Mathew of Aquasparta.[98]

The origin of this tradition Tillich attributes to Augustine's adaptation of neo-Platonism to Christian thought. Tillich understands Augustine to have made a major contribution to the Western conception of religious humanity when he solved the dual problems of our search for certitude and for happiness by uniting the resolution of both in our unity with the God of our interiority. Augustine, Tillich explains, did this by reversing the dynamism of neo-Platonic philosophy from its direction toward union with God beyond the world to a union with God in the depth of the soul itself.[99] The import of this reversal is captured in Augustine's dictum that his, and, by implication, the Christian's, only interest is "with God and the soul."[100] The latter is the *locus* where the former is encountered.

On this point Tillich's conception of Augustine's anthropology echoes Jung's identification of the soul or psyche as the *temenos* of our experience of God. Tillich, in this matter, would seem to proffer an interpretation of Augustine's thought on humanity as religious which would be supportive of Jung's reference to Augustine as a seminal thinker who has preceded him in pointing to the archetypes of the soul as of such an importance in human, and specifically, religious awareness. If Jung can be read to affirm that the entry of God into our consciousness is through the unconscious, he would seem to share Tillich's endorsement of Augustine's dictum about the most fruitful and immediate direction to be taken in our search for God, "Do not go outside; go into yourself."[101] It is this immediacy of God to the soul that leads Tillich to describe himself as an Augustinian in the matter of understanding God's immanence and so to describe himself negatively as "anti-Aristotelian and anti-Thomistic."[102]

2) The Ontological Argument

Tillich, like Jung, understands the immediately sensed presence of an absolute to human consciousness as the core experience giving rise to the various formulations of the ontological argument which existed both before and after its most sophisticated expression by Anselm.[103] In a line of argument reminiscent of Jung's treatment of the same point, Tillich denies that the ontological argument is an argument or a "proof" for the existence of "a" or "the" God conceived of as a supreme object or being over against the world thought of in its turn as the sum total of objects other than God.[104] Here Tillich would seem to be taking a stance identical with Jung's when the latter states that the ontological argument is neither "an argument nor a proof" but an expression of a *consensus gentium*.[105] Tillich too contends that when the ontological argument is true to its own best interests it simply leads the mind to an awareness of the pre-existence of an absolute or unconditioned and in so doing is unassailable. But when it oversteps these bounds and goes on to prove the existence of a God as a discontinuous object beyond the mind it falls subject to its rightful dismissal by Guanilo, Aquinas and Kant. Tillich also makes the point in this context that any alleged proof of God's existence which includes God in the subject-object split and any religiosity which might attend it reduce God to one object among many, however grandiose the predications attributed to this object, and is rejected by an atheism inspired paradoxically by respect for the dignity of God.[106] In his efforts to make cogent again for his times the force of the ontological argument, Tillich makes clear he is not concerned with winning an argument but with the much more important issue of preserving our awareness of the precondition of religious experience, namely the presence of God in and to our being, so that the human ability to ask the question of God might be preserved.[107] Here he implies most strongly that certain logical proofs of God's existence may appear more cogent at one level but fail to communicate any experience of that which they prove, just as institutional religion may provide answers to questions which humanity no longer asks and, worse, may be growing incapable of asking.[108] In this matter not only Tillich's understanding of the ontological argument but even his motivation in reviving it would seem to coincide with Jung's concerns inasmuch as both men associate its demise with the demise of human religious awareness itself. Both consider this a serious loss.

3) The Thirteenth Century

All commentators agree that the thirteenth century was of unusual significance in the development of Western Christian thought. It is precisely in the exercise of the issue of the relationship of immanence to transcendence that Tillich locates the significance of this century in the debate that then occurred between the representatives of the traditional Platonic-Augustinian ontology and anthropology and the newly emerging forces of Christian Aristotelianism.[109] Tillich, like many historians, sees Aquinas' adaptation of Aristotle as the greatest theological event of the century but views it as a dubious accomplishment. In Tillich's view, Aquinas, to accommodate Aristotle, had to deny the dialectical unity of God and humanity that lay at the heart of Augustine's anthropology and the mystical tradition as such. In this context Tillich, like Jung, approves of the profound intimacy in shared being between human beings and God which Eckhart spoke of and alleges that Aquinas had to deny this intimacy due to his allegiance to Aristotle.[110] In this denial Aquinas "cut the nerve of the ontological argument" and so denied that point in human beings in which the opposites of humanity and divinity, the finite and the infinite, coincide.[111] This theological option on Aquinas' part constituted, in Tillich's estimation, the substance of the theological opposition to him in his own time and thereafter. In particular the Franciscan representatives of the older Augustinianism pointed to the implicit split in Aquinas' theological framework. The human mind and spirit is made totally autonomous and God becomes extraneous to life. All religious and theological truth come to receive their ultimate sanction in authority, either that of God or Church, and both are considered to be beyond life in the sense that the truth they mediate has no basis in the fabric of the soul itself but comes totally from without.[112]

Despite these inadequacies Tillich concedes that the Aristotelian theology with its cleavage between humanity and God carried the century. The split that Aquinas made theoretically possible in the thirteenth century was made real by Scotus and Ockham in the fourteenth.[113] Ultimately this movement came to the double truth theory of two positivisms wherein an autonomous mind held its own areas of self-sufficiency and competence in the philosophical, phenomenal and scientific field while an authoritarian church mediated a heteronomous revelation received from beyond. The link between the two spheres needed to overcome a schizoid duality between the human and the religious was lost, and, in Tillich's mind, has yet to be regained. Here again Tillich and Jung seem to join in an agreement based upon a very similar analysis of the past when they concur in affirming that the scientific and the mystical-religious aspects of the human psyche have disengaged themselves in the Western tradition in a way injurious to the wholeness of the humanity of those who stand in the tradition. Both seem anxious to relieve the pain caused by the loss of this wholeness by showing how seemingly disparate and opposite sides of the human possibility might come together in new and powerful harmonies.

4) The Reformation and Enlightenment

Tillich understands the split between religion and culture to have been a significant factor among the forces which generated the Reformation. In Tillich's estimation, the Church, as an increasingly authoritarian mediator of a revelation for which there was no onto-logical or psychological and, hence, experiential basis in life, came to lose its capacity to confer on humanity a convincing sense of a gracious, forgiving and accepting God.[114] In Luther's genius Tillich discerns a profound reaffirmation of human experience of divine acceptance in the face of and in spite of his continued dialectical awareness of his own sinfulness.[115] Luther's initial experience was intensely subjective and, after a period of Protestant scholasticism in which its subjectivity and power were muted in the interests of the preservation of the Protestant gain, re-emerged in the doctrine of the inner light. In turn the sense of divine immediacy pertaining to the inner light developed, on the one hand, into religious pietism, and, on the other, into the Enlightenment when this inner light was identified with reason.[116] In this way Tillich contends that pietism and the enlightenment shared much in common. Whether the inner light was considered a religious reality as with the pietist or as the power of reason as with the people of the Enlightenment, both were convinced of the immediacy of truth to the mind or spirit of humanity. In this way, too, Tillich can show the intimate connection that he assumes to exist between scientific reason and mysticism inasmuch as both are convinced of the effective presence of the ultimate within humanity.

In this manner does Tillich relate the spiritual origin of the Enlightenment to the Reformation as its secularized offspring. He argues, in effect, that the God of the Enlightenment became autonomous human reason which satisfied its religious demands by positing a totally transcendent God beyond the world, the God of deism, so that it might have a free hand in ordering the world along the pattern of residual human reason in the name of the distant divine. It was precisely this deistic transcendent God to whom Kant denied reason any significant access and so brought the Enlightenment to doubt seriously its own philosophical and theological premises by showing the rather dubious relationship between the mind and that God in virtue of whose rationality the created mind strove to impose a rational order on humanity.[117] Tillich goes on from this analysis to a position again reminiscent of what has been seen in Jung's thought on Kant. Tillich contends that while Kant destroyed the mind's over-confident conviction that it could grasp and handle deity through an exclusively rational and theoretical process, nevertheless Kant introduces the possibility of an immediate access to and experience of the reality of divinity in his second critique wherein humanity's universal sense of a divinely sanctioned ought operated effectively as an experience of God.[118] Thus Kant as the initiator of modern philosophical and theological thought may not have severed the immediate links between human beings and God quite so thoroughly as his first critique and a very real part of his own thought might at first sight indicate.

5) The Modern Period

Tillich and Jung evidence certain similarities in their understanding of the reaction of the philosophical-theological mind to Kant. Both see Hegel as leading the effort to transcend Kant. Tillich, while much more appreciative of and possibly more deeply affected by Hegel's response to Kant, also feels that Hegel was guilty of a certain *hubris* in authoring an essentialism incapable of seriously accommodating the negativities in reality which led to a too easy and

unqualified unification or coincidence of the divine and human realities.[119] Tillich, in fact, is more impressed by a second effort to unite
more harmoniously the divine and human realities in the face of
Kant's constrictions of the mind's capacities and of his reduction of
religion to morality. Friedrich Schleiermacher, a contemporary and
colleague of Hegel in his Berlin period, located in human beings a
universal experience of God cast in terms of their "feeling of absolute dependence." Tillich occasionally admits that his own central
conception of ultimate concern as descriptive of humanity's universal endemic standing in a faith concern owes much to Schleiermacher.[120]

However, Tillich goes on to admit that the great synthetic
efforts of Schleiermacher and Hegel made in the interest of re-es-
tablishing the fractured unities between the divine and human failed
to satisfy the religious and philosophical spirit.[121] First Schelling,
then Kierkegaard, rejected Hegel with an existentialism grounded
on a strong sense of the unreconciled and still alienated nature of
human existence and, at least in the case of the latter, on the accompanying anti-synthetic proposition that the divine and human have
no being in common. Hence relations between the two are wholly
from without and initiated in a wholly gratuitous way by a transcendent God.[122] This was the ultimate undoing in principle of Hegel's
attempt to show the coincidence of the opposites of the divine
and human.

Despite its failure in the nineteenth century Tillich is insistent
that the effort of synthesis be taken up again. If Hegel and Schleiermacher have lost their audience in the twentieth century, nevertheless the search for unity which empowered their efforts must continue.[123] Otherwise we are doomed to a schizoid life of unreconciled
opposites wherein the religionist is severed from his humanity by a
truncating fundamentalism and the humanist and scientist are separated from their religious depths by an equally truncating rationalism
often imbued with its own absolute. Tillich goes on to sketch the
nature of the new synthesis. In terms of a negative critique Hegel's
essentialism would be rejected at one extreme as an overstatement of
the unity between the human and the divine. Kierkegaard's and,
later, Barth's transcendentalism would be rejected at the other extreme as so distancing God and humanity as to deny the possibility

that any significant and truly humanizing unity could ever be realized. In a more positive vein Tillich's own synthesis would affirm
that God is that power at the basis of life which makes life possible
and increasingly richer by bringing into ever greater harmonies the
opposites or polarities which make up the dynamic and structure of
life.[124] Thus, like Jung, Tillich would be very open to the idea of
grace as a balanced, though painful, growth toward an ever more
widely embracing self-realization and consciousness. Yet, for Tillich, and in this Jung also may share his spirit, life remains forever
ambiguous and fragmentary since no life process can ever exhaust its
possibilities, grounded as they are in its participation in divine fecundity. And thus the greatness of being human and so susceptible to
infinite growth is also its tragedy inasmuch as this growth can never
be fully realized in existential life and unequivocal unity with the
essential or divine remains beyond its ambit.

Yet the presence of God in life is the very power that works to
whatever fullness, wholeness and extension we acquire. And so, for
Tillich, Kierkegaard's existentialism which separates the divine and
human and theologies based upon it remain unaware of the direction
from whence the salutary and the wholemaking enter life and so may
make it more difficult for us to engage with them. Tillich felt strongly
that the task of theology in the twentieth century was to build again
for its time a synthesis which would make credible and cogent for
modern human beings the source of a new and fresher life within life.
Such a synthesis would re-establish the reality of God as the basis of
life at the ground of life enlivening it from within. In his efforts to
construct such a model of God's presence for modern humanity
Tillich has identified his ancestry clearly. He has stated that "... his
spiritual father was Schleiermacher, his intellectual father was Schelling, and his grandfather on both sides was Jacob Boehme."[125] But
even further back looms Augustine and Augustine's Platonic anthropology wherein all creative expressions of the human spirit are ultimately expressions of the one God within and so common to all. It is
to a revivification of this sense of God's immanence to the psyche of
human beings that Tillich points in his effort to heal the painful
breach which now exists between the adherents of the various expressions, disciplines and viewpoints that this one psyche has produced. Thus his concerns are more than academic when he writes:

The ontological approach to philosophy of religion as envisaged by Augustine and his followers, as reappearing in many forms in the history of thought, if critically reinterpreted by us, is able to do for our time what it did in the past, both for religion and culture: to overcome as far as it is possible by mere thought the fateful gap between religion and culture, thus reconciling concerns which are not strange to each other but have been estranged from each other.[126]

IV. CONCLUSION

In conclusion, three principles can be stated, from a study of the historical reflections of Jung and Tillich, which illuminate their conception of the nature of religion and also contain the norms which they use in evaluating religious developments.

These principles are the following:

1. Religion is an inescapable and *a* (if not *the*) most important dimension of life.
2. To the extent that religion is understood to rise out of an experience based upon the reality of God as immanent within life it enhances life ontologically, spiritually and psychologically. This principle would not deny a sense of divine transcendence but would make it a function of the experience of divine immanence.
3. To the extent that religion relates humanity to God conceived of as wholly extrinsic to life it tends to divest human beings and creation of ontological value and consequently of psychological and spiritual well-being and energy.

Expanding on the first principle, Tillich and Jung hold religion to be inevitable because of the manner in which they relate human consciousness ontologically to the being of God in the human psyche. Tillich in his understanding of God as the ground of being affirms the dialectical participation of each existent in the being of God in such a way that neither any existent nor their sum total can ever by equated with God but in such a way that none of them are divested of the reality of God's being within them. Jung seems to argue, with admitted nuances and disclaimers about being a metaphysician, that the collective unconscious, in which each individual consciousness participates, is the psychogenetic basis of all religious experience. The religious experience, which Jung closely relates to the movement of life toward balance, completeness and wholeness, would seem to coincide, then, with his understanding of the individuation process. In this sense the very process of individuation would be "religious" in the wider sense that Jung's categories can give to the term. In short Jung's thought strongly implies that the working of the unconscious toward human wholeness is itself religious. It is this sense of the religious process which Jung would seem to have in mind in his famous statement that all the problems in his clients in the latter part of life were religious and ultimately resolvable only in a religious manner.[127] Thus the first principle simply states that human beings who participate in the ground of being, to use Tillich's idiom, and whose consciousness is in living dialogue with the collective unconscious, to use Jung's, are constitutionally and unavoidably religious.

The last two principles explicate the first. Both thinkers regard God as a power or dynamism operative in the depths of life on behalf of life goading it from within to ever widening configurations of the integration of the apparently disparate. In this sense God is the constant source of life within life offering it an ever greater fullness. With neither thinker does such an implication imply some hidden form of the pleasure principle. Both Tillich and Jung can easily be construed to be talking, from differing perspectives, about the cruciform nature of life and growth in which powerful opposites and polarities must be reconciled in such a way that their seeming contradictory truth is preserved. Holding to this tension is the price of growth. Thus Tillich understands the pattern of life to be trinitarian or dialectical in which the ego is driven to relate itself to ever wider perimeters of life and so to grow into an ever wealthier interplay with reality but at the price of its passing through many forms and configurations. Jung also speaks of the universal truth of sacrifice in the psychic process and has likened the growing process of the integration of the unconscious to the Catholic theme of the Mass wherein Christ is priest and victim in so much as in the individuation process ego and unconscious must sacrifice each other as they grow into a more vital intimacy.[128] In so much as the individuation process is the substance and meaning of life Jung could argue from psychic grounds that every human being is destined to be both priest and victim.

Nevertheless, the centrality of the sacrificial in the thought of each should not be allowed to disguise the positive and even optimistic depths of their thought. In spite of its difficulties, the sacrificial dimension of growth and the forces which trigger it are ultimately benign and all true suffering is in the interest of the expansion of life through a more intense unity with the source of life in its depths. In this sense Jung and Tillich see the goal of growth and life as an increased unity with the God within. Moreover, Jung pictures this process in such a way that every advance in the growth of consciousness through the actualization of the unconscious, that is, every realization of human potential, can be termed an incarnation since it makes real in consciousness the unity of that consciousness with its depths from which the divine proceeds into it.[129] From this imagery one gains a sense of the importance that Jung and also Tillich attach to the immanental tradition. The realization of human growth in consciousness is intimately connected with the reality of God among human beings. Hence any devaluation of human potential is a devaluation of God's concretization in creation.

The third principle is simply the reversal of the second. If the reality of God as the ground not only of being but value is wholly extrinsic to created life, it is impossible to escape the conclusion that the latter and so also the psyche is void of intrinsic worth.[130] Moreover, even if created life should be somehow later validated by a recuperative divine saving action in the second instance, so to speak, this consequent validation cannot hide but simply overlays the intrinsic worthlessness of creation and human life processes. Tillich is explicit in terming such an approach to creation from beyond by a God who is no way within it as demonic. Such a God would be unfortunately compelled to violate and manipulate in his revelational and redemptive activity the very structures he authors as creator.[131] In Locke's idiom each instance of the making of the prophet would be an unmaking of the human being. This is Tillich's heteronomous God who in revealing himself remains a stranger and so intensifies rather than alleviates our estrangement.[132]

Jung, too, especially in some of his later writings complains that Christianity in placing God wholly beyond life or, in Jung's terms, "too much outside" has removed human worth from human beings and so also depreciated their soul.[133] Jung then argues against exclusively transcendentalist positions because in them there is always an implied denial of the value of human potential and so of the divine basis of this potential in the soul. If, as we have seen him state above, Jung considers the realization of human potential as an incarnation, the position that the achievement of growth in consciousness is not incarnational nor a realization of the divine would come to be the ultimate sin against the spirit and the process of life itself. This absence of the divine in the created and in human life both Jung and Tillich agree to be the heart of the Marcionite heresy. Both locate its error in the split it drives between a creation divested of the being of God and redemption in which God addresses creation in the manner of an intrusion and both see it implicit in all theologies of absolute transcendence.[134]

The burden of this paper has been to show that Tillich and Jung read the Western religious development as one in which the true sense of religion has gradually been lost in ways that are injurious to modern society. We have tried to show how both proposed a revitalization of our sense of God's immediate and immanental presence to our soul or psyche to counter his loss and to contribute to a fuller humanity once again in greater resonance with its inner resources.

This brings us to a concluding question which all practitioners of those disciplines related to humanity may be increasingly driven to face. Jung and Tillich so intensely link the being of God and the being of humanity, and so closely connect our depth experience of ourselves with our experience of God, that they ground the genesis of human mythology, religion, metaphysics, theology, spirituality and psychology in a common matrix. From this sense of their origin from a common source one would be able to see that every theological and metaphysical position would have its accompanying psychology or spirituality in the mind of its adherents. This would mean that no longer could theology exempt itself from psychological scrutiny or become engaged in arguments to the effect that good theology might be bad psychology so that adherence to "revealed" truths or to certain theological systems might have a "religious" or "supernatural" validity though they would be capable of inducing widespread neurosis or other forms of illness at the purely "natural" or "human" level. In the integrated view of Tillich and Jung bad theology would inevitably produce bad psychology and accompanying forms of sickness. The proposal of inhumanity in the name of religion is excluded in principle.

The implications from the viewpoint of psychology are equally impelling. Psychology in the face of the thought of Jung and Tillich may be forced to explicitate more fully the nature and locations of the healing powers on which it draws. Jung and Tillich would seem to imply in their own ways that within the depths of life with which the psychologist deals there are operative those healing and restorative powers the experience of which human beings have commonly called God. Such a proposition should draw psychologists into a continuous dialogue with religious disciplines on the nature of healing and with themselves on the question of their relationship to the healing resources they hope to activate in their efforts to bring about a fuller humanity in those with whom they deal. In this process of inter-disciplinary discussion into which the collective human mind may now be entering, the atmosphere may already be such that no discipline or group of them can ever hope for an unconditional victory or the surrender of all to any. Rather some cooperative model must be adopted wherein all are ready to admit that they deal from varying perspectives with a common mystery in the depths of humanity and that each of them is but one expression of this creative depth and possesses but a limited capacity to illuminate the mystery which gave it birth. As this effort proceeds, the modern mind will remain indebted to such spirits as Tillich and Jung for compelling it to shoulder its responsibilities and to face this issue, as well as for providing it with the wider sensitivities in which the new task must be carried out. It will also remain indebted to both men for their humble sketches of the structures and dynamics of the depths of the human mystery to which all the humanities must now address themselves if they are to remain faithful to their name.

Notes

1. Cf. Paul Tillich, "The Two Types of Philosophy of Religion," *Theology of Culture,* ed. by Robert C. Kimball (New York: Oxford University Press, 1964), pp. 12, 25; *A History of Christian Thought,* ed. by Carl E. Braaten (New York and Evanston: Harper and Row, 1968), pp. 186–189; C.G. Jung, *Collected Works,* Vol. II (New Jersey:

Princeton University Press, 1969), "Psychology and Religion," p. 43, par. 75; "On 'The Tibetan Book of the Great Liberation'," p. 497, par. 794; "Foreword to 'Introduction to Zen Buddhism'," p. 553, par. 903.

2. C.G. Jung, *Collected Works*, Vol. 11, "A Psychological Approach to the Trinity," p. 188, par. 280.

3. C.G. Jung, "A Psychological Approach to the Trinity," p. 192, par. 285; P. Tillich, *Dynamics of Faith* (New York: Harper and Row, 1957), pp. 8–12.

4. C.G. Jung, *Collected Works*, Vol. 11, "Answer to Job," p. 456, par. 740; p. 464, par. 752; pp. 468–469, par. 757.

5. P. Tillich, *Systematic Theology*, Vol. I (Chicago: University of Chicago Press, 1951), pp. 79–81, 115–118.

6. P. Tillich, "The Two Types of Philosophy of Religion," *Theology of Culture*, p. 10.

7. P. Tillich, *Systematic Theology*, Vol. I, p. 139.

8. C.G. Jung, *Collected Works*, Vol. 9, ii, "The Psychology of Christian Alchemical Symbolism," p. 181, par. 282; *Collected Works*, Vol. 9, i, "Archetypes of the Collective Unconscious," p. 23, par. 49; "Psychology and Religion," pp. 87–88, par. 144; P. Tillich, *Dynamics of Faith*, pp. 2–4.

9. P. Tillich, *Dynamics of Faith*, pp. 11–12.

10. Ibid., II, pp. 30–40.

11. P. Tillich, *A History of Christian Thought*, p. 120; *The Religious Situation* (Cleveland and New York: Meridian, 1956), pp. 176–178.

12. C.G. Jung, *Collected Works*, Vol. 9, i. "Archetypes of the Collective Unconscious," p. 23, par. 49.

13. P. Tillich, "The Two Types of the Philosophy of Religion," pp. 12–16, 29; *A History of Christian Thought*, pp. 111, 185.

14. P. Tillich, *Perspectives on 19th and 20th Century Protestant Theology*, ed. by Carl E. Braaten (New York and Evanston: Harper and Row, 1967), pp. 76–82; *Systematic Theology*, Vol. I, pp. 191, 237.

15. P. Tillich, *Systematic Theology*, Vol. I, pp. 61–62, 256.

16. C.G. Jung, *Collected Works*, Vol. 11, "On 'The Tibetan Book of the Dead'," pp. 517–518, par. 845.

17. C.G. Jung, *Collected Works*, Vol. 11, "Transformation Symbolism in the Mass," p. 277, par. 419; "On 'The Tibetan Book of the Dead'," p. 490, pars. 781, 782; "On 'The Tibetan Book of the Great Liberation'," p. 495, par. 790.

18. C.G. Jung, "Psychology and Religion," p. 59.

19. C.G. Jung, *Collected Works*, Vol. 12, "Introduction to the Religious

and Psychological Problems of Alchemy," p. 17, par. 20; p. 27, par. 32.

20. C.G. Jung, "Foreword to 'Introduction to Zen Buddhism'," p. 553, par. 903.

21. C.G. Jung, *Memories, Dreams, Reflections,* ed. by Aniela Jaffe (New York: Vintage Books, 1961), pp. 200–201; *Collected Works,* Vol. 12, "Introduction to the Religious and Psychological Problems of Alchemy," p. 23, par. 26; pp. 33–34, par. 40; *Collected Works,* Vol. 9, ii. "Background to the Psychology of Christian Alchemical Symbolism," p. 173, par. 267.

22. C.G. Jung, *Collected Works,* Vol. 11, "Transformation Symbolism in the Mass," p. 292, par. 444.

23. C.G. Jung, *Collected Works,* Vol. 12, "Introduction to the Religious and Psychological Problems of Alchemy," pp. 35–36, par. 41; "The Psychic Nature of the Alchemical Work," pp. 243–245, pars. 343–346; p. 258, par. 361; pp. 266–267, pars. 375, 376; "Religious Ideas in Alchemy," pp. 427–428, par. 511; p. 482, par. 564.

24. C.G. Jung, *Collected Works,* Vol. 12, "Individual Dream Symbolism in Relation to Alchemy," p. 112, par. 144; "Religious Ideas in Alchemy," p. 304, par. 412; p. 306, pars. 414, 415; pp. 312–313, par. 420; pp. 354–355, par. 452.

25. C.G. Jung, *Collected Works,* Vol. 12, "Introduction to the Religious and Psychological Problems of Alchemy," pp. 8–9, par. 9; p. 11, par. 12, and fn. 6; "Individual Dream Symbolism in Relation to Alchemy," pp. 98–102, par. 126; p. 112, par. 144.

26. C.G. Jung, *Collected Works,* Vol. 12, "Individual Dream Symbolism in Relation to Alchemy," p. 112, par. 144; "Religious Ideas in Alchemy," p. 306, pars. 414, 415; p. 313, par. 421; pp. 322–323, pars. 431, 432; p. 355, par. 452; p. 477, par. 557.

27. C.G. Jung, *Collected Works,* Vol. 12, "Religious Ideas in Alchemy," p. 348, par. 450; "Individual Dream Symbolism in Relation to Alchemy," p. 112, par. 144.

28. C.G. Jung, *Collected Works,* Vol. 6, "The Problem of Types in the History of Classical and Medieval Thought," pp. 36–37, pars. 54–55.

29. Ibid.

30. Ibid., pp. 63–64, pars. 94, 95.

31. Ibid., pp. 41–43, pars. 61, 62.

32. Ibid., p. 42, par. 62.

33. Ibid., pp. 45–46, pars. 66, 67.

34. Ibid., pp. 51–52, pars. 77, 78.

35. Ibid., pp. 45–46, par. 67.

36. P. Tillich, *Systematic Theology*, Vol. I, p. 206.
37. C.G. Jung, *Collected Works*, Vol. 6, "The Problem of Types in the History of Classical and Medieval Thought," p. 45, par. 66; Theodore M. Greene, "The Historical Context and Religious Significance of Kant's *Religion*," in I. Kant, *Religion Within the Limits of Reason Alone* (New York: Harper and Row, 1960), pp. lxv–lxxi.
38. C.G. Jung, *Collected Works*, Vol. 6, "The Problem of Types in the History of Classical and Medieval Thought," pp. 45–46, par. 67.
39. P. Tillich, *Dynamics of Faith*, Ch 1, pp. 1–29; *Systematic Theology*, Vol. III, pp. 130–131.
40. P. Tillich, *Systematic Theology*, Vol. I, "The Possibility of the Question of God and the So-Called Ontological Argument," pp. 204–208.
41. C.G. Jung, *Collected Works*, Vol. 6, "The Problem of Types in the History of Classical and Medieval Thought," p. 52, par. 78.
42. Ibid., p. 52, par. 78; p. 59, par. 85.
43. C.G. Jung, *Collected Works*, Vol. 6, "The Type Problem in Poetry," p. 242, par. 409.
44. G.W.F. Hegel, *Lectures on the Philosophy of Religion*, Vol. 1 (London: Kegan Paul, Trench, Trubner, 1895), trans. by E.B. Speirs and J.B. Sanderson, pp. 217–218.
45. Teilhard de Chardin, "Mon Univers," *Science et Christ* (Paris: Editions du Seuil, 1965), p. 114; "Comment Je Vois," *Les Directions de l'avenir* (Paris: Editions du Seuil, 1973), pp. 211, 213.
46. C.G. Jung, *Collected Works*, Vol. 6, "The Type Problem in Poetry," p. 249, par. 422.
47. Ibid., pp. 252–253, par. 427; p. 255, par. 430.
48. Ibid., p. 254, par. 429.
49. Ibid., p. 248, par. 421; p. 255, par. 431.
50. C.G. Jung, *Letters*, Vol. 1, 1906–1950, ed. by A. Jaffe and G. Adler (Princeton: Princeton University Press, 1973), p. 540.
51. C.G. Jung, *Memories, Dreams, Reflections*, ed. by Aniela Jaffe (New York: Vintage Books, 1961), p. 69.
52. C.G. Jung, *Letters*, Vol. 1, p. 317.
53. P. Tillich, "The Two Types of Philosophy of Religion," pp. 17–19; *A History of Christian Thought*, pp. 184–189.
54. Cf. Thomas Aquinas, *Summa Theologiae* (Rome: Marietti, 1952), I, q. 2, art. 1, corp., p. 10; I. q. 12, art. 12, corp. pp. 61–62.
55. C.G. Jung, *Collected Works*, Vol. 11, "On 'The Tibetan Book of the Great Liberation'," p. 492, par. 785; "The Psychology of Eastern Meditation," p. 559, par. 908; *Collected Works*, Vol. 6, "The Type Problem in Modern Philosophy," p. 304, par. 512.

56. Thomas Aquinas, *Summa Theologiae*, I, q. 2, arts. 2 and 3, corp., pp. 11–13; I, q. 1, art. 1, corp., pp. 2–3.

57. C.G. Jung, *Collected Works*, Vol. 6, "The Type Problem in Poetry," p. 257, par. 433; *Collected Works*, Vol. 9, ii, "The Fish in Alchemy," p. 150, par. 235; *Collected Works*, Vol. 11, "Psychology and Religion," p. 49, par. 86.

58. C.G. Jung, *Collected Works*, Vol. 11, "Psychology and Religion," p. 21, par. 33; pp. 48–49, par. 86.

59. C.G. Jung, *Collected Works*, Vol. 11, "Psychoanalysis and the Cure of Souls," pp. 352–353, par. 548.

60. C.G. Jung, *Collected Works*, Vol. 11, "Psychology and Religion," p. 49, par. 86; "Psychoanalysis and the Cure of Souls," p. 350, par. 543.

61. C.G. Jung, *Collected Works*, Vol. 11, "Answer to Job," p. 465, par. 754.

62. C.G. Jung, *Collected Works*, Vol. 11, "Psychology and Religion," pp. 46–47, par. 82.

63. C.G. Jung, *Collected Works*, Vol. 11, "Answer to Job," p. 463, par. 749; pp. 466–467, par. 754.

64. P. Tillich, *The Protestant Era*, trans. by James Luther Adams (Chicago: Chicago University Press, 1957), "Author's Introduction," xix–xx; "The Idea and the Ideal of Personality," pp. 131–135; "The End of the Protestant Era," p. 228.

65. P. Tillich, "The Permanent Significance of the Catholic Church for Protestantism," *Protestant Digest*, III (Summer, 1941), pp. 23–31.

66. C.G. Jung, *Collected Works*, Vol. 11, "Answer to Job," p. 458, par. 743; p. 461f, par. 748f.

67. P. Tillich, *Systematic Theology*, Vol. III, pp. 292–294.

68. C.G. Jung, *Collected Works*, Vol. 11, "On 'The Tibetan Book of the Great Liberation'," p. 505, par. 819; *Collected Works*, Vol. 6, "The Type Problem in Modern Philosophy," pp. 304–305, par. 512.

69. I. Kant, *Critique of Pure Reason* (New York: St. Martin's Press, 1965), Second Division, Transcendental Dialectic, pp. 297–570.

70. C.G. Jung, *Collected Works*, Vol. 6, "The Type Problem in Modern Philosophy," p. 304, par. 512; *Collected Works*, Vol. 11, "Transformation Symbolism in the Mass," p. 245, par. 375.

71. C.G. Jung, *Collected Works*, Vol. 6, "The Type Problem in Classical and Medieval Thought," p. 45, par. 66.

72. C.G. Jung, *Collected Works*, Vol. 8, "On the Nature of the Psyche," p. 169, par. 358.

73. Ibid. Cf. also *Letters*, Vol. 1, p. 194.

74. Ibid., pp. 169–170, pars. 358–360.

75. Ibid., p. 170, par. 359.
76. Ibid.
77. P. Tillich, *Systematic Theology*, Vol. II, pp. 25–44.
78. C.G. Jung, *Collected Works*, Vol. 8, "On the Nature of the Psyche," pp. 169–172, pars. 358–362.
79. P. Tillich, *Perspectives on 19th and 20th Century Protestant Theology*, pp. 141–152.
80. Cf. S. Kierkegaard, *Philosophical Fragments* (New Jersey: Princeton University Press, 1967), *passim.*
81. C.G. Jung, *Collected Works*, Vol. 9, i, "Archetypes of the Collective Unconscious," p. 8, par. 11; *Collected Works*, Vol. 11, "On 'The Tibetan Book of the Great Liberation'," p. 482, par. 772; *Letters*, Vol. 1, pp. 231, 332–333.
82. K. Barth, *Epistle to the Romans* (London: Oxford University Press, 1968), pp. 10, 99.
83. C.G. Jung, *Letters*, Vol. 1, p. 58.
84. Ibid., p. 332.
85. C.G. Jung, "Reply to Buber," *Spring*, 1957, p. 6.
86. Cf. as typical C.G. Jung, *Collected Works*, Vol. 11, "Psychology and Religion," pp. 5, 6, pars. 2, 3.
87. C.G. Jung, *Collected Works*, Vol. 11, "Foreword to 'Introduction to Zen Buddhism'," p. 552, par. 899; *Collected Works*, Vol. 9, ii, p. 34, pars. 64, 65.
88. C.G. Jung, *Collected Works*, Vol. 11, "Answer to Job," p. 468, par. 757; "On 'The Tibetan Book of the Great Liberation'," p. 482, par. 771; p. 488, par. 779.
89. C.G. Jung, *Collected Works*, Vol. 11, "On 'The Tibetan Book of the Dead'," pp. 517, 518, par. 845.
90. Cf. note 1.
91. Cf. note 14.
92. Cf. note 1.
93. P. Tillich, *A History of Christian Thought*, pp. 7–9, 29–32, 55–57, 59–63; *Systematic Theology*, Vol. III, pp. 284, 288, 290.
94. C.G. Jung, *Collected Works*, Vol. 11, "Transformation Symbolism in the Mass," p. 277, par. 419.
95. P. Tillich, *A History of Christian Thought*, p. 36.
96. Ibid.; *Systematic Theology*, Vol. 1, pp. 95–96, 153–154.
97. P. Tillich, *A History of Christian Thought*, pp. 111–115.
98. Ibid., pp. 141–144, 158–191; "The Two Types of Philosophy of Religion," pp. 11–16.
99. P. Tillich, *A History of Christian Thought*, pp. 108–109.

100. Ibid., pp. 111–112.
101. Ibid., p. 113.
102. Ibid., p. 111.
103. Ibid., pp. 162, 164; "The Two Types of Philosophy of Religion," pp. 14–16.
104. P. Tillich, *Systematic Theology*, Vol. I, pp. 204–208.
105. C.G. Jung, *Collected Works*, Vol. 6, "The Type Problem in Classical and Medieval Thought," pp. 41–43, pars. 61–62.
106. P. Tillich, "The Two Types of Philosophy of Religion," pp. 18, 25.
107. P. Tillich, *Systematic Theology*, Vol. I, p. 208.
108. P. Tillich, *A History of Christian Thought*, pp. 186–187.
109. Ibid., p. 141; "The Two Types of Philosophy of Religion," pp. 16–20.
110. P. Tillich, "The Two Types of Philosophy of Religion," pp. 14–15.
111. Ibid., p. 17.
112. Ibid., pp. 17–18; *A History of Christian Thought*, pp. 185–187.
113. P. Tillich, "The Two Types of Philosophy of Religion," p. 19; *A History of Christian Thought*, 186–188.
114. P. Tillich, *A History of Christian Thought*, pp. 188, 201.
115. Ibid., pp. 248–249.
116. Ibid., pp. 286–287; *Perspectives on 19th and 20th Century Protestant Theology*, p. 21.
117. P. Tillich, *Perspectives on 19th and 20th Century Protestant Theology*, p. 66.
118. P. Tillich, *Systematic Theology*, Vol. I, p. 206.
119. P. Tillich, *Perspectives on 19th and 20th Century Protestant Theology*, pp. 131–133.
120. Ibid., pp. 75, 94–104.
121. Ibid., p. 91.
122. Ibid., pp. 148–152, 171–176.
123. Ibid., p. 91; *Systematic Theology*, Vol. I, p. 86.
124. P. Tillich, *Systematic Theology*, Vol. I, "The Ontological Elements," pp. 174–186.
125. P. Tillich, as quoted in, "Tillich and the Nature of Transcendence," by Nels Ferre, *Paul Tillich Retrospect and Future* (Nashville and New York: Abingdon Press, 1966), p. 11.
126. P. Tillich, "The Two Types of Philosophy of Religion," p. 29.
127. C.G. Jung, *Collected Works*, Vol. 11, "Psychotherapists or the Clergy," p. 334, par. 509.
128. Ibid., "Transformation Symbolism in the Mass," pp. 201–296.
129. C.G. Jung, *Collected Works*, Vol. 12, "Religious Ideas in Alchemy," p. 312, par. 419; "The Lapis-Christ Parallel," p. 355, par 452.

130. Ibid., "Individual Dream Symbolism in Relation to Alchemy," pp. 98–102, par. 126.
131. P. Tillich, *Systematic Theology*, Vol. I, pp. 116–117.
132. P. Tillich, "The Two Types of Philosophy of Religion," p. 10.
133. C.G. Jung, *Collected Works*, Vol. 12, "Introduction to the Religious and Psychological Problems of Alchemy," pp. 9, 11, pars. 10, 12; "Individual Dream Symbolism in Relation to Alchemy," pp. 98–102, 126.
134. C.G. Jung, *Collected Works*, Vol. 12, "Individual Dream Symbolism in Relation to Alchemy," p. 102, par. 126.

Naomi R. Goldenberg

A Feminist Critique
of Jung

Feminist scholarship in religious studies has explored the reasons why many women feel estranged from traditional religious institutions. Rejecting conventional views of what their subordinate place in the world should be, women can hardly be content with theological formulations which both reflect and justify that place.[1]

Portions of Jungian theory may prove helpful in the search for new formulations. Jung hypothesized that there is a religious process in every human being which dreams, symbols, and myths manifest. He saw such religions as Christianity, Judaism, and Buddhism as elaborate communal ways of organizing a basic religious progression. He thought a person quite lucky if she or he could be a devout follower of an inherited religion, for then the road would be easy, well planned, and secure. In *The Collected Works* Jung often states that his first effort in therapy is to try to connect patients to their native religions, since many of his patients did not suffer from a sense of the impossibility of coping but, rather, from a sense of the meaningless, barren quality of life. Contact with "religion" could help in their cure. If the connection with the native religion could not work, the patient had to become expert in listening and being guided by her or his own religious authority and adept in seeing a basic process within.

However, Jungian psychology particularly warrants a feminist critique because it has largely become a form of patriarchal religion itself. The first step in such a feminist critique is to question the veneration of Jung himself. He is regarded as a "prophet" by the vast majority of Jungians, whose self-assigned role is to teach and explicate the Jungian opus.[2] Most "original" Jungian works simply extend Jung's assumptions without questioning any premises. Erich

Neumann, for example, assumed the archetypes as already proven and then arranged them in succession.[3] Marie Louise von Franz looked at the archetypal truth of various fairy tales.[4] Even a work such as Ann Belford Ulanov's study of *The Feminine in Jungian Psychology and Christian Theology* does not in any way disagree with Jung in the classification of the concept of the feminine.[5] Given such attitudes, Jungians tend to overlook the several contradictory statements Jung may make within a single work, to veil his complexities and failures in an effort to make everything simple, cohesive, and inoffensive.[6] They will not admit that his statements were often misinformed, ignorant, or just plain prejudiced. (To paraphrase one unpublished seminar, for example, Jung virtually equated the Negro with the gorilla.)[7]

More important, feminist scholars must confront the sexism of Jung's theories which has also been glossed over by his followers. In fact, it is often argued that, in comparison with Freud, Jung valued the feminine and therefore valued women more. To look at a characteristic statement of Jung's on women, however, is to gain a very different impression:

> Woman is compensated by a masculine element and therefore her unconscious has, so to speak, a masculine imprint. This results in a considerable difference between men and women, and accordingly, I have called the projection-making factor in women the animus, which means mind or spirit. The animus corresponds to the paternal Logos just as the anima corresponds to the maternal Eros. But I do not wish to give these two intuitive concepts too specific a definition. I use Eros and Logos merely as conceptual aids to describe the fact that woman's consciousness is characterized more by the connective quality of Eros than by the discrimination and cognition associated with Logos. In men, Eros, the function of relationship, is usually less developed than Logos. In women, on the other hand, Eros is an expression of their true nature, while their Logos is often only a regrettable accident.[8]

Despite his caveats that his "intuitive concepts" should not be taken too literally, Jung is certain that women are characterized by Eros, an ability to make connections, while men are oriented toward Logos, the function of analytic thought. It is true that Jung genuinely values woman for her remarkable and all too often overlooked Eros, but it is equally true that he confines her to this sphere. Once she moves into a Logos arena, she is not only at a great disadvantage but is behaving unnaturally as well. Jung is not content to stay on a symbolic or harmlessly vague level with his ideas of "feminine" and "masculine." Like all the thinkers that Mary Daly describes who subscribe to a concept of the "Eternal Feminine," he gets around to making "dogmatic assertions" about what should or should not be the role of "existing individuals."⁹ Jung writes in his essay "Woman in Europe,"

> No one can get around the fact that by taking up a masculine profession, studying and working like a man, woman is doing something not wholly in accord with, if not directly injurious to, her feminine nature. She is doing something that would scarcely be possible for a man to do, unless he were a Chinese. [Note the racism.] Could he, for instance, be a nursemaid or run a kindergarten? When I speak of injury, I do not mean merely physiological injury, but above all psychic injury. It is a woman's outstanding characteristic that she can do anything for the love of a man. But those women who can achieve something important for the love of a thing are most exceptional, because this does not really agree with their nature. Love for a thing is a man's prerogative.¹⁰

Beyond the overt sexism in Jung's concept of the feminine, a feminist critique must examine the inequity of the anima-animus model of the psyche, which is never challenged by any of his immediate circle of followers.¹¹ The theory clearly favors men, even though it has been praised as a liberating concept because it supports that marvelous unseen creature—the "androgyne."¹² The anima-animus theory postulates a contrasexual personality in each sex. In men this personality would be female—in women, male. The word "personality," however, is too light; in Jungian thought, "anima" and "animus" conjure up associations to the unconscious and the soul. In fact, "anima" and "animus," like "Eros" and "Logos," are never clearly defined and are often used with different connotations, a slippery quality common to most Jungian concepts that serves to insulate them from much questioning. The only certain element is that an anima is man's picture of his female other side, while an animus is woman's picture of her other. Jung writes,

Since the anima is an archetype that is found in men, it is reasonable to suppose that an equivalent archetype must be present in women; for just as the man is compensated by a feminine element, so woman is compensated by a masculine one. I do not, however, wish this argument to give the impression that these compensatory relationships were arrived at by deduction. On the contrary, long and varied experience was needed in order to grasp the nature of anima and animus empirically. Whatever we have to say about these archetypes, therefore, is either directly verifiable or at least rendered probable by the facts. At the same time, I am fully aware that we are discussing pioneer work which by its very nature can only be provisional.[13]

The hesitation, the assertion of probability, and the mention of "pioneer work" at the end of the paragraph reveal Jung's uncertainty. But the key statement is the first sentence: *"Since the anima is an archetype that is found in men, it is reasonable to suppose that an equivalent archetype must be present in women."* The presence of the animus in women certainly seems to have been deduced from Jung's contention about an anima in men. He hypothesized the former to balance the latter. According to Jungian stereotypes of masculine and feminine, however, this gives women and men qualitatively different kinds of unconscious (or soul)—an enormous assertion based on little "evidence." It is not surprising, then, that Jung never developed the idea of the animus to the same extent as the anima; in my view he was forcing a mirror image where there was none. The anima-animus model is clearly more beneficial to men than to women. Barbara Charlesworth Gelpi correctly states that Jung "is primarily concerned with the integration, or, within the tradition of the myth [of androgyny], reintegration, of the feminine into the masculine psyche."[14] Jung's theory simply exemplifies the sort of androgyne Gelpi labels "the masculine personality fulfilled and completed by the feminine. . . ."[15] For women, Jung's particular model militates against change in the social sphere. While men can keep control of all Logos activities and appropriate just whatever Eros they need as a kind of psychological hobby, women are by no means encouraged to develop Logos, since they are thought of as handicapped by nature in all Logos arenas. Thus the anima-animus theory does not lead to the integration of the sexes but, rather, to more separatism.

Admittedly, it is good to urge men who have been afraid of experiencing Eros or anima because they think it is inappropriate to their sex to develop their contrasexual element. But the Jungian model functions with and sustains decidedly masculine and feminine stereotypes. I would argue that it makes far more sense to postulate a similar psychic force for both sexes. Freud did this regularly when he spoke of the "repudiation of femininity" as the task of successful psychoanalysis for men *and* women.[16] The current theology of women's religions argues positively for contact with female energy as the end toward which both sexes should strive.[17] It is less important, in my view, whether the basic human drive is labeled "male" or "female"; what matters is that the *same* primary impetus in human libido exists for men and women alike. In future work this model might be developed more profitably than the petty anima-animus division of the psyche.

To Jungians the anima, the animus, and their verbal handmaidens Eros and Logos are "archetypes," by definition, what is unchanging and unchangeable. This concept of archetype allows Jungians like Erich Neumann and Esther Harding to write studies on the "archetypal" nature of the feminine psyche which are based on their subjective selection of mythological material to document preordained conclusions.[18] Feminist scholars must examine the very idea of archetype in Jungian thought if sexism is ever to be confronted at its base.[19] Indeed, if feminists do not change the assumptions of archetype or redefine the concept, there are only two options: either (1) to accept the patriarchal ideas of the feminine as ultimate and unchanging and work within those or (2) to indulge in a rival search to find female archetypes, ones which can support feminist conclusions.

I have several reservations about this second alternative, which some feminists have chosen. Elizabeth Gould Davis's *The First Sex,* for example, is an essentially imaginative work—which claims to be "science."[20] It proclaims matriarchy as an *empirical* absolute, the very same kind of proclamation that men have made to justify the subjugation of women. I do see the great use in recovering lost, buried images of women; but if we establish these images as archetypes that define the proper experience of women, we are in danger of setting bounds to that experience. I see this as a new version of the Eternal Feminine enterprise which could become just as restrictive as the old Eternal Feminine ever was.

Instead of a new search for absolutes, feminists could abandon the idea of absolutes altogether. We could, further, renounce the Jungian idea of separating archetype from its expression in images, that is, the absolute, transcendent ideals of which our changing experiences, which usually appear visually in the mind and are expressed actively in the world, are only inferior copies.[21] This separation leads to a distinction between the ideal form out there in archetype land and the expressed content in here, in the activities, dreams, and mediations of individuals.[22] It is this separation of absolute from experience which lies at the base of all patriarchal religion: women are the way they are because they are conforming to something out there which can never change. It is such a concept which allowed much of Jungian thought to become racist, sexist, and closed to experience.

Rather than rival absolutes or superior-inferior paradigms, we could begin to equate image with archetype. This would put much greater value on what is happening in the individual psyche. Images are, after all, our psychic pictures of action, our imaginal depictions of the behavioral patterns we are continually enacting and continually modifying. All imaginal activities, all images, could then be understood as archetypes to the degree that they move things and partake of what we might want to call "numinosity." *Archetypes therefore would refer to the imaginal or religious process itself rather than to past documents of that process.* With this sort of notion, we can stay open to all the data of experience and cease looking for authority words to label that experience archetypal, mythological, or religious.

I am suggesting nothing less than breaking down the hierarchy of mind—to which all other hierarchies and authority structures are linked—whether political, economic, or religious. Since feminists have suffered more than most others from these hierarchies, I propose this as the task of the feminist scholar concerned with the psychology of religion. Like the patients Jung described who saw too much hypocrisy and too little relevance in native religion, feminists are both cursed and blessed—cursed because they cannot refer to any established text or doctrine to make the way easier and blessed because their religious innovations have a chance of being more creative.[23]

Notes

1. See esp. Sheila D. Collins, *A Different Heaven and Earth* (Valley Forge, Pa.: Judson Press, 1974); Judith Plaskow and Joan Arnold Romero, eds., *Women and Religion* (Missoula, Mont.: Scholars' Press, 1974); and Rosemary Radford Ruether, ed., *Religion and Sexism* (New York: Simon & Schuster, 1974).

2. See, e.g., Frieda Fordham, *An Introduction to Jung's Psychology* (London: Penguin Books, 1954); and Jolande Jacobi, *The Psychology of C.G. Jung* (New Haven, Conn.: Yale University Press, 1971). Thus in bookstores one will see rows of books summarizing Jungian thought.

3. Erich Neumann, *The Origins and History of Consciousness,* trans. R.F.C. Hull (Princeton, N.J.: Princeton University Press, 1954).

4. Marie Louise von Franz, *Creation Myths* (New York and Zurich: Spring Publications, 1972); *Interpretation of Fairy Tales* (New York and Zurich: Spring Publications, 1970); *The Problem of the Puer Aeternus* (New York and Zurich: Spring Publications, 1970); and *The Feminine in Fairy Tales* (New York and Zurich: Spring Publications, 1972).

5. Ann Belford Ulanov, *The Feminine in Jungian Psychology and in Christian Theology* (Evanston, Ill.: Northwestern University Press, 1971). Ulanov begins to raise questions in the appendix to "A Note on Eros and Logos," pp. 335–41. One can only wish she had carried such questions further.

6. Philip Rieff has pointed out some of the worst features of Jung's style in *The Triumph of the Therapeutic* (New York: Harper Torchbooks, 1968), pp. 44–45.

7. All of the seminars consist of notes transcribed by some of Jung's students. These notes cannot yet be directly quoted in print; one can only report on their contents. I discovered this reference to Negroes while editing a seminar for possible publication in Zurich.

8. C.G. Jung, *The Collected Works,* ed. G. Adler et al., trans. R.F. Hull, 2d ed. (Princeton, N.J.: Princeton University Press, 1968), 9, pt. 2:4.

9. Mary Daly, *The Church and the Second Sex, with a New Feminist Post-Christian Introduction by the Author* (New York: Harper Colophon Books, 1975), pp. 148–49.

10. Jung (2d ed., 1964), 10:117–18.

11. Jung's immediate circle of followers, in fact, were and are prone to emphasize it to an even greater degree than Jung himself. Dr. Jolande Jacobi, one of the most successful female members of the second generation of Jungians, insisted that, "just as the male by his very nature is uncertain in the realm of Eros, so the woman will always be unsure in the realm of Logos . . ." (pp. 117–18). The fact that her very

successful career as author and lecturer in the realm of "Logos" seemed to contradict this statement never bothered her at all.

12. I believe that, if there is a modern-day unicorn, it has to be the androgyne. It is said to be out there somewhere, running around but nearly impossible to catch. Cynthia Secor has envisioned the androgyne as a unicorn also ("Androgyny: An Early Reappraisal," *Women's Studies* 2, no. 2 [1974]: 163). Catharine Stimpson has seen it as another species of chimera ("The Androgyne and the Homosexual," *Women's Studies* 2, no. 2 [1974]: 242–43).

13. Jung, 9, pt. 2:14.

14. Barbara Charlesworth Gelpi, "The Politics of Androgyny," *Women's Studies* 2, no. 2 (1974): 158.

15. Ibid., p. 151.

16. Sigmund Freud, *The Standard Edition of the Complete Psychological Works*, trans. James Strachey (London: Hogarth Press, 1964), 23:252.

17. From a class given in the Wicca by Star Hawk, High Priestess of the Compost coven in San Francisco, December 1975.

18. Erich Neumann, *The Great Mother: An Analysis of the Archetype*, trans. Ralph Mannheim (Princeton, N.J.: Princeton University Press, 1972); and "The Psychological Stages of Feminine Development," trans. Rebecca Jacobson, *Spring* (1959); and Esther Harding, *Women's Mysteries* (New York: Bantam Books, 1971).

19. See my article entitled "Archetypal Theory after Jung," *Spring* (1975), pp. 199–219.

20. Elizabeth Gould Davis, *The First Sex* (Baltimore: Penguin Books, 1973).

21. James Hillman pointed this out in relation to instinct in his "Essay on Pan," in *Pan and the Nightmare*, by James Hillman and Wilhelm Roscher (Zurich: Spring Publications, 1972), pp. xxiii–xxvi.

22. Toward the end of his life, Jung toyed with the idea of a psychoid continuum on which our action in the world, our images of that action, and the ideal spiritual "archetype" were linked. Although he continued to insist on the transcendence of archetypes, he was beginning to join them to the material world of experience in images. See Jung, "On the Nature of the Psyche," in *Collected Works* (2d ed., 1970), 8:159–237.

23. See esp. Jung (1970), vol. 11; and "The Meaning of Psychology for Modern Man," in *Collected Works* (2d ed., 1964), 10:134–56.

Demaris S. Wehr

Religious and Social Dimensions of Jung's Concept of the Archetype: A Feminist Perspective

In recent years, feminist discussion of the usefulness of C.G. Jung's theories, notably the theory of archetype, has been wide-ranging, with some of the most intense debate taking place in the field of religion. Conferences and journals have been the usual forum for this debate. Feminist authors like Carol Christ and Naomi Goldenberg have criticized Jung's psychological model from a feminist perspective, and Jungians have responded by either updating the theory or defending Jung against what they perceive to be mis-interpretations of his theory.[1] This essay is my contribution to the debate.

Using a methodology informed by feminism and drawn from the sociology of knowledge, specifically the work of Peter Berger, I will examine the religious and social dimensions of Jung's concept of the archetype. This broad sociological emphasis allows us to un-cover the central problem and the potential value of this concept. The central problem is this: Jung ontologizes what is more accu-rately and more usefully seen as socially constructed reality. Even though Jung and Jungians at times describe the archetype as simply a propensity or a predisposition to act or image in a certain way, the category of archetype is often used as a category of Being itself. Thus Jungian theory can function as quasi-religious or scientific legitimation of the status quo in society, reinforcing social roles, constricting growth, and limiting options for women. Seen for what they actually describe, however, in other words, deontologized, Jung's archetypes can be useful.

I. A PARADIGM FOR UNDERSTANDING: SOCIOLOGY OF KNOWLEDGE

The sociology of knowledge is a subfield of sociology that emphasizes the role of institutions (religious, psychological, scientific and others) in molding human behavior and emotions. It also stresses the enormous human need for the ordering principles that institutions provide and the seemingly exorbitant price paid by individuals who defy established boundaries. Although human beings have created these institutions, the institutions have acquired an objective character, hiding the fact that they were created by humans in the first place. People collude with these structures because of the suffering they would incur if they did not and also, more importantly, because the very structures of consciousness itself come to be isomorphic with the social structures. By a similar process, one which Jung seems to have overlooked, the archetypal images of the collective unconscious and social structures, institutions, and roles also become congruent with one another.

In *The Social Construction of Reality,* written with Thomas Luckmann, and *The Sacred Canopy,*[2] Peter Berger has elaborated his sociology of knowledge as it applies to the individual in society. In *The Sacred Canopy,* a sociological study of religion, Berger concentrates on the interaction between a human being and society and on the role of religion in ensuring that society's mandates gain the necessary, sacred legitimation that will ensure their enforcement. Berger emphasizes that a society is nothing but a human product, and yet this product attains an objective status which allows it to "continuously act back upon its producer."[3] While it is obvious that society is a human product, it is perhaps not so obvious that each human being is also a product of society, and not merely in a simple and benign sense; for society is not only an objective reality but also a coercive force in the lives of individuals. Although human beings are entirely responsible for creating institutions, they come to perceive institutions as something that can act over and against them. Their role in the creation of these institutions becomes entirely lost to them and their relationship to institutions is thus characterized by alienation and even self-deception. The socialization process occurs in three phases—externalization, objectivation, and internalization:

Externalization is the ongoing outpouring of human beings into the world, both in the physical and the mental activity of men. Objectivation is the attainment by the products of this activity (again both physical and mental) of a reality that confronts its original producers as a facticity external to and other than themselves. Internalization is the reappropriation by men of this same reality, transforming it once again from structures of the objective world into structures of the subjective consciousness.[4]

Externalization, the first phase, takes place almost on the level of instinct. It is an "anthropological necessity." Human beings, by definition, must pour themselves and their activities into the world and, by so doing, create the world. This necessity springs from the unfinished character of human beings and the "relatively unspecialized character of our instinctual structure."[5]

Objectivation, the second phase, refers to the process by which the human outpouring of activity in the world attains an objective character so that human products come to confront human beings over and against themselves. These products then seem to have what Berger calls a "facticity" outside of the factor of human agency. "The humanly produced world becomes something 'out there.' It consists of objects, both material and non-material, that are capable of resisting the desires of their producer."[6]

The third phase, internalization, is the process whereby human beings come to be determined by society. Internalization refers to the "reabsorption into consciousness of the objectivated world" so that the structures of the world and the structures of consciousness are isomorphic. In other words, society produces people with structures of thought that coincide with the social institutions people created in the first place. "Internalization, then, implies that the objective facticity of the social world becomes a subjective facticity as well."[7]

Berger uses the metaphor of a conversation to explain the socialization process. He says that socialization is an ongoing conversation between significant others and the individual. World-maintenance, Berger points out, is a precarious affair and depends on this ongoing conversation with other people who live within the social structures and institutions and take them for granted, thereby giving them legitimacy. If this conversation is disrupted, the world begins to lose its "subjective plausibility." "In other words, the subjective reality of the world hangs on the thin thread of conversation."[8] The reason we do not recognize either the necessity of maintaining the conversation or the precariousness of the socially created world is that most of the time the conversation goes on undisrupted and unnoticed. The maintenance of this continuity is one of the most important imperatives of social order: "The socially constructed world is, above all, an ordering of experience. A meaningful order, or nomos, is imposed upon the discrete experiences and meanings of individuals."[9]

For Berger, two of the strongest structurers of human experience are language and religion. Religion is the "sacred canopy" which lends sacred status to socially constructed reality. Language is a strong reinforcer of social reality because it bestows an objective and apparently permanent status on humanly produced institutions, making them resistant to change. Descriptive language becomes prescriptive and helps to ward off change, thus maintaining and protecting our fragile social existence. Drawing heavily on Alfred Schutz's view that language is rooted in everyday life, Berger situates language within the stage of objectivation since it has the qualities of objectivity and coerciveness. Language tells us what is and religious language tells us what is in the realm of the sacred or the inviolable:

> All legitimation maintains socially defined reality. Religion legitimates so effectively because it relates the precarious reality constructions of empirical societies with ultimate reality. . . .
>
> Religion legitimates social institutions by bestowing upon them an ultimately valid ontological status, that is, by locating them within a sacred and cosmic frame of reference.[10]

As we will see later, the mythological language used by Jung and Jungians locates the archetypes within a sacred and cosmic frame of reference. Furthermore, since the language of Jung's psychology contains both scientific propositions and religious overtones, it fits well within Berger's framework.

Jung and the Jungians seem to think that by seeing irrational modes of behavior as being "possessed" by an archetype, or by viewing social role definitions as archetypes of the feminine, that is, by "seeing archetypally," they have freed people from the power of stereotypes. As feminists we claim that precisely the opposite effect occurs.[11] Using Berger's paradigm, we see that the third phase, internalization, is the phase at which the problem is no longer recognizable by us, the phase at which we are almost self-deceived, or alienated. When religious or scientific language names the world, it bestows an objective and sacred validity and fits Berger's second phase, objectivation. Such language is the tool of the most powerful legitimating process: the creation of a symbolic universe which gives us a matrix of meaning.

Seeing certain modes of behavior and role definitions as symbolic is especially dangerous when archetypal images of the collective unconscious serve to legitimate and perpetuate painful experiences in the world. Consider the prostitute, for example. Were such a woman to consult a Jungian analyst, the analyst's goal would be to free her from an identification with this archetypal image. But there is danger in archetypalizing her experience in the first place. It is not far-fetched within the Jungian framework to describe her experience as a living-out of the archetype of the fallen woman, a form of the Hetaira archetype, and thus lend her socially created role a kind of sacred status:

> Being given over to the concern with individual feeling, with its everchanging fluctuations, this type of woman may find it difficult to commit herself to any permanence in outer relationships. Indeed she may, like her male counterpart, the *puer aeternus,* shy away from any concrete commitment and forever lead a provisory life of emotional wandering. The mythological images which express this type are the love deities, hierodules and priestesses dedicated to the service of love; the seductresses, nymphs, beautiful witches and harlots also express its unadapted aspect.[12]

Surely there is a problem with a psychology that identifies certain ways of being in the world as archetypal and then makes no real distinction between types of archetypal experiences. If an experience is "numinous," it is archetypal and in some way partakes of divinity. This elevation has the effect of cosmic endorsement. The

Jungian framework, while it gives us a way to integrate unconscious and conscious contents, shows very little awareness of the social conditions that have created certain character types and offers no explicit criticism of traditional female and male roles.[13]

Another hazard in understanding certain experiences, psychic images, or behaviors as archetypal is that one thereby excludes the possibility of any real freedom from these compulsions. Jung said, in discussing the mana personality:

> It is indeed hard to see how one can escape the sovereign power of the primordial images. Actually I do not believe it can be escaped. One can only alter one's attitude and thus save oneself from naively falling into an archetype and being forced to act a part at the expense of one's humanity.[14]

II. JUNG, JUNGIANS, AND DEFINITIONS OF THE ARCHETYPE

Jung's understanding of the archetype evolved during his lifetime and his conceptualization of it became clearer. His use of the term remained persistently ambiguous, however, because he failed to distinguish between "archetype" and "archetypal image." His lack of precision in using these two terms led to frequent attempts at clarification by his disciples and students. In the beginning, a certain fuzziness, as Jung formulated his concept, was perhaps natural. Also, Jung seemed to be motivated by a strong desire to be accepted by the scientific community. This may account for his use of medical language, equating archetypes with instincts. The instincts, he said, "form very close analogies to the archetypes, so close, in fact, that there is good reason for supposing that the archetypes are the unconscious images of the instincts themselves, in other words, that they are patterns of instinctual behavior."[15] While the biological model may have been useful in legitimizing Jung's theories, the analogy with instincts has not added clarity to the concept of the archetype, which continued to be associated with images.

When associating the archetype with motifs from literature, myth, and folklore, Jung arrives at a much clearer definition:

The concept of the archetype . . . is derived from the repeated observation that, for instance, the myths and fairytales of world literature contain definite motifs which crop up everywhere. We meet these same motifs in the fantasies, dreams, deliria, and delusions of individuals living today. These typical images and associations are what I call archetypal ideas. . . . They impress, influence, and fascinate us. They have their origin in the archetype, which in itself is an irrepresentable, unconscious, pre-existent form that seems to be part of the inherited structure of the psyche and can therefore manifest itself spontaneously anywhere, at any time.[16]

This definition makes a distinction between archetype and archetypal image (idea), a distinction so crucial to Jung's thinking that it is unfortunate that he was not careful to speak of "archetypal images" every time he meant them, rather than lapse into the linguistically simpler "archetypes." Even if this distinction had been maintained, however, the concept of the archetype is still problematical in ways having to do with Jung's particular use of "numinosity"—a quality attributed to the experience of the archetype. As Jolande Jacobi explains in her study of the archetype, the archetype has a "dynamism which makes itself felt in the numinosity and fascinating power of the image."[17] In another book, Jacobi follows Jung in linking the archetype to the biological model, which she calls the "concern of scientific psychology." She distinguishes between the biological aspect of the archetype and the picture of the archetype when viewed from the inside, where its most important aspect is its numinosity, "that is, it appears as an experience of fundamental importance."[18]

III. ON NUMINOSITY: JUNG AND OTTO

Jung borrowed the concept of numinosity from Rudolf Otto's *The Idea of the Holy* (1923). There are some interesting implications of this borrowing. Otto's premise is that the rationalist conception of God lacks something essential, leading to a "wrong and one-sided interpretation of religion."[19] Otto thought that orthodox Christianity had failed to recognize the value in the non-rational and hence had kept that element out of its interpretation of God. His aim was to restore to the understanding of God the element of the non-rational. Thus Otto brings us to the category of the "holy" or "sacred." He calls the "holy" a category of interpretation and locates it squarely within the sphere of religion.

Otto suggests that there is something special about the "holy" which is "above and beyond the meaning of goodness." To describe this something, he uses a word, "numinosity," coined from the Latin "numen." Numinosity implies first of all, for Otto, creature-feeling. "It is the emotion of a creature, submerged and overwhelmed by its own nothingness in contrast to that which is supreme above all creatures."[20] The numinous is felt as objective and outside the self; it is the "Wholly Other." It also carries with it the feeling of *mysterium tremendum*. Otto is poetically eloquent in his description of this feeling, comparing it to the "sweeping of a gentle tide" or the bursting "in sudden eruption up from the depths of the soul with spasms and convulsions."[21]

The numinous also has an element of awefulness. Otto associates the kind of awefulness that accompanies the numinous not only with the perfectly familiar and "natural" emotion of fear but with a particular kind of fear. "Its antecedent stage is 'daemonic dread'. . . . It first begins to stir in the feeling of something uncanny, 'eerie' or 'weird.' "[22] This fear of the *mysterium tremendum* is accompanied by shuddering, which "is something more than 'natural,' ordinary fear. It implies that the mysterious is already beginning to loom before the mind."[23] The numinous, too, is characterized by *majestas*, which means "might, power, absolute overpoweringness." Otto connects the qualities of creature-feeling, awefulness, dread, a sense of the weird or uncanny, and the element of overpoweringness with mysticism and its annihilation of the self and understanding of the transcendent as the whole and entire reality: "One of the chiefest and most general features of mysticism is just this *self-depreciation* . . . and the estimation of the self, of the personal 'I', as something not perfectly or essentially real."[24]

The numinous contains an element of energy or urgency: "It [the numinous object] everywhere clothes itself in symbolical expressions—vitality, passion, emotional temper, will, force, movement, excitement, activity, impetus."[25] The numinous also has the power to fascinate:

The daemonic-divine object may appear to the mind an object of horror and dread, but at the same time it is no less something that allures with a potent charm, and the creature who trembles before it, utterly cowed and cast down, has always at the same time the impulse to turn to it, nay even to make it somehow his own. The "mystery" is for him not merely something to be wondered at but something that entrances him. . . . he feels a something that captivates and transports him with a strange ravishment.[26]

Throughout his descriptions of the numinous, Otto is talking about the experience of God. Jung applies the notion of numinosity to the experience of archetypal images residing in the collective unconscious, but his use of the term remains very close to Otto's. In carrying over a concept that pertains to the experience of the Divine and applying it to human (psychological, mythological, imaginal, fanciful, and social) interaction, is Jung divinizing the human psyche, or at least part of it, the unconscious? His use of the word "numinous" to apply to an experience of the archetype is congruent with Otto's description of an experience of the "holy," a category of interpretation and valuation peculiar to the sphere of religion.[27]

Jung is careful in some of his statements to separate the psychological and theological dimensions of inquiry, claiming that theologians are the only ones who can legitimately speculate about Reality or the Beyond. He states that as a psychologist he can only speak of human psychological experience and claims only to have demonstrated that a God archetype exists in the human psyche. In his theoretical explanation of the concept of God, however, he comes close to collapsing the distinction between the psychological and theological realms. In the following passage Jung gives religious legitimation to irrational behavior such as "an inexplicable mood, a nervous disorder, or an uncontrollable vice" by equating "autonomous psychic contents" with what has previously been labeled in our culture as divine, or even daemonic.

When, therefore, we make use of the concept of a God we are simply formulating a definite psychological fact, namely the independence and sovereignty of certain psychic contents which express themselves by their power to thwart our will, to obsess our consciousness and to influence our moods and actions. We may be outraged at the idea of an inexplicable mood, a nervous disorder, or an uncontrollable vice being, so to speak, a manifestation of God. But it would be an irreparable loss for religious experience if such things, perhaps even evil things, were artificially segregated from the sum of autonomous psychic contents. . . . If we leave the idea of "divinity" quite out of account and speak only of "autonomous contents," we maintain a position that is intellectually and empirically correct, but we silence a note which, psychologically, should not be missing. By using the concept of a divine being we give apt expression to the peculiar way in which we experience the workings of these autonomous contents. We could also use the term "daemonic," provided that this does not imply that we are still holding up our sleeves some concretized God who conforms exactly to our wishes and ideas. . . . by affixing the attribute "divine" to the workings of autonomous contents, we are admitting their relatively superior force.[28]

In the following passage Jung goes even further in conflating psychology and theology:

It is only through the psyche that we can establish that God acts upon us, but we are unable to distinguish whether these actions emanate from God or the unconscious. We cannot tell whether God and the unconscious are two different entities. Both are border-line concepts for transcendental contents.[29]

The admission by Jung of a possible fusion, or at least a possible confusion, of God and the unconscious is crucial for our understanding of how the collective unconscious can serve to legitimate socially constructed roles for women.

On the negative side: the quarrel I have with Jung is with his willingness to consider archetypal phenomena as manifestations of the Divine and with his assertion that we lose something valuable psychologically if we do not see them as such.[30] While a plunge into Jung's theology is outside the scope of this essay, it is enough here to note that Jung's theory confers religious and ontological status on behaviors, moods, and even uncontrollable vices, which can be explained on other grounds. These grounds do not involve us in categories of the sacred as we try to understand ourselves and others, to change our behavior, and to become free from stultifying roles and compulsions.

On the positive side: although the theological underpinnings of Jung's psychology are fundamentally flawed in this way, and although he mixes the levels of psychology, ontology and theology to a confusing degree, his *method* of differentiating oneself from unconscious contents has much to recommend it. It gives us a greater awareness of the unconscious pulls operating on us—greater self awareness in other words—and a measure of freedom from those irrationalities. The consequent absence of moralistic condemnation as a response to the evil in ourselves is also valuable, and indeed, is the first step toward self-acceptance and transformation.

Jung's perception of the numinosity of certain moods and the irresistible pull of certain psychic responses is convincing. There is no doubt that our inner world often contains powerful compulsions and Jung describes very well the inner experiences, fantasies, moods, compulsions, pulls, that beset us in our daily lives. Nor is there any doubt that we experience these things as autonomous, coming from somewhere other than our own conscious will. In fact, our own conscious will alone is insufficient to free us from them. The process which Jung called individuation (both the goal and the natural outcome of life) is one in which we become more truly ourselves. It demands that we increasingly differentiate our conscious selves from a sort of murky identification with unconscious contents. In other words, we become more aware of moments when inner voices, archetypal images, or complexes, are pulling on us and we learn not to identify with them. We can also engage with them, as personifications (shadow, animus and anima) and gain the benefit of their perspectives. As individuation proceeds, we become increasingly free of such compulsions, since we perceive them as autonomous, collective, and impersonal. Archetypes, used in the sense of a compulsion, mood, or psychic pull, are part of a vast sea of mental influences, from which the process of individuation gives us at least some measure of freedom. That element of Jung's description is part of the genius of his psychology.

IV. ANIMUS AND ANIMA

Our understanding of archetypes can illuminate the way women's and men's psyches both reflect and conflict with images of women and men given to us by a patriarchal society. In particular, the experience of "being possessed by an archetype" (acting out of an unconscious identification with an archetypal image, so that a man acts like the anima and a woman acts like the animus—both of which are inferior "feminine" and "masculine" ways of acting), when viewed in cultural context, exposes the human tendency to internalize imprisoning and oppressive images. But understood ontologically, as archetypes often are, Jung's concept has the capacity to imprison us further. Because of his gift for grasping fantasy and dream images, Jung offers a more imaginal description than Freud does of the inner world of women and men bound by a patriarchal culture. Women caught in seemingly isolated individual struggles are acting out the culture-wide struggle of all women to realize their full humanity (one that includes, for example, a strong intellect) in a society which devalues them and offers no complete vision of their possibilities of empowerment.

The anima and the animus are two especially powerful archetypes. Both Emma and Carl Jung used the terms anima and animus to indicate the unconscious contra-sexual element (the anima being the feminine component of the male psyche and the animus the masculine component of the female psyche) in the male and female personalities. These are lopsided concepts given that the cultural positions of men and women differ, with men generally having and women generally lacking, power and respect. This inequality is not discussed by the Jungs, although Emma Jung comes close to recognizing it. Jung summarizes the distinction between anima and animus as follows:

> If I were to attempt to put in a nutshell the difference between man and woman in this respect, i.e., what it is that characterizes the animus as opposed to the anima, I could only say this: as the anima produces *moods,* so the animus produces *opinions.*[31]

Emma Jung's version of the animus was clearer and less pejorative than C.G. Jung's. She describes the animus in terms more likely to resonate with women's inner experience. For example, with respect to the way in which the animus functions within the female psyche, Emma Jung says:

The most characteristic manifestation of the animus is not in a configured image (Gestalt) but rather in words (logos also means word). It comes to us as a voice commenting on every situation in which we find ourselves. . . . As far as I have observed, this voice expresses itself chiefly in two ways. First, we hear from it a critical, usually negative comment on every movement, an exact examination of all motives and intentions, which naturally always causes feelings of inferiority, and tends to nip in the bud all initiative and every wish for self-expression. From time to time, this same voice may also dispense exaggerated praise, and the result of these extremes of judgment is that one oscillates to and fro between the consciousness of complete futility and a blown-up sense of one's own value and importance.[32]

Had Emma Jung gone one step further in her analysis, she would have realized that the animus can emerge as harsh self-criticism in a male voice and that this internal, critical voice is an accurate reflection of the culture's derogatory view of women's motives, intentions, and self-expressions.[33] Since, from a Jungian standpoint the psyche operates by compensation, the animus's exaggerated praise is the opposite of devaluation. The woman's inner evaluation of herself swings back and forth between these two extremes. But this phenomenon, too, reflects the polarized images of women that our society offers. As many scholars have noted, images of women presented by modern media, as well as in fairy tales, myths and religious stories, tend to be extreme rather than balanced, fragmented rather than holistic.[34]

Emma Jung describes another facet of the animus:

And now we come to the magic of words. A word, also, just like an idea, a thought, has the effect of reality upon undifferentiated minds. Our Biblical myth of creation, for instance, where the world grows out of the spoken word of the Creator, is an expression of this. The animus, too, possesses the magic power of words, and therefore men who have the gift of oratory can exert a compulsive power on women in both a good and an evil sense. Am I going too far when I say that the magic of the word, the art of speaking, is the thing in a man through which a woman is most unfailingly caught and most frequently deluded?[35]

Again, without a sense of the social dimension, Emma Jung did not realize that women are spellbound by the power of the word precisely because that is the power which has been denied them. An awareness of this double bind is essential if women are to be liberated from their sense of powerlessness. Mary Daly's description of the problem is characteristic of the large body of feminist theory about women and the power of the word.

> Women have had the power of *naming* stolen from us. We have not been free to use our own power to name ourselves, the world, or God. The old naming was not the product of dialogue—a fact inadvertently admitted in the Genesis story of Adam's naming the animals and the woman. . . . To exist humanly is to name the self, the world, and God. The "method" of the evolving spiritual consciousness of women is nothing less than this beginning to speak humanly—a reclaiming of the right to name. The liberation of language is rooted in the liberation of ourselves.[36]

A positive contribution of Jung's concept of the anima is that it offers us a unique view of the inner world of the male who struggles to accept a side of himself which is devalued by society. It is interesting that no devaluation of the man by his anima like that of the woman by her animus is presented. Rather, the anima in men appears to work primarily by seduction (again, a replication of the way in which society has encouraged women to behave). This seduction takes many forms—bewitchment, frozen feelings, dangerous fascination—but it is seduction nevertheless, and not devaluation. There are many examples of the anima's gentle art of seduction in Emma Jung's article on the animus and anima. Here is one:

> But swan maidens and nixies are not the only forms in which elemental feminine nature shows itself. Melusine is scolded by her husband for being a "serpent," and this figure, too, can embody the primal feminine. It represents a more primitive and chthonic femininity than the fish does, for example, and certainly more than the bird, while at the same time cleverness, even wisdom, is ascribed to it. Moreover, the serpent is also dangerous. Its bite is poisonous and its embrace suffocating, yet everyone knows that despite this dangerousness the effect that it exerts is fascinating.[37]

While Emma Jung's treatment of the anima and animus arche-types may be offensive to some feminists because it starts from an assumption of differing feminine and masculine natures, it is inter-nally consistent and speaks of the necessity of integrating the other side of one's nature. Unlike female followers of Jung such as Toni Wolff and Ann Ulanov, Emma Jung does not make the mistake her husband does of identifying real women with the anima.[38]

Carol Christ has astutely observed that "the strength of [Jung's] theory lies in its insight into the psyches and psychic tasks of edu-cated (and culture-creating) white males in Western culture."[39] Christ feels that Jung's eros/logos model does seem to account for white males' underdeveloped eros function and highly developed intellect, and suggests that the model be kept as a "useful tool for analyzing white males and the culture they have created."[40] I agree with Christ here, and I also think that the archetypal model of the psyche has some value for understanding women as well as men if the model is seen in relationship to society and its values, in other words, if it is contextualized and hence deontologized.

Jung and the Jungians omit from their descriptions of the animus and anima three crucial elements: the ubiquitous nature of patriarchy, the equally ubiquitous and persistent problem of misog-yny, and the dialectic relationship between the individual and soci-ety.[41] If these three phenomena are explained and incorporated in the Jungian system, we discover a useful description of our culture as it is *experienced inwardly,* and as it is reflected by the psyche in dreams, fantasies, and moods.

Jung not only ontologizes a socially constructed reality, his emphasis on religion, religious experience, and the numinosity of the archetypes gives divine sanction to psychological experiences that are culturally-based. These psychological experiences, or images, need to have the divine sanction removed from them.

Naomi Goldenberg has suggested that the Jungian concept of the archetype as an absolute must be discarded or revised.[42] None-theless, she thinks that there is much of worth in the Jungian schema, particularly Jung's understanding of the symbolic reality of religion and of the religious value of inner experience. Goldenberg is helpful in directing our criticism to the concept of the archetype, the central Jungian concept. Without it the Jungian system loses its very foundation.

Feminist readers have asked, "Why retain the Jungian model at all?" "Why bother about its 'uniqueness' if the theory is corrupt?" Part of the answer is that Jung's psychology does give us a workable view of the unconscious. Jung's understanding of the unconscious is positive and creative in many respects. That this concept has been used, like many others, to reinforce existing stereotypes about women does not warrant throwing out an idea which gives the study of soul some of its soulful dimension. Our understanding of what the unconscious is can be rescued from the notion that it is a stagnant, static eternal entity. Furthermore, the volumes and volumes of work Jung did on the collective unconscious do illustrate the ways in which it mirrors the culture. Assimilation and integration of archetypal images can be understood as an experience of wrestling with the demons of a sexist culture. Gender-linked archetypes can be seen as inner representatives of socially sanctioned, seductive but oppressive roles and behavior patterns.

V. THE ANIMA AND THE FEMININE: TWO ARCHETYPAL IMAGES ILLUSTRATED

The socially constructed nature of the archetype as it affects women is best illustrated by comparing the concepts of the anima and the feminine. The anima is a component of male psychology, and the feminine a component of female psychology. Although both terms seem to refer in some way to women, "anima" is not synonymous with "the feminine." The anima is the soul-image of men's imaginations which they often project onto real women. Men must disentangle themselves from the anima in order to be able to relate to real women and to allow real women the space to be themselves. The feminine, on the other hand, is a way of perceiving and being in the world as lived out by women. The latter is a social role definition, although it becomes archetypal in Jungian thought. This essential distinction between the anima and the feminine is not always made by Jungians.[43]

Men's experience of the quality of their own souls, according to Jung, is primarily a "feminine" experience; that is, it has an emotional quality that reminds them of what they think women are like. Jung intends to make it clear that the anima is a part of male psychology. This "soul-imago" is composed of three elements. The first is the experience of real, adult women whom the particular man has known; this experience is registered as an "imprint" on his psyche. The second is the man's own femininity, usually repressed; the more repressed his own femininity, the more traditionally feminine his soul-image will be and the more likely it is that the women he is attracted to will carry that projection. ("Carrying the projection," in Jungian terminology, means being the one on whom the image is projected.) The third is an *a priori* category, an archetype, an inherited collective image of women.[44]

Though Jung placed the anima in the male psyche, he frequently mixed a discussion of the anima with a discussion of the psychology of women:

> Woman, with her very dissimilar psychology, is and always has been a source of information about things for which a man has no eyes. She can be his inspiration; her intuitive capacity, often superior to man's, can give him timely warning, and her feeling, always directed towards the personal, can show him ways which his own less personally accented feeling would never have discovered.[45]

This quotation is taken from the chapter "Anima and Animus" (*CW* VII) in which Jung attempts to explain the way the feminine soul-imago is formed upon the male's experience of real women. Jung fails to acknowledge, however, that what he has written is *his* experience of women, a reflection of *his* anima, and, no doubt, that of many men. While attempting only to describe the anima in men, he has attributed all of its characteristics to "woman."

A similar mixing of levels arises when Jung explains man's own repressed femininity:

> It seems to me, therefore, that apart from the influence of women there is also the man's own femininity to explain the feminine nature of the soul-complex. There is no question here of any linguistic "accident," of the kind that makes the sun feminine in German and masculine in other languages. We have, in this matter, the testimony of art from all ages, and besides that the famous question: *habet mulier animam?* [Does woman have a soul?] Most

men, probably, who have any psychological insight at all, will know what Rider Haggard means by "she-who-must-be-obeyed," and will also recognize the chord that is struck when they read Benoit's description of Aninea. Moreover they know at once the kind of woman who most readily embodies this mysterious factor of which they have so vivid a premonition.[46]

This last sentence again illustrates Jung's confusion of the anima and all women. In discussing "man's own femininity" he has lapsed into talking about actual women. No wonder later readers have had such a hard time deciphering the meaning of the anima. Jung himself alludes to the difficulty of the concept: "I do not expect every reader to grasp right away what is meant by animus and anima."[47]

With respect to the third component of the anima, the *a priori*, or inherited, collective images of women, Jung does not slip into a discussion of real women, but keeps to the issue at hand:

> As we know, there is no human experience, nor would experience be possible at all, without the intervention of a subjective aptitude. What is this subjective aptitude? Ultimately it consists in an innate psychic structure which allows man to have experiences of this kind. Thus the whole nature of man presupposes woman, both physically and spiritually.... The form of the world into which he is born is already inborn in him as a virtual image. Likewise parents, wife, children, birth, and death are inborn in him as virtual images, as psychic aptitudes. These *a priori* categories have by nature a collective character; they are images of parents, wife and children in general, and are not individual predestinations. We must therefore think of these images as lacking in solid content, hence as unconscious.[48]

While Jung in this passage does not equate women with male projections onto them, he does take an androcentric perspective. Female psychology, while mentioned frequently in his writings, always has a clearly derivative character.

Another Jungian, Marie Louise von Franz, in *The Feminine in Fairytales*, provides an example of the way Jungians have confronted and rationalized inconsistencies in Jung's theory such as the ones noted above. Unlike Jung, von Franz seems at least to recognize the mixing of levels as she describes the feminine in fairytales:

The authors of these religious writings are men known to us. Under such circumstances, we can say that the figure of Sophia represents certain aspects of the man's anima. At other times, however, we could just as well say that the figures represent feminine psychology. The whole problem becomes in one way more, in another less, complicated if we try to concentrate on how the psychology of the feminine and the psychology of the anima are intertwined. . . . Thus some women give in entirely to the anima projection. . . . If he only likes her as an anima figure, she is forced to play the role of the anima. This inter-reaction can be positive or negative, but the woman is very much affected by the man's anima figure, which brings us to a very primitive and simple and collective level where we cannot separate the features of anima and real women. Frequently they are mixed to some extent and react upon each other.[49]

Von Franz's description has the advantage of clarity on one level— she is undoubtedly correct about the effect of male projections on female behavior and attitudes—but this passage shows the same androcentric bias found in Jung's writings. Neither does it account for the social element in this interplay. There do not seem to be any accounts of the man's character being shaped and formed by women's animus projections, other than the descriptions of the man who has been plunged into an anima mood because of conversing with a woman's animus.

Like Emma Jung in *Animus and Anima,* von Franz failed to realize that men's projections shape female character and behavior to the great extent they do because women are relatively powerless in society. As Jean Baker Miller shows in *Toward a New Psychology of Women,* dominants have very different psychological characteristics from subordinates, and subordinates absorb much of the dominants' viewpoint because it is the norm. "Tragic confusion arises because subordinates absorb a large part of the untruths created by the dominants."[50]

Much about "women's nature" has crept into what is reputedly a discussion of a component of male psychology, the anima. This mixing means not only that readers must make a continual effort to clarify Jung's ideas, but also that the usefulness of the anima as a concept is seriously undermined. Disparaging comments about women can be found throughout Jung's writing and feminists who examine Jung's theory of the anima in its present state will reject all Jungian statements about female psychology.

If we consider Jung's concept of the anima in light of Otto's description of the numinous, we see that the effect of the numinous is remarkably similar to the feeling of being gripped by an archetypal image. The element of fear, whether it takes the form of dread, awe, horror, or fascination, is important in both. The experience of the anima in men seems to contain all of these elements, and parallels men's attitudes toward women in our culture and toward the feminine element in themselves. In our society men are often alienated from their own emotions and from relationships generally.[51] In this condition, they do indeed project onto women both exalted and debased images of the kind Jung describes and then are captivated by these projections.

The crucial element in these descriptions is fear. Fear (awe, dread, horror, bewitched fascination) must surely be the basis of misogyny and misogynistic projections such as the devouring mother. Fear functions in the psyche as an agent of distortion, preventing one from truly seeing the other, as of course, Jungians know. Yet their descriptions of the anima contain these very distortions of women's nature. The concept of the anima can still be useful, however, if it is recognized for what it is: a picture of romantic alienation in men, or, to put it another way, a psychological response arising from men's ambivalence toward women, which is a form of fear.[52]

The archetypes of the feminine were first elaborated by Toni Wolff, a member of Jung's inner circle. Drawing on Jung's own description of feminine archetypes, Wolff names and describes them: the Mother, the Hetaira, the Amazon, and the Medium. For Wolff, these four archetypal images represent the major ways in which women experience the world. Ann Ulanov explains this tetralogy in *The Feminine in Jungian Psychology and Christian Theology:*

> These fundamental archetypal forms of the feminine are described in the myths and legends of all cultures throughout history, as for example in the recurrent tales of the princess, the maiden, the wise woman, the witch, etc. In our everyday speech, when we describe women we know or know about, we often resort to typing them, unconsciously using archetypal imagery.

Common examples are the references to a woman as "a witch," "a man-eater," and so forth. The archetypal forms of the feminine describe certain basic ways of channeling one's feminine instincts and one's orientation to cultural factors. They also indicate the type of woman one is or the type of anima personality a man is likely to develop.[53]

Notice that in this passage certain social categories are unquestionably accepted as categories of Being. The feminine, a social role definition and a way of relating to the world, has acquired ontological status. Moreover, archetypes of the feminine, with their aura of the numinous, have entered the dimension of religious experience.[54] They have become part of the meaningful order, or nomos, that is "imposed upon the discrete experiences and meanings of individuals. . . ." "It may now be understandable if the proposition is made that the socially constructed world is, above all, an ordering of experience."[55] Role definitions and behavior as well as neurotic character types have become legitimated by their relationship to the sacred.

According to Berger's framework, it is impossible for human beings to live without a nomos, or an ordering principle in their lives. Society is just such a giver of order, and it follows that socially defined roles which order and legitimate our lives in the social realm also partake of the character of the nomos. Berger's dialectic shows that an individual becomes that which she or he is addressed as being by others. On the other side of the dialectic of identity formation and society lies "anomy," a word Berger took from Durkheim's "anomie" but spelled in the Anglo-American manner. "Anomy" means "loss of order." At its most extreme, anomy leads to disintegration, fragmentation, and chaos; on an individual level this can mean mental illness, suicide, or extreme anguish. These are the consequences, Berger believes, of trying to live outside of the social order (nomos). To criticize, doubt, or otherwise threaten the identity-creating conversation with others is to risk anomy, but anomy must be risked if social change is to be effected and the truth about our institutions be known.

The concept of the archetype protects and shields us from the terror of anomy. This concept gives order to our experience, giving archetypal experience the blessing of the gods. Yet a confrontation with nothingness, Mary Daly tells us, is essential if women are to become authentic: "This becoming who we really are requires existential courage to confront the experience of nothingness."[56] Speaking of a space set apart from the prevailing "nomos": "it is important to note that this space is found not in the effort to hide from the abyss but in the effort to face it, as patriarchy's prefabricated set of meanings, or *nomos*, crumbles in one's mind. Thus (this space) is not 'set apart' from reality, but from the contrived nonreality of alienation."[57] Many societies punish members who dare to live outside the prescribed roles. However, the confrontation of anomy is the first step in creating not only an authentic self but a new social order.

A possible way of confronting the experience of nothingness is to attempt to live outside nomic structures which legitimate damaging or limiting social roles and identity concepts. The experience of nothingness to which Mary Daly refers must surely be the consequence of stepping outside the parameters of the ongoing conversation. In spite of the risk of anomy, feminists must dare to step outside of the nomizing conversation. On the other hand, all of the works cited, as well as Jung's, understand the inherent human need for order. Feminists, being human, do not escape this need.

What, then, is a possible solution? Goldenberg suggests the breaking down of mental hierarchies; Daly proposes the radical bond-breaking bonding between women; Miller stresses the need for the courage to embrace conflict with men, with other women, and with outworn self-images whose fraudulent hold on our psyches nonetheless exerts a formidable grip. All of these are sign-posts. None of these is a total solution. We do not and cannot know the full direction in which we are moving, as we continue to see through and reject nomic solutions with sexist implications.

From the point of view taken in this essay, Jung's and Jungians' explanations of archetypes of the feminine and of the anima are descriptively, and also prescriptively, limiting images of women in a patriarchal society. There *is* room, however, within the theory for a creative working-through of one's relationship to certain archetypal images. This working-through must be done with awareness of the patriarchal imprint which the archetypal images bear.[58] Jung's and the Jungians' explanations of archetypes of the feminine and the anima, therefore, are not useful to women unless deontologized and they may be dangerous as originally conceived and presented.

Archetypal images are really considered by Jung to be the stuff of which revelation is made. They also constitute the symbolic language of the unconscious. Jung is concerned with our increasing symbolic impoverishment and the consequences of this for human life and relationships; many feminists share this concern. The problem, then, lies in the divine status which is given in Jungian theory to certain symbolic expressions.

I see gender-linked archetypal images as inner compulsions, psychic pulls, to be part of a collective view of women and men. My evaluation of Jung's concept of the gender-linked archetypes finally rests on two bases: one negative and one positive. On the negative side, it carries the potential for lending sacred legitimation and ontological status inappropriately to neurotic behaviors. The ontological-theological language about archetypes paradoxically serves to reinforce existing stereotypes about women and men rather than freeing us from them. Seen ontologically, the concept is stultifying and romantically compelling; it tends to make social change difficult. On the positive side, the method of differentiation is useful and the concept of the collective unconscious with its archetypal images is ingenious, original, and unusually effective in describing people's inner states. When it is deontologized and seen as a reflection of cultural taboos and fears, the concept of gender-linked archetypes is a very helpful one. As a way of understanding the manner in which our psyches wrestle with socially constructed images of women and men, it is liberating.

Notes

1. See Naomi Goldenberg, "A Feminist Critique of Jung," *Signs: Journal of Women in Culture and Society* 2, No. 2 (1976), 443–49. Also see Goldenberg, "Archetypal Theory after Jung," ibid., 443–49; Carol Christ, "Some Comments on Jung, Jungians and the Study of Women," *Anima* 3, No. 2 (Spring Equinox 1977), 68–69; Goldenberg, "Feminism and Jungian Theory," *Anima* 3, No. 2 (Spring Equinox 1977), 14–18. Responses to Christ and Goldenberg can be found in *Anima* 4, No. 1 (Fall Equinox 1977).
2. Peter L. Berger and Thomas Luckmann, *The Social Construction of*

Reality: A Treatise in the Sociology of Knowledge (Garden City, N.Y.: Doubleday, 1967); Berger, *The Sacred Canopy: Elements of a Sociological Theory of Religion* (Garden City, N.Y.: Doubleday, 1976).

3. Berger, *Sacred Canopy*, 3.

4. Berger, *Sacred Canopy*, 4.

5. Berger, *Sacred Canopy*, 5.

6. Berger, *Sacred Canopy*, 8–9.

7. Berger, *Sacred Canopy*, 17.

8. Ibid.

9. Berger, *Sacred Canopy*, 19.

10. Berger, *Sacred Canopy*, 32–33.

11. Thanks are due to one of my students at Harvard Divinity School, Lorna Hochstein, for sharing this insight with me.

12. Edward C. Whitmont, *The Symbolic Quest: Basic Concepts of Analytical Psychology* (Princeton, N.J.: Princeton Univ. Press, 1969), 179.

13. It does offer social criticism in some other areas, however, such as war, which is seen as the corporate "shadow projection" of one nation unto another.

14. Jung, *The Collected Works* VII, pars. 389–90. (*The Collected Works of C.G. Jung*, trans. R.F.C. Hull, are published by Princeton University Press in the Bollingen Series XX and are hereinafter cited as *CW* with volume and paragraph numbers following.)

15. Jung, *CW* IX, Part I, par. 91.

16. Jung, *Memories*, 392–93.

17. Jacobi, *Complex, Archetype, Symbol*, 37.

18. Jacobi, *Psychology of C.G. Jung*, 41.

19. Rudolf Otto, *The Idea of the Holy* (New York: Oxford Univ. Press, 1958), 1.

20. Otto, *Idea*, 10.

21. Otto, *Idea*, 12–13.

22. Ibid.

23. Otto, *Idea*, 14–15.

24. Otto, *Idea*, 21.

25. Otto, *Idea*, 23.

26. Otto, *Idea*, 31.

27. In an article entitled "Religion and Modern Thinking" which appeared in the German periodical *Merkur* (February 1952), Buber criticizes the religious nature of Jung's thinking. Buber says Jung oversteps "with sovereign license the boundaries of psychology in its most essential point" (Martin Buber, *Eclipse of God*, New York: Harper & Bros, 1952, p. 104). Buber defines Jung's psychology as a modern form of Gnosticism, primarily because Jung conceives of God as a *conjunctio*

oppositorum in which good and evil are bound together. Buber's reply is close to my own criticism of Jung's divinization of the human psyche:

> The psychological doctrine which deals with mysteries without knowing the attitude of faith towards mystery is the modern manifestation of Gnosis. Gnosis is not to be understood as only a historical category, but as a universal one. It—and not atheism, which annihilates God because it must reject the hitherto existing images of God—is the real antagonist of the reality of faith. Its modern manifestation concerns me specifically not only because of its massive pretensions, but also in particular because of its resumption of the Carpocratian motif. This motif, which it teaches as psychotherapy, is that of mystically deifying the instincts instead of hallowing them in faith. (175–76)

28. Jung, *CW* VII, pars. 400, 403.
29. Jung, *Memories*, 395.
30. Much as Jung disavowed himself as a theologian, he did consider theological matters to a great extent in his work. The entire concept of the collective unconscious rests on Jung's understanding of the way the Divine is manifested in human life. Jung's major theological point is that the Christian concept of God as all-good and all-powerful is erroneous. Jung's theology and psychology mutually derive from and reinforce one another. Jung was preoccupied with theological problems from an early age, especially the problem of evil and its coexistence with an omnipotent, good God. From an early religious experience (the cathedral vision, at age eleven) Jung took comfort in what he felt God had revealed to him: that God, too, has an evil side and that God had willed Adam and Eve to sin. God's evil accounted for the evil in humanity, since people are created in the image of God. Since God contains both good and evil, Jung reasoned, He needs human evolution in order to evolve Himself more fully. The placing of good and evil on the same level—ontologically, psychologically and theologically—is the fundamental Jungian tenet that allowed Jung to elevate to the level of the Divine so many opposing and neurotic interhuman and intrapsychic phenomena.
31. C.G. Jung, *CW* VII, par. 331. Many feminists have seized on such extreme statements as the following:

> A woman possessed by the animus is always in danger of losing her femininity, her adapted feminine persona, just as a man in like circumstances runs the risk of effeminacy. These psychic changes of sex are due entirely to the fact that a function which belongs inside has been turned outside. . . . With regard to the plurality of the animus as distinguished from what we might call the "uni-personality" of the anima, this remarkable fact seems to me to be a correlate of the conscious attitude. The conscious attitude of woman is in general far more exclusively personal than that of man. Her world is made up of fathers and mothers, brothers and sisters, husbands and children. The rest of the world consists likewise of families, who nod to each other but are, in the main, interested essentially in themselves. The man's world is the nation, the state, business concerns, etc. His family is simply a means to an end, one of the foundations of the state, and his wife is not necessarily *the* woman for him (at any rate not as the woman means it when she says "my man"). The general means more to him than the personal; his world consists of a multitude of co-ordinated factors, whereas her world, outside her husband, terminates in a sort of cosmic mist. (Jung, *CW* VII, par. 338)

32. Emma Jung, *Animus and Anima: Two Essays* (Zurich: Spring, 1974), 20.
33. Of course, from a Jungian standpoint the collective unconscious, by definition, cannot be a reflection of the surrounding society. Jung is quite clear on this point:

> Looked at from the outside, the psyche appears to be essentially a reflection of external happenings—to be not only occasioned by them, but to have its origin in them. And it also seems to us, at first, that the unconscious can be explained only from the outside and from the side of consciousness. It is well known that Freud has attempted to do this—an undertaking which could succeed only if the unconscious were actually something that came into being with the existence and consciousness of the individual. But the truth is that the unconscious is always there beforehand as a system of inherited psychic functioning handed down from primeval times.

> Consciousness is a late-born descendant of the unconscious psyche. (Jung, *CW* VIII, par. 676)

On the question of which level is causative—the psychic (or spiritual, as Jung also calls it) or the material level—Jung is clearly, although not philosophically, idealist. He sees the psyche as causative and would have to say that culture derogates women *because* of an archetype (the animus or negative anima) and not the other way around. More recent scholarship on the psychological characteristics of minority and oppressed groups, however, suggests that the concept of internalized oppression, rather than innate inferiority or a propensity toward self-devaluation, accounts for their self-derogation. Furthermore, our everyday observations tell us that no one, male nor female, comes equipped with enough self-confidence to value himself or herself properly without encouragement from outside.

34. See, for example, Sarah Pomeroy, *Goddesses, Whores, Wives, and Slaves* (N.Y.: Schocken, 1975) and Sheila M. Rothman, *Woman's Proper Place* (New York: Basic Books, 1978).
35. Emma Jung, *Animus and Anima*, 19.
36. Mary Daly, *Beyond God the Father: Toward a Philosophy of Women's Liberation* (Boston: Beacon, 1973), 8.
37. Emma Jung, *Animus and Anima*, 76.
38. She flirts with such an identification, but she actually avoids making it. For examples of Emma Jung's relative caution on this issue, see *Animus and Anima*, 55, 59. Ulanov does not do this, either, in her recent book *Receiving Woman: Studies in the Psychology and Theology of the Feminine* (Philadelphia: Westminster, 1981).
39. Christ, "Some Comments," 68.
40. Ibid.
41. Jung and Jungians are not totally unaware of these three social facts. For them, however, social reality is always derived from the psychic (i.e. archetypal) level and is always of secondary importance.
42. Goldenberg, "Feminist Critique."
43. Some of the authors who do make the distinction are Christ, "Some Comments," Whitmont, *Symbolic Quest,* and Ann Ulanov, *The Feminine in Jungian Psychology and in Christian Theology* (Evanston, Ill.: Northwestern Univ. Press, 1971).
44. Jung, *CW* VII, pars. 296–301.
45. Jung, *CW* VII, par. 296.
46. Jung, *CW* VII, par. 298.
47. Jung, *CW* VII, par. 340.
48. Jung, *CW* VII, par. 300.

49. Marie Louise von Franz, *The Feminine in Fairytales* (Zurich: Spring, 1972), 1-2.

50. Jean Baker Miller, *Toward a New Psychology of Women* (Boston: Beacon, 1976), 11.

51. They do not rate relatedness high on a scale of values. See Carol Gilligan, "In a Different Voice," *Harvard Educational Review* 47, No. 4, 481-516.

52. Carol Christ has already spoken of the way the anima functions in the psyches of men, in an appropriate application of the anima theory.

53. Ulanov, *The Feminine*, 195.

54. Of course, this very fact illustrates a thorny aspect of Jung's psychological and theological thinking. While he claims to be an empiricist, and neither a metaphysican nor a theologian, in his own use of the categories Jung fails to distinguish consistently between ontological and psychological dimensions—even though he makes this distinction theoretically, as illustrated by his statement, "The religious point of view understands the imprint as the working of an imprinter; the scientific point of view understands it as the symbol of an unknown and incomprehensible content" (quoted in Ulanov, *The Feminine*, 125). Yet, even Ulanov admits that: "For Jung, 'God' designates a psychic, not an ontological reality, even though he does not always make this clear. The empiricist is limited to what is observable; beyond that resides mystery, which he does not presume to classify. For the empiricist, metaphysical truth and religious experience are essentially psychic phenomena, that is, they manifest themselves as such and must therefore be investigated, criticized, and evaluated from a psychological point of view. . . . A serious criticism of Jung's insistence on separating the empirical from ontological statements is that his own theories and results do not support the separation. . . . Ontological assertions are unavoidable because one's mode of approach in all its details is itself a piece of the reality one perceives as well as one of the means of giving it its shaping and identifying qualities" (126-27).

55. Berger, *Sacred Canopy*, 19.

56. Daly, *Beyond God*, 23.

57. Daly, *Beyond God*, 156.

58. See for example Christine Downing's essay, "Coming to Terms with Hera," *Quadrant, Journal of the C.G. Jung Foundation for Analytical Psychology*, 12, No. 2 (Winter 1979), 26-47.

Ann Belford Ulanov

The Objectivity of Subjectivity:
The Feminist and Spiritual
Strengths of Psychoanalysis

I. DEPTH PSYCHOLOGY

The psyche is the departure point for depth psychology.[1] It is the urtext, not the scriptures, not the oral or written documents of history, not a set of theological doctrines or liturgical rituals, but simply the human psyche. To say this so boldly is to feel how depth psychology pushes us to the borderlands, close to the dangerous frontiers of the unknown. Why this is so derives from several hard facts.

The first fact is that the text to be studied in depth psychology —the psyche—is a living presence. This is what is researched and interpreted—the psyche's dreams and fantasies, its symptoms and obsessions, its compulsive behavior and relationship with others, its longings and impulses. This psyche of ours is a living document and it speaks back, indeed yells, if poorly treated or misunderstood.[2]

To say that the text that depth psychology studies is the living psyche is also to say that it is *our* psyche, not someone else's, not "theirs." Hence much of the training in depth psychology means working on our own psyche directly often for years, sometimes for a lifetime. For the fact that we are trained to treat the psyches of others does not mean that we can escape the tasks set by our own psyches. For working with others means working with our own reactions, fantasies, failures, in the responses of what we call countertransference. We go on learning how to use our reactions to others for their benefit, as well as for our own continuing education.

One of the first borders we are brought to when the psyche is the text is the wavery line where subjective and objective are somehow to be distinguished. Then we can cross the borderline into another country where distinctions between subjective reactions and objective facts no longer announce themselves in accustomed ways. Part of what we do to ascertain the objective facts of another person's psychic history is to use subjective reactions, our own and the other's. To be specific about the topic of feminism means using precise examples of these kinds of reactions. I will use illustrations from women's experience and men's responses to the feminine.

For example, in a particular case history the question may arise in an analyst's mind: Was this woman to whom she has been listening intently raped as a child? The woman cannot remember. The facts are gone, extinct, repressed. She, the patient, experiences the event as not existing, not there to be found even when looked for. But objective evidence may exist that suggests the need for such a question—symptoms that arise and cripple her now, many years after the event, when she wants to enjoy her sexuality. She may be assaulted by images of violent, even of murderous wishes toward her partner, or of overwhelming feelings of a withering contempt. Anxiety may steal her sexual responses from her, so they simply are not there at her disposal. But even these symptomatic reactions may be blocked and not registering consciously. Instead, they may turn up in the analyst's responses to the woman. For the analyst may herself be invaded by fantasies of murderous impulses, or contempt, or intense anxiety. Whose emotion is the analyst experiencing, her own, or the woman's?

Sometimes the first way that a lost event, an objective fact, makes its way to subjective consciousness is through the subjectivity of another person. Subject and object get all mixed together, sometimes so muddled that the old categories of separation do not hold. That mixing is a great and constant danger in the work of depth psychology and it is unavoidable. We can catch things from each other, patient and analyst. The complex that bedevils one person can take up residence in the other. All that we know with certainty in this area is the objectivity of the subjectivity that we share. But that is, in fact, a great deal, for we know that that is so across all the differences between us, differences of experience, of background, race, creed, color, sex, education, physical health, or illness.

A second fact about this text that is the psyche is that it is particular and personal—our own.[3] The psyche is never abstract but always specific, and yet its particularity is formed by others, shaped and influenced by the communities and collectivities in which all of us live. When we think about depth psychology as a resource for feminism and for spirituality we must ask about the experience of being a woman, our actual housing or abandoning of our femaleness. But again, our experience depends on others and cannot be pulled loose from them.

Many maps exist to guide our journey into the borderlands of the psyche. Many interpretive schemes offer aid in approaching the psyche as text. The object relations school of depth psychology makes much of the significant others in our lives, especially before our egos were mature and strong. Whom did we take into ourselves? Who became our introjected objects of the womanly, the feminine? What do we see as good and bad about being feminine? What kind of family setting, social setting, natural setting—in farm or city—influenced how we understand the feminine?[4]

My patient's childhood in wartime was terminated at twelve, she said, when the hospital where she was being treated for a broken arm was hit by a bomb. She, as the oldest child on the pediatric ward, became the adult leading the "children" to the air raid shelter. She lost her girlhood right there, she said. From then on she coped—she had to—whether it was foraging for food, hiding in the countryside, or caring for her mother grieving over the loss of her husband, the patient's father. She grew up to become a nun, to go on serving others. Eventually she had to leave her order because she had lost her self, her particular connection to the center, to the spirit and to the feminine. In her fifties, she set out to find her lost girlhood and the womanhood that was lost with it. The feminine was as distant from her as the grain goddess of Sumer who so aroused her awe and reverence. In such soil, she felt, her soul could root and grow into rich feminine life, both personal and professional.

How different from a man of the same generation who was also victimized as a child in war. He both feared and despised the feminine and all things female. For him they were filled with the disgust he had felt as a little boy who had to wear his sisters' stockings to keep warm. He still felt the despair he had known trying to be the man of the family for his mother, sorrowing and made distant by the sudden loss of his father, and for his five sisters, a task intensified by the fact that he was the youngest in the family. He had been over-whelmed by terror and depression. As an adult, he still found the feminine overwhelming, a force which unmanned him, and yet one upon which he felt dependent.

We are shaped by those who love us, those who leave us, by what happens right around us in our family and town and country. The spoken and unspoken rules, the teaching, the politics and the weather all go into us. This is what we take in—introject: our cultural setting, the temper of the times, the languages and social images of the sexes. All these "objects" not only help to form our images of the feminine and the spirit, but take up permanent residence in ourselves. They are what comprise our interior life.

This is as true for bad as for good images. A woman who grew up in the south came to detest the kind of coercive religiosity, steeped in sentimentality, with which she grew up in her family and community. She summed it up in a few angry words, which she spat out: "Jesus is not pink!"

When we see that the psyche's text is particular to us, highly personal, not at all general, or abstract, we find ourselves moving toward another borderland. For what is particular and most personal is in fact also shared. The particular is touched by the general too; the personal is also tied to the collective. The borderland of public and private, inside and outside, mine and ours, is now to be crossed. The categories of separation are insufficient. Mixing is the point here.

The object-relations map outlines this clearly. Our interior life is made up of bits and pieces of others—the objects that we have taken into ourselves and combined with our emotions, body feelings, perceptions. What is inside is certainly ours—it is after all inside "us"—but it is comprised of bits of "them," not only specific other people, but also images of our culture and historical time. That is why psychological terrorism is so devastating. We can damage so many layers in the interior of another person, another sex, another people. And that is also why prejudice is so hard to uproot. Its roots go down deep, out of sight, twined around internal images of self and other that must be radically changed if the prejudice is to be excised. If we have taken in and lived with the conviction of a parent, as a patient of mine did from her father, of an image of the female as unalterably second-class, we may find ourselves fixed in low self-esteem and in great trouble in our relations to men. We may also find ourselves full of anger for this contemptuous inner father.

Our burden here, conscious and unconscious, is heavy. It may suddenly hit us in what may seem an unrelated area, as church liturgies change and women come into the sanctuary. These things are not just matters of consciousness, but reach far into the unconscious, when they touch a host of internal objects and our ties to self and other and thus to community.

Jung's analytical psychology stresses a whole additional set of images and feelings that arise from unconscious depths of the psyche, collective images and feelings that the small personal ego must confront. That is, I think, the third fact about the psyche as text. Both the object relations school and the Jungian concern themselves with inner objects, but the first puts its emphasis on those objects that originate outside ourselves while Jungians stress those objects that spontaneously emerge from the layers of the unconscious which Jung calls collective or objective.[5]

In a woman's case, conscious ego images of the female are invariably introjected from significant women in her life, mother, older sister, teacher. Images of woman come to her too from her culture, for example the pencil-thin feminine figure that our fashion magazines have so long held out as ideal. But much older, archetypal images of woman and the feminine also arise in her, in dreams and fantasies.[6] What happens if these images, primordial ones, present visions of the feminine absolutely opposed to those of a woman's cultural experience? What if, for example, a woman dreams of the female body as a Venus of Willendorf whose might, powerful presence, and fecundity are bodied forth in her plenitude of flesh while still, consciously, she feels compelled to achieve a pencil-thin figure? How is a woman's ego to find her way through these strong opposites, both collective, both impersonal, that operate within her person? Some eating disorders, both anorexic and bulimic, involve just such a task of coming to terms with opposing images of the feminine and setting the ego in right relation to them.[7]

Some feminists misunderstand Jung's notion of archetype as another stereotype enjoined upon us, another dubious image of the ideal feminine to which a woman must accommodate.[8] The direct experience of archetypal images is the answer to that misunderstanding. The real thing is not a mental concept but a living presence to which we must work out relationship. This we do by putting together live bits from our personal biography, from images in our

culture, and from the archetypal images that emerge from the unconscious. The archetype confers a readiness to respond, not a set
content. The Willendorf image, for example, is just one of many
ways to envision the feminine, and its sudden emergence in archetypal dream or fantasy reminds us of the wealth of possibilities of the
feminine. Which image appears and why and when depends on
biographical, cultural, or historical circumstance. Working out relation to archetypal images means just that—working it out, in detail,
over some time, with a kind of improvisatory attitude, not slapping
on labels or set contents to which women must conform.

This example, of the opposition of conscious object-related
images of a pencil-thin female figure and the archetypal Willendorf
figure, suggests another more basic tension between a woman's ego
and her self. She may well ask: Who is in charge of my psyche? Is it
my ego version of how I should look and want to look? Or is it this
crazy alien dream image?[9] Is it possible that both of these images are
collective? Do I have to work out my own way of being and appearing female all over again?

For simplicity's sake, I have contrasted the ego and the unconscious, the object-related image and archetypal. The opposition is
not often that precise. For the woman involved, both sets of images
carry an archetypal punch. She feels equally compelled to match her
culture's fashion image and its opposite looming from her unconscious. She cannot just sit down and decide between the choices. She
must work out relations to the conflicting images and the opposing
powers of ego and self. Archetypal images, it must be stressed again,
are just not set contents of new coercive forces in our lives. On the
contrary, archetypal images and our efforts to relate to them—which
also may mean changing them according to idiosyncratic conditions
of personality or epoch—offer antidotes to the stereotypes so persistently laid upon women.[10]

Jungian psychology points to the danger of the collective ab-
sorbing the ego from within as well as from without. We can lose
our soul by being swept off into identification with an archetypal
image from within just as much as we can be carried off into identification with outer cause or mass movement. The poor souls in the
back wards of mental hospitals for thirty years or more, or the
mentally-ill homeless yelling at us on our city streets, now attest to
this. They have intense visions, perhaps of their being the new

Christ or anti-Christ or mother of God. The visions rise up and carry their egos far beyond the known boundaries. Visions die and rise up again endlessly. Egos in such ill people either drown or float forever, with no grounding in concrete earth.

Mental hospitals or city streets are not the only places this happens. It happens too in our churches and our political groups. It can threaten any of us in one of those powerful gripping moments which mark our lives, which bring a kind of manna, accompanied often by an image of almost numinous force. Do we receive these images? Do we become them?

A specific area that Jung concerns himself with more than other depth psychologists is our God-image. What if God is a goddess? An animal? How do we receive this odd impulse without becoming identified with it? How do we relate that to the God-image of Judeo-Christian tradition? Do we replace the old one with the new? Can we, in our little egos, talk and listen to both? Can we find a personal standpoint of devotion and integration rather than just being pushed this way and that by inner and outer forces and a welter of images? There are, after all, such things as psychic infections and contamination. The Jonestown massacre offers a frightening example; Nazi ritual, a still more terrifying one. Here God-images got loose and caught up millions into identifying with them, with no grounded, embodied ego-stance to provide anchor or resistance.[11]

Thus another threatening borderland is crossed and recrossed. God-images from collective tradition, the God-images of our group, pull us to one side. The God-images that well up from unconscious collective imagery pull us to the other side. Our small ego, caught between these pulls, needs not only to cross back and forth but finally to come back to firm earth, to find and create a path of spiritual life and devotion, in its individual life and in its community. How do we house the collective and personal images of God and connect them? This central, spiritual and cultural task includes the psyche.[12] Jung's words ring true: neurosis is our failure to discover religious values; we fall ill for lack of spiritual meaning in our lives.

When we take the psyche as our text we see the psyche in its particularity and as part of the collective. We see that it pulls us across the borderlands of subjective-objective, personal-collective, traditional and personal God-images. The psyche as text is embodied, concrete; it is here and now in space, in relationship; it reaches through its concreteness to touch the unknown. Thus we come to another borderland, the one that strikes between known and unknown, between the clearly circumscribed and a vast boundarilessness.

Depth psychology, looked at in this way, leads us to claim our psyches in their concreteness so that we know who and where we are well enough to risk crossing borders into what is unknown, is disembodied, unlived. For in the living text that is the psyche there is also an unwritten text, a text yet to be written and to be read—the unconscious. Really to experience the known is to be led into the unknown.

The unknown can be frightening. Most people, Jung thought, will do almost anything not to go there. Only necessity drives us there in most cases. Our problems, our sufferings, our ruptures with other people, our unhealed wounds, force us toward the unknown. We know, for example, that we are caught in addictive forms of behavior—smoking, overeating, gossiping, anxious complying with others, compulsive combat with others—and we know we should stop. We tell ourselves all the reasons as we reach for another cigarette, another cookie, another argument.

Our conduct, once embodied this way, outruns our reason. Our repeated wounds and hurts drive us farther into ourselves to find the unlived life hiding there that is pressing us to be lived, and lived consciously. When a woman pastor weeps, for example, about the emptiness of a spiritual life that is devoid of a real, live presence and about an accompanying compulsion to eat, we see two kinds of hunger right in that borderland between known and unknown. The soul's hunger embodies itself in the body's hunger to press forward the unlived spirit that seeks open entrance into the woman's life and work.

That sort of example is easy enough to give but very hard to live through. The frightening area between madness and sanity seems closer than we thought. It feels crazy to be caught in such compulsive behavior. Obsessive eating is bad enough, but what if what happens is more like the experience of a man who ejaculated spontaneously whenever he saw a mother with a young child. This could happen on a bus, a street, a subway. It was as if he were compelled to pay homage to a madonna image, a Great-Mother image, to go out of himself to her in this startling body behavior because he had not consciously accepted her numinosity. Such wounds feel mad and do indeed make us crazy. And yet it is clear that we must go into these wounds. They are a central part of our embodied selves, rather like dark passageways that lead to the pieces of our missing life, not unlike darkness of the spiritual life. Here we are the object of another subject, obviously not in control, driven, afraid.

God feels in such experience like the pursuing hound, even the author of our failures or the bully who overpowers us, not tender, friendly, or clear, but willful, capricious, dangerous. For those who question that God can be so near and so negative, those who want to correct us by saying God is transcendent and never mixed up in our neuroses, I want to ask: Where else can God find us but in the darkness and dirt of our psychic stable, the prison of our compulsions, the outcast places in ourselves?

Our religious tradition really is about salvation and a God who enters our suffering, who takes up our ridiculous small problems. In those problems, we become the lame, the halt, and the blind, held fast in our compulsions by powers beyond our control. This God—so fierce, so intimate, so pursuing—reaches right to those wounded places, sufferings which mirror all the other sufferings, sufferings taken right to the mystery of the cross.

The fact of the psyche, present as living text in all of us, cuts across the divisions of age, class, sex, creed, race, culture, and epoch. We do not all fear the same mental life, for we are shaped by our differences, but we have much in common in the way we lead the life of the psyche. The text that it provides and the effort of depth psychology to read it offers us together a splendid hermeneutic and an undeniable one. We cannot get around the psyche; it is there in all that we do. It reflects the influence of culture, even when it inverts culture, or transcends it. It is not confined to introjecting it.

II. FEMINISM

If we think of feminism as the name given to those who support women and want to see them supported in all their diversity, in all their needs and skills and deserts, where does it cross paths with depth psychology?

The task of depth psychology can be described as to put the parts of a person together. Most of us who seek therapy are suffering from missing or lost parts or parts yet to be uncovered. Depth psychology brings to feminism a consciousness of such parts in women and the psychic necessity to gather the parts, not just those we know about or want.

First among these is the body, the first and continuing basis of the ego, the foundation of the psyche, the book in which the psyche's text is written. Here we enter an area of tension. Freud emphasized the body, yet in a restrictive way for women, illustrated by his often disparaged statement about women that anatomy is destiny. Of course, I must reject his conclusion. It takes one part for the whole. But I would not reject the part itself, as some have tried to do. Whatever body we possess—tall, short, stout, emaciated, healthy, sick, formed, deformed, able, unable—helps shape us and remains a major source of our fantasies and visions, of our female consciousness and spirit. As Elizabeth Petroff points out, some women saints feel attached to the wound in Christ's side, and not only in the communion ritual, making Christ, not Mary, the nursing mother for their souls. They also see Christ's blood as representing his femininity: the blood is milk; his wound, a womb. These saints seem to suggest that Christ's blood is menstrual blood, heretofore ritually impure, a part left out, now fully gathered into spiritual life.[13]

For all his projections onto the female, Freud himself recognized the special departure-point of female psychology in a female body, saying we needed not only a different content to meet it but a different mode of apprehension. We must go to women themselves, he suggested, and to poets.[14] Thus it was Freud who inaugurated the study of the female as different from the male—or perhaps I should say, this is my reading of Freud's own unconscious and the part it has played in his own studies of women and others—one very different from his conscious efforts to understand the female as the obverse of the male. We can see in Freud's theories about women his own experience of the feminine in himself, his anima, to use Jung's term, which he in turn projected onto the women around him. His was an ambivalent attitude to the feminine, evident also in the contrast between his theories about female psychology and the number and range of brilliant, talented, unconventional women who gathered around him to do so much of the work of psychoanalysis. They were mavericks as well as pioneers. For none of them was anatomy destiny!

Whatever our approach to its material, depth psychology insistently reminds us that the body in each case is central to our sexual, spiritual, personal, shared life. We must reckon with it. Depth psychology says to feminism: Look to your body, do not skip over it; house in your awareness all that your body means, its seasons, its cycles, its fecundity.

A good case in point is the abortion issue. Depth psychology says, in effect, that a decision here, whether for or against abortion, has psychological roots which must be unearthed and worked through. It is within the power of consciousness to do so, but it remains hard work, because the roots are far down in the unconscious. In one set of roots, we discover the symbolic significance of pregnancy as the power to carry being, to incarnate a living spirit. How, we must ask, are we connected to that capacity? Do we fear it? Disown it? Another set leads to our feelings about our mothers and motherhood. Another reaches to our feelings about our childhood and to our present inner psychological child, the part in us that has not yet grown up, the damaged and neglected child. Is this child, unknown or disowned, behind our pregnancy? We would not acknowledge or mother it, would not hear its pain, so that the only way its psychic content could get our attention was to implant itself as a real child growing in our womb. Or is this inner child a symbol of our potential wholeness and future life? Have we ignored that forward thrust of our impulse toward life, toward the unknown, so that again the only way a living psychic urge could reach our awareness was for its symbolic spiritual life to become literal in pregnancy? Are we pregnant because we wanted to prove our power to conceive a life or because we skipped over our wish to do so? And what about the antecedent question about all the different forms of contraception open to us? Why is unwanted pregnancy on the rise? The answers lie in these hidden roots. They must be uncovered, sorted through, understood for a woman facing abortion.

The feminist movement has had salutary effects on depth psychology on precisely this area of decision. Earlier psychological literature claimed that a woman deciding for abortion would suffer lifelong guilt because she was opposing maternal instinct. She would never get over it. I see that position as a kind of bullying, out of the fear that arises from a still unconscious identification of the feminine with maternal instinct. The women's movement has helped expose this unconscious assumption. We make our own decision about our hunger and aggressive instinct. We call it differentiation of our relation to these instincts. The same can be true with the maternal instinct. But it takes work. Depth psychology learned that and its more recent literature speaks out of that awareness. We can put the point more boldly: Are we to be identified with this instinct any more than with our sexual instinct? Are we not to house it, to relate to it, to find our own embodied way to deal with it, to know the potentials of motherhood?

It may be possible for a woman to choose abortion and not be dogged by guilt, but only if she can gather all the parts of her psychic reactions to maternity, abortion, and pregnancy, and try to know all her embodied feelings and fantasies, conscious and unconscious.

We cannot be sure ahead of time where we will come out. We may discover that in fact we have two different views. We may feel strongly that the right to choose abortion should be afforded women and then discover that we ourselves cannot make that choice. Or we may feel strongly that abortion is wrong and should be outlawed and then, when we are in a particular situation, suddenly find ourselves choosing abortion. The choice is particular and embodied. Depth psychology reminds us to leave space for the diversity of persons and reactions, conscious and unconscious.

Depth psychology supports feminism's emphasis on women's actual experiences rather than what women are told they should be, or might wish they were. Depth psychology recognizes the differences between the sexes, standing against all those, including those feminists who would skip over the facts of different bodies, different cultural conditioning, different psychic configurations and clusters of symbols around the female and the feminine. Depth psychology rejects reductionist positions, whether biological—anatomy is destiny—or cultural—all can be traced to conditioning. What does the text say? What is the living experience? What has it been for you or her or me?

Depth psychologists look, on the whole, to root out the confusion that results from equating difference with discrimination. Some feminists criticize Jung here, misunderstanding the symbolic concepts of anima and animus to indicate a set content of masculine and feminine characteristics that invariably impose themselves on living persons.[15] That is a misguided reductionism, this time into dogmatic abstraction. Animus and anima are Jung's names for living people's experiences of being brought deep inside themselves and far outside themselves simultaneously whenever they risk intimate engagement with another person, the embodied "other." Not only do sexual fires ignite them, but spiritual ones, too. In these meetings of self and other, of ego-world and self-world, we feel found out, discovered, unearthed, set free it may be, brought face to face with what we are willing to live for, what quickens our enthusiasm for being, and sometimes what we are willing to betray for, even to die for.[16] Anima and animus stand for the readiness to respond to otherness, not through a set content, not in the abstract, but in the face and body and presence of another person, or in the astonishment at finding another point of view, with its own definite characteristics, inhabiting our own body and life.

In depth psychology, we discover that we cannot get rid of sexual differences without leaving out the body which is the foundation of the psyche, its housing, the shaping force of identity.[17] It recognizes women as distinct from men and not to be made into copies of men. Jung's recognition of feeling as a rational function, for example, is echoed in Carol McMillan's work in philosophy where she says reason's paradigms traditionally have been defined as "masculine" modes of abstract cognition and analytical logic, leaving "feminine" to be associated with intuition and emotion as if they were inferior, less grown-up modes of moral discourse. McMillan shows that emotion and intuition also have their cognitive and rational aspects. Evelyn Fox Kellar finds a similar bias in the history of science, exposing as simply one among several possible approaches the objective, analytical, abstract mode of investigation usually identified as masculine and rated as superior. In psychology, Carol Gilligan sets alongside the accepted stages of moral development a different "feminine" way which goes at a set problem by asking different questions and thus arriving at different conclusions. This differentiation of departure point, if left unrecognized, leaves a little girl who is working from it to be scored as inferior on tests of moral development. All she is doing is seeing problems differently. Caroline Walker Bynum studies the ways that women, over the centuries, have tended to interpret religious symbols very much in contrast to men. Continuity, paradox, connectedness stand out for women; contradiction, opposition, confrontation emerge as dominant in the "masculine" mode of approach.[18]

Depth psychology acts as a resource for feminism by distinguishing real women from what is projected upon them. This may be a complicated procedure at times, for as with any human endeavor, depth psychology often succumbs to the vice of its virtue. Depth psychology has made its own dubious contributions to the psychic stuff projected onto women. But still one finds somewhere in all its theorizing and clinical work an underlying critique against any system, including its own, that would substitute rhetoric for the living text of the psyche, that would substitute common cause for particular experience, or ideology for persons. There exists in depth psychology a radical hermeneutic applied to all positions, including its own. Jung describes it as both reductive and prospective.[19]

The reductive side of the hermeneutic unmasks unconscious motives by always asking: What are the parts of this view? What is the psychic origin of the view? Where has it come from? What is its hidden agenda? Are you, for example, rejecting women as priests because you are in thrall to a mother complex? Are you appeasing a feminist who is angry because you live in terror of the angry rejecting mother who could swat you down like a fly? Are we so angry in the service of our cause of justice for women because we are retaliating against a father who failed to love us? Are we insisting on a collective group against an individual because we have so little hold on our own ego that its unformed state needs group boundaries to secure it? Are we rejecting the group and overprizing the individual because we carry scars from being always the one left-out at school? Are we ignoring men, or saying that they are all that matters, because we are avoiding the wounds we suffered from men in the past? Are we just discarding this part of ourselves rather than coming to terms with it? Are we calling men pig-headed tyrants because there is a man inside us who behaves that way, judging our every effort as inferior, so that we must project that force onto actual men in order to put it somewhere outside ourselves? Is part of our attraction to a goddess-image a way of venting anger at a church or synagogue system? Is part of our allegiance to an inherited theology a way of avoiding the numinous force of the feminine?

These are challenging questions, maybe even harsh ones, looking to the underside of our beliefs and positions. This particular
reductive hermeneutic is a knife that cuts all ways, even through our
own most prized psychological defenses, so that we do not become
identified with our own point of view and then project all our
missing and defective parts onto our neighbors. This exposure of
our unconscious identifications is a central function of depth psychology. It addresses our commitments to social causes, intellectual
positions, and hermeneutical methods. It cuts across the usual distinctions of class, race, culture, education, creed, and sex. These are
psychic issues that belong to all of us and all of us must struggle with
them in our great community of strugglers and sufferers.

The prospective part of the hermeneutic asks a different set of
questions. Where is this view leading? What is struggling to come
into consciousness? What psychological processes are hidden here?
The prospective hermeneutic asks not just where a view comes from
or what is missing and hidden in it, but where it takes us, and what
new parts are to be uncovered and brought into being.

The prospective hermeneutic leads beyond self and group, or,
to put it another way, into the deeper dimensions of self and groups.
This is what Jung calls the archetypal world, which is close to Karl
Popper's third world, to Ernst Cassirer's world of symbolic forms
and organs of spirituality, to D.W. Winnicott's transitional space,
and to Marion Milner's domain of psychic creativity. Specifically, in
relation to our subject of feminism, this prospective view brings us
to the archetypal dimensions of the feminine, to those clusters of
images and numinous symbols which gather round themselves powerful affects and behavioral patterns that are in turn bodied forth and
made perceptible in a large variety of images of the feminine and all
parts of the feminine, light, dark, negative, positive, bountiful, devouring, life-promoting, life-destroying. Here we find huntress and
hag, both wise and aggressive, good mother and wicked witch, seer,
prophet, artist, pioneer, snake woman, siren, goddess of fertility and
the one who blights or makes impotent.

These images of women in the concrete and the abstract are as
varied as they are numerous. The archetypal content that addresses
us is equally varied, unfixed, and delivered through the living text of
our lives with all our personal problems and experiences, our social
setting, the Zeitgeist. None of us lives out all of these images and

contents. The images, and all else that our unconscious presses upon us, may change across the years. But in our finitude, we usually discover that only a few of these images and issues are what we have struggled with in the living text of our psyches. That is one reason women need each other. They embody for each other parts of the feminine beyond the reach of talent or time on earth of any one woman.

In the archetypal realm we find numinous images of the feminine with a potency so distinctly female, so eminently of woman in her many forms, that only a vast imaginative and spiritual space can hold them all. Depth psychology pushes feminism beyond group identification as it probes the symbols of the feminine. It supports the true meaning of "sisterhood" in emphasizing the many different ways women and men come to terms with the feminine in themselves and others and find that way access to spirit.

In the most concrete terms, connection to this level of the psyche's text opens us to glimpses of how personal struggles contribute to a larger human struggle so that, for example, personal guilts may be assuaged, or, where they cannot, can be better carried rather than be projected onto one's neighbors. Sharp dichotomies between the personal and public, between service to the deepest truth within ourselves and service to others, between personal love and love of God, are exposed as false. The psyche's text is revealed as bigger than our ego-concerns.

One set of examples, drawn from fearful mothers, of how the prospective hermeneutic pleads for the archetypal dimension will demonstrate what I mean. A mother fears she has failed her child, because the child, now grown up, suffers such serious problems— food addiction, hostility, grave uncertainty, neurotic lack of confidence or even ease in being herself. This may be a heavy burden of guilt for a mother. In a collective way, we may reassure ourselves: such guilt simply comes with mothering. But for the individual parent, recognition of failure, repentance, the hope of making reparation, prove a grim struggle. Interpreting the particulars of such struggle from a prospective viewpoint leads us to archetypal mothering. Here a mother is no longer identified with an ego's view. The archetypal image of mother reaches to all the parts, failures as well as successes, as intrinsic to mothering. Negative acts are inevitably part of the psyche's text as well. The ego tries to edit them out, saving just the positive bits. The archetype of the good mother is less defensive; it always brings the opposite into play—the witch, for example, who wants not to feed but to eat up the child, not to welcome dependency but to challenge it with trickery and guile. But, by just that opposition, the absence of support, the witch contributes to a child's development.[20] Moreover, seeing things in this archetypal perspective gives us glimpses into powers, negative and positive, that bring mother and child into strong relation to each other. This perspective reminds us that what a mother does or fails to do is not the whole story, thus counteracting the moralizing undertone of psychological theories of mother-child relationship which so quickly place burdens of guilt on mothers.

A fragment from the dreams of a mother of a grown-up daughter illustrates the contaminating power of a witch-complex and the insight that freed the dreamer to make good sense of the witch force. The dreamer reports: "I dream my daughter is mad at me, full of reproaches and recriminations because I do not know things about her and her feelings. I say to my daughter: 'But you never told me those things, so how could I be sensitive to them?' I am angry. She pauses and sees the point but then sweeps on, saying something about how I control her through food. I can feel I want to thrash it out but will only get caught if I do so, feeling she is voracious, that no matter what I give, she will say it is not enough. She seems like a voracious witch to me. But she sees the witch in me too."

On waking, the dreamer meditates on how both of them can experience the other as witch. The one is never satisfied, eats up everything given to her and then is full of reproaches: it is never enough. The mother has an answering feeling of being victimized. The daughter criticizes her for using food to control her. She had always liked her mother's food, yet here in the dream, giving turns out to be as bad as not giving. At that thought an insight jumped into the dreamer's mind. She sees that giving is not the point at all. Another force is involved. She should not thrash it out with her daughter, or with the daughter that remains inside. The dreamer—the mother—is also a daughter. She has felt for a long time the same way about her own mother. Mother and daughter share a wound. Both feel in some essential way unmothered.

The insight brought a surprising question, Where do the daughter's complaints fit the case? The answer was swift: they go back to life's earliest moments, when an infant daughter relies on a mother's knowing what she feels without having to tell her so. In the nursing couple the infant needs and expects a mother attuned empathetically to her needs.[21] The dreamer saw she had not been able to give enough of that because she did not have it: it had not been given to her. She and the daughter were bonded in a new way, through shared suffering. Rather than antagonists, they were sisters in their woundings. Perhaps they could help each other reach to when they were wounded. The witch, by the very absence of good mothering, had made a good-mothering presence possible.

This example, showing that the psyche's text includes the negative as well as the positive, also may caution us against the tendency to idealize all things feminine in our zeal to recover all aspects of the female and the feminine. It is only too easy to see feminism as all light, moving only toward justice, and females always as innocent victims of blind, ignorant, power-hungry males and masculine forces. Depth psychology takes us to the borderland of the fearful, forceful, demonic within ourselves individually and within the feminine as a whole. Insisting on the symbolic dimension, as well as the reality of the world, of which it is such a vital part, depth psychology leads us to see forces within the feminine that include initiatory acts of hate as well as love, to see that mothering includes coming to terms with envy and the savage power to dismiss and turn away from children, even those held dear. Depth psychology forces us to see that the feminine cannot be equated with nurture alone, but must be seen to house its opposites as well: challenge, confrontation, a devilish originality—taking for oneself and discarding the other like a meaningless rind. Depth psychology calls us again and again to look at these forces within ourselves and to come to terms with them, not to project them onto the opposite sex nor onto other women who do not identify with our point of view, nor other periods or cultures. This is our struggle and these are our forces to tame, to forge into abilities at our disposal. If we fail to do this we shall be at their disposal, swept along, acting out the patterns of archetypal maenads in modern dress.

Depth psychology works to bring into consciousness all the parts of the psyche's text, presses us to face the fullness of the feminine, even where we may hate and fear it, even that possible sexist inside ourselves, so much like the one outside ourselves we criticize so bitterly. Such consciousness will take us to the border-land again, where we may discover we are not all that sure about things, where we no longer pray like the Pharisee thanking God we are not like other women. For in fact we are. We can come to enjoy and profit from that likeness only if we make room for unlikeness. We will feel contained in our sameness only if the container is spacious enough to house our differences. Depth psychology holds feminism to its true size, large enough for all women—no Cinderella consigned to the ashes here.

III. SPIRITUALITY

By spirituality, I mean the life of the soul, that doorway to God that reaches through many levels of the psyche's text to find its own vocabulary. Augustine talks about the voice of our prayer which is different from our public voice and even from our private one. It is a distinct voice, all its own, and not to be reduced to the words we say, nor conscious intent in praying.[22]

A systematic life of the soul involves us in exercises to build up spiritual muscles and psychic strength tough enough to withstand the consequences of being open to God. Such spirituality always involves us in attentiveness to the soul's currents, needs, and long-ings for God. The soul learns that God is like a hidden leaven in the lump of us, a spark of Christ in the darkness of us, that needs further stirring. For the Spirit that touches our souls has its own autono-mous life; it is not subject to our rules or our needs. We do not get it simply because we want it. It comes; it speaks or it is silent. There are no "rights" here, only a gift given. To take up and be taken up by the spiritual life means to recognize its otherness, in ourselves, and in the ways it focuses upon others and otherness.

We find ourselves asking who it is that comes through that doorway into us. Who is this other? Who is it that talks back, talks first or last? In the Judeo-Christian tradition the figure of the divine and human Jesus comes through a two-way door, entering our hu-manity and pulling us into the currents of divinity. People who develop their spirituality best are those for whom the soul's life is central. These are passionate people who always want more and more connection to the center. Ana-Maria Rizzuto notes that religious people are those for whom the god-representation goes on developing as a principal concern their whole lives.[23] It is also true, I think, that such religious people are also always close to unconscious life, with its greeds, and desires, its primary colors of hunger and aggression, its excesses and dartings outside the lines. No pale pastels here. Such people go at God with full heart, mind, body, and strength. They want to love; they need to do so.

In this want and need, they welcome an altered sense of self. They find themselves willing to bring to each moment every hidden resource of theirs. They are drawn to essentials. Trivia, inconsequential events, fall away. They are willing to be pushed to new departure points, to live as close as possible to the centers of being. Passion moves them to outpourings, to an order of love that transcends ordinary awareness and actions.

The first insight depth psychology brings to the spiritual life is the certainty that the psyche is the spirit's flesh as much as the body is. We cannot skip over it as irrelevant. We cannot get away from it. To reach to the profoundest levels of our being, feminine being, masculine being, we must make use of all the parts. We must begin exactly where we are, attend to those images which reveal where we are.[24] They will not be easily translated into action or word. We cannot use them to coerce others. They must be received, pondered, circled round in our meditations. We can only grow our way toward them. Then God's spirit will be implanted, we will be rearranged, raised to the cross, and resurrected.

A dream may foster religious experience or gather up threads of experience which push us toward a central soul-life. Here is a woman's decisive dream of this kind: "A priest tells a story to a group of women about the spiritual life. There is a man who goes down to the edge of the sea to celebrate Mass (he might be a king). He has a golden chalice with odd words on it. One woman tells of research into the derivation of the words which seem to describe a belt with a secret compartment. This fits. The man takes a small bit of consecrated host and hides it in the compartment of a belt he is wearing, and then goes off to battle in the world. He is a warrior. I understood all this. One woman asks, 'But what about the women? How does it work for them?' The priest agrees this is important, saying that the man he learned this story from spoke of it only as it pertained to men. I said, 'That's the crux of the problem. It's not

possible for women to go from one—the spiritual life—to the other
—fighting in the world. It's not possible for women to do both. The
way for men won't work for women; it doesn't take women's psychology into account.' " The dreamer added: "I awoke crying and
had a vivid image of myself weak and dying at the edge of that sea,
with nothing to eat. I prayed to God for help. A big bird, a pelican,
got me a fish, and dropped it, alive and wriggling, at my face. But
there was no way to clean it, prepare it for eating. It had to be full of
scales and sand."

The dreamer was very upset by this dream. She did not want to
be cut off from the familiar words and procedures of the eucharist
and yet she felt keenly what her dream-self said, that somehow the
mixture envisioned for kings and warriors neglected to take
women's psychology into account. It seemed an either/or way to
her, separating what could not be separated—the spiritual and the
worldly, the hidden and the public. She felt life could not be split up
that way. Yet the seeming answer—a squirmy, sandy fish—what
good was that? But what about the fish with all its symbolic meaning
of the living Christ, and the pelican, symbol of a motherly Christ-
figure who wounds her own breast to feed her young, all tossed right
to her, in response to her plea for help? These were certainly living
God-images. In more than one sense, it would take her time and
work to house and understand them.

In the emphasis of depth psychology on the embodied spirit, on
the psyche as the flesh in which God incarnates, there is to be found
a hermeneutic that will add to our understanding of spiritual events,
as this dream does. Living images like these reach across personal
symbols such as the pelican and the fish were for this woman, and
across the borders of officially defined religious meanings, to fall
upon us, at our feet, say, or, like the fish in the dream, at our face at the
edge of an oceanic fullness of feeling. Symbols like these will necessarily be obscure, for they express, as Dorothy Emmet put it, the
ambivalence of the finite experiencing the infinite: "Such ambiguity
is not the result of pious vagueness or of confusion of thought. . . . It
is a precise way of conveying the fundamental dilemma of religious
symbolism, which presents an analogue of the transcendent in the
forms of the phenomenal, of the infinite in the finite."[25] We point
beyond the human but only through the terms of the human. The
psyche accomplishes this by modes of experience that transcend ego

limitations, such as dreams or visions that seem to address the ego from the beyond.

We must not dodge what a symbolic event, such as this dream, can mean to a dreamer. It is talking to her, in this case, about missing parts of herself that she has allowed to pass by, to fall away to the other side, so to speak. She needs now to explore her neglected sexuality as a woman, her sharp division between masculine and feminine routes of understanding. The dream shows her that the man has his own womb-like secret compartment in his belt. She needs to ask why she is unable to reconcile these modes of being in herself. Using a prospective hermeneutic, *we* have to ask what the pelican stands for. There it is, a blunt, even crude presence that plops a fish before the dreamer, rough, sandy, scaly. Here is no handsomely articulated symbol of procession, with robes, defined role and ritual. The fish is alive, a pulsing thing, facing the dreamer with basic questions. It points somewhere, not only to her specific problems of the past but toward a growth into the future.

Through such dreams we are brought a new sense of the living Christ, bold, if awkward, a mother-figure feeding her young from her wounds. Thus, although this is just one woman's dream, it speaks through her to others. It offers the dreamer and the hearers of the dream a new look at old religious symbols. It should evoke in us the long hard stare of contemplation, to inspect what the soul embodied in the flesh of the psyche can hand us, for our spiritual life, for our life in the world. This is clearly no religion, split off from embodied experience. It is an asceticism of feeling purged of hyperactivism and withdrawn passivity. It draws us away from a religion of doing for others that is no more than a defense against deficits in our own being. A wry observation of Freud is relevant here: he said he never felt so much sadism that he had to make excessive use of the reaction formation against it by dedicating himself to serve humanity.

To experience soul addressing us through psyche is to be commanded to stand back and look at our actual experience of the spirit, not substituting for it either moralizing or sentimentalizing. What is it that is really there? Who addresses us? Is it a silence? If it is, begin there. Nothing? Then begin there. It will come to us in its own particular concrete way, influenced by, embodied in, our own particular history, social context, in our psychological colors, complexes, turnings to and turnings away, in virtue, in sinful denial. Are we like the barren woman? Are we like the Queen of Sheba making a long journey across desert wilderness to ask our questions? Are we like Anna, waiting a lifetime to see God in our midst? Considering how much life-stuff God has to get through to get to us, it is a wonder that we are addressed at all and can hear any of it.

Taking seriously the way the soul addresses us through the psyche means learning that God comes to the neighbor inside us as well as outside. This inner-neighbor whom we cast off, this possibly virtuous part of us that we do not trust or even imprison, may convey God to us. God reaches us through our God-images too, however odd, scary, ornamental, whatever—claiming us, gathering us into a people. This means God can even reach us through our revilings of neighbors and God, acts of injustice, crucifyings. Sin does not require an outer act. Neither does goodness. No place is excluded. Nothing is too hidden. God finds us everywhere, even at the far borders of the psyche where sanity and madness blur. Depth psychology puts before us, for our contemplation, those who would love the spiritual life, those who would attend to the life of the soul, those who will take up the task of including the psyche's flesh with the soul's spirituality.

A second resource that depth psychology offers the life of the spirit is a hermeneutic of reductive and prospective directions. Through this instrumentation, we inquire into the psychological meaning of spiritual images for women and the goddess for example, and the meaning for women of collective events, such as the rituals of feminism.

Applying the reductive interpretation to the goddess image, depth psychology would ask such a question as: What psychological materials and experiences are evoked by goddess imagery?[26] The answer might be that what is stirred up is pre-oedipal material, of affect and instinct, of multiple longings and meanings not yet clearly enough differentiated from each other to be organized into specific agencies of id, ego, and superego. Depth psychology might ask in what ways an image empowers a group, giving it expression and goal, and what it compensates for. The very evocation of a pre-oedipal passion answers that last question, for the kinds of experiences goddess-imagery puts us in touch with compensate for a too dry, too schizoid and rationalistic a distortion of religion, one too distant from embodied experience with all its pushes and pulls and mixtures of conscious and unconscious. Such imagery affirms the dignity of the body, and the female body in particular, as an originating residence of new life and an affirming of the energies of feminine will.

In this reductive hermeneutic, depth psychology always points to what is missing. Thus it asks those who advocate goddess imagery: What are you leaving out? Are you omitting the figure of Jesus and a history of two thousand years of a religion that established the value of the human person? The image of the goddess portrays the female in terms of blood, milk, fertility, not as a person. Is a symbolic equation in operation instead of a symbol, where image, deity, and person are equated? Is a split-off religion forming, in the opposite direction, from what went before, where we will fall into identification not with words and rationalism but with images, affect, and unconscious instinct? What has happened to the transcendent God different from every thing in our language and imagery? What has happened to our ways of looking at God, at God's self, for God, for God's self? Are we restricted now to seeing how God functions for us and our group?

The prospective side of interpretation is never a restricted seeing. For it, the psyche's symbols look forward, evoke into being, call into clear form what is at first only dimly apprehended. Here the numinous imagery of the feminine points toward inclusion, not exclusion, toward the essential. Here are evoked feminine modes of being and becoming, styles of perceiving and apperceiving that place us in the midst of things instead of abstracted from and merely gazing at them. Here the great images of the feminine depict the modes of being human that are embodied, concrete, particular, in contrast to generalized, abstract, would-be universal categories. Here apprehension is downward, toward the hidden, covered, the ambiguous in contrast to an upward movement toward a simplifying clarity and discrete definitions. Here we get at what is, not pre-defined goals, relating and knowing through identification and inclusion, as against knowing through exaggerated differentiation and ultimate separation. Female imagery by including what has been left out—the numinosity conveyed by female experience and symbols— moves toward a vision of completeness. It gives up a goal of perfection that arrives at its end by eliminating what is imperfect, however much it may characterize us and our world.

We might look at the women's movement symbolically in both these reductive and prospective hermeneutics. In a reductive way the movement is an amassing—in the concrete numbers of women involved. It is a stressing of the female presence in our midst to compensate for the unclaimed, undervalued feminine in both men and women. It offers support in the group to claim the missing anger, the missing honoring of the female, unrecognized female identity, lost experiences, the validation of the female by the female. Depth psychology presses on us to see the forward thrust in such reductive interpretation. Prospectively, we must ask if this regression to an all-female world, which is a necessary and valid stage but not a final one, will not turn out to be, if arrested there, a major loss of opportunity. Will we not then fail to grasp what the psyche offers to consciousness of both feminine and masculine, of the transcendent as in fact both and neither, fully male and female and quite beyond them? Regression embraced becomes part of the flow into the future. Indeed, it is often the secret way through which the unguessed future will flow.

We might imagine and speculate what it would take us to develop the other side of the traditional speaking of God as Father, Son, and Spirit. The unspoken side of that configuration pictures us as feminine—as mother, as beloved, as all that the pronouns "she" and "her" can possess. Masculine names have traditionally been used to discover and describe God. What would it mean boldly to embrace and uncover all of us whom God loves as feminine? World, earth, people, society, soul are largely feminine, are God's feminine containers. Psychologically, this would mean reaching to the profoundest layers of feminine being, in women, in men, as in my patient's dream where the man kept the host in a secret pocket in a belt tied around his waist. Spiritually, it would mean developing a vocabulary of the spirit close to the changing tides and periodic cycles of human emotion and perception embodied in a woman's sexual cycle.

But that is not all. There are group-images too. How are the living texts of psyche defined by sex, race, creed, devotion to specific ideals, and the texts of scripture? How do these things, these institutions, these texts relate? What are the bridges between them? How do we receive that divinity that is more than psychic experience, indeed, that breaks our dead or sterile psychic images for God, male, female, animal, vegetable, mineral? We do not get to God by subtraction, by leaping over the living text of the psyche. But God is not our psyche, even our unconscious psyche. What happens in that space where all the bridges collapse? Are we not led to a still more remote borderland in the psyche? We climb a ladder of images to God only to see our ladder stop suddenly, utterly, completely, delivering us into the spacelessness mystics call the wilderness, the dark night of the soul.

This is a third contribution depth psychology makes to spirituality, this deliverance right to the boundaries of human perception. Depth psychology unshackles us, so that we cannot avoid, repress, defend against, intellectualize, politicize or psychologize the fact that the transcendent exists beyond categories. Depth psychology brings home to us the full experience of being finite, contingent, transitory, fragmentary. Our images and names for God, so precious and so empowering, so real as images, are only images. Our impulses toward charity and justice, so important to human community, are impulses only. We are brought to the breaking of the law in the operation of new creative forces that transmute goals into momentary stages in which we can glimpse the unseen that is beyond goals and stages. Depth psychology brings us to the borders of our religious territory where we struggle to give form to a knowledge of the transcendent which can hold together negation and affirmation, to know in the parts of our lives that can only be parts some sense of the whole.

One essential part is the female part, so long neglected, undervalued, unclaimed. Though women represent an ancient constituency for the spiritual life, they still need to be fully claimed, they and their ways. Female mystics and saints crafted their own ways of getting at God out of the stuff of their lives, including all the restrictions, on education, on activity, on position and power. Their spiritual experiences not only altered the ways open to the women who came after them, but also shaped new perceptions of God to include recognition of feminine experiences in the life of the human with the Divine.[27] They accomplished this by taking account of all the parts of themselves—their rebellion, their aggression, their love, their madness, their ambition, their childishness, their intuition, their wish to serve in the world, their awareness of their own bodies and psyches. Here is the way women are present, as women, not as men in disguise, not in imitation of men, but as their own persons asserting their intrinsic womanhood. This identity, so rooted in personal experience and through it to the transpersonal, is the feminine way.

Depth psychology and spiritual life meet in a shared emphasis upon disidentifying from what lives in us, whether consciously, or unconsciously, in order to gather all our parts and to house them. For it is through these parts that God touches us and pulls us beyond them into that terrifying and liberating space where we know not to identify God with any of the parts. God, we learn this way, is not the God of our projections, though God meets us and finds us in them. God is not to be identified with any of our symbols, though we are found in them—and by God.

Thus, we know that we do not have to reach anything all by ourselves. That is the life of the spirit—everything does not depend on our ego efforts. We rest upon others, too—their efforts, their experiences, their breakthrough. And we rest upon God. We are ourselves the parts that make up the whole. We have each other. God has us. We are consoled by the presence of the Holy Counselor that quickens this awareness, out of the psyche and soul in concert, that no image, no movement, no dogma is to be equated with God.

Notes

1. This article is based on lectures given at Union Theological Seminary and at the University of Virginia in 1984. All examples cited from persons' lives are taken from my psychoanalytic practice, with gratitude to the people who allowed me to use their material.

2. In conversations with biblical scholars I have felt a longing for a written text. I imagine a simpler, or at least a clearer, task with a written text. It stays on the page in black and white. You can examine it according to an historical critical method of interpretation or a method of literary form criticism or of sociological analysis. These methods promise more distance between oneself and what is studied and hence a chance for a clarifying perspective. A written text does not jump up and plunge around the room in an agony of tears or an explosion of anger the way a person may act. But this view may be simply a case of the grass looking greener on the other side of the disciplinary fence, because, after all, a text can shut up against you, or defy your every effort to reach its meaning, or even infect you with its power, for good or for ill.

3. Jung links the question of whether or not we are related to the infinite to the fact of being bound in our own finite selves. We are only this self, and from that particular departure point our relation to the infinite is formed.

> The feeling for the infinite, however, can be attained only if we are bound to the utmost. The greatest limitation for man is the "self". It is manifested in the experience: "I am *only* that!" Only consciousness of our narrow confinement in the self forms the link to the limitlessness of the unconscious. In such awareness we experience ourselves concurrently as limited and eternal, as both one and the other. In knowing ourselves to be unique in our personal combination—that is, ultimately limited—we possess also the capacity for becoming conscious of the infinite. But only then!

C.G. Jung, *Memories, Dreams, Reflections*, ed. Aniela Jaffe, trans. Richard and Clara Winston (New York: Pantheon, 1963), p. 325.
4. For a fascinating discussion of how much we introject and are shaped by the non-human environment, see Harold Searles, *The Non-Human Environment* (New York: International Universities Press, 1960).
5. Ana-Maria Rizzuto gives a good description of how internal objects influence our pictures of God. See her *The Birth of the Living God* (Chicago: University of Chicago Press, 1979), chapter 4.
6. See Rosemary Gordon, "Narcissism and the Self: Who Am I that I Love?" *The Journal of Analytical Psychology*, 1980, Vol. 25, No. 3, 247–265.
7. For detailed discussion of eating disorders in relation to the ego and the self, see Ann Belford Ulanov, "Fatness and the Female," *Psychological Perspectives*, Volume 10, Fall 1979.
8. See articles in this volume by Naomi Goldenberg and Demaris Wehr.
9. For discussion about relating to this "voice" and not just ceding all authority to it, see C.G. Jung, "A Psychological View of Conscience," in *Civilization in Transition, Collected Works*, vol. 10, trans. R.F.C. Hull (New York: Pantheon, 1964), p. 447 (paragraph 844).
10. For fuller discussion of archetype as answer to stereotype, see Ann and Barry Ulanov, *The Witch and The Clown: Two Archetypes of Human Sexuality* (Wilmette: Chiron, 1987), chapter I.
11. For discussion of God-images in relation to tradition, see Ann Belford Ulanov, "Picturing God," in *Picturing God* (Cambridge: Cowley Press, 1986). For a discussion of the dangerous power of God-images,

see Ann Belford Ulanov, "The God You Touch," *Christ and the Bo-dhisattva,* eds. D.S. Lopez and S.C. Rockefeller (Albany: State University of New York Press, 1987).

12. For a discussion of the ego's task and the church's task of housing all these God-images, see Ann Belford Ulanov, *The Wisdom of the Psyche* (Cambridge: Cowley Press, 1988), chapter I.

13. See Elizabeth Petroff, *Consolation of the Blessed* (Millerton, NY: Alta Gaia Society, 1979), pp. 67, 73–76. See also Ann Belford Ulanov, *The Feminine in Christian Theology and in Jungian Psychology* (Evanston: Northwestern University Press, 1971), chapter 9, for a description of kinds of feminine consciousness and spirit that issue from woman's body.

14. See S. Freud, *New Introductory Lectures on Psychoanalysis,* trans. James Stracey (New York: Norton, 1965), p. 135. See also Paul Roazen, *Freud and His Followers* (New York: Knopf, 1975), chapter 9, for a description of the professional women who gathered around Freud.

15. See note 8.

16. See Ann Belford Ulanov, *Receiving Woman, Studies in the Theology and Psychology of the Feminine* (Philadelphia: Westminster, 1981), chapter 6, for a discussion of the animus function. See also the forthcoming study by Ann and Barry Ulanov on the anima and animus (Princeton University Press).

17. The ego begins as a body-ego, according to Freud, originally derived from body sensations. I leave to the side for this discussion the fascinating notion of the subtle body (Jung) and the resurrection body.

18. See Carol McMillan, *Women, Reason and Nature* (Princeton: Princeton University Press, 1982). Evelyn Fox Kellar, *Reflections on Gender and Science* (New Haven: Yale University Press, 1985). Caroline Walker Bynum, "Introduction: The Complexity of Symbols," in *Gender and Religion,* eds. Caroline Walker Bynum, Stevan Harrell, Paula Richman (Boston: Beacon, 1986), chapter I. See also Carol Gilligan, *In a Different Voice* (Cambridge: Harvard University Press, 1982). In 1971 I described this different mode of approach as feminine and, in contrast to Gilligan who tends to identify it as belonging to girls, I found the feminine mode inhabits boys and men too. See *ibid.,* pp. 25, 171, 173, 174. See also Ulanov, *The Feminine,* pp. 37–40, 166.

19. See C.G. Jung, *Two Essays in Analytical Psychiatry, Collected Works,* vol. 7, trans. R.F.C. Hull (New York: Pantheon, 1966), Part VI.

20. See Ann and Barry Ulanov, *The Witch and The Clown,* pp. 31–44.

21. See D.W. Winnicott, *Through Paediatrics to Psycho-analysis* (New York: Basic Books, 1975), p. 99.

22. See Ann and Barry Ulanov, *Primary Speech: A Psychology of Prayer* (Philadelphia: John Knox of Westminster, 1982), pp. 1, 137.

23. See Ana-Maria Rizzuto, *The Birth of the Living God,* passim.
24. Similar advice is given to the beginner in prayer: Begin where you are, God will show you how. See *The Cloud of Unknowing,* trans. Clifton Wolters (Baltimore: Penguin, 1970), p. 92 (chapter 34).
25. See Dorothy M. Emmet, *The Nature of Metaphysical Thinking* (London: Macmillan, 1957), p. 105.
26. Kathleen Raine's poem "The Goddess" wonderfully displays such an image:

> She goes by many names; Diana of the sacred wood
> With manifold breasts like acorns on an oak
> And primitive features, image of the joy men take
> In her, all powerful where in caves and shadows lie
> These mortal beasts, her offspring and her prey.
>
> We have known her as archaic mother Eve.
> The earth is all her cradle
> Where we awake from our first sleep to see
> Her flower-face bending over us
> The sky, the rowan, and the elder-tree.
>
> Some worship her as queen of angels, Venus of the sea,
> House of gold, palace of ivory,
> Gate of heaven and rose of mystery,
> Inviolate and ever-virgin earth,
> Daughter of time and mother of eternity.
>
> Lover, in your true love's body lie
> The sacred darkness of Diana's grove,
> Hers are the careful arms that Adam's children hold,
> And in her heart the cause of joy, the house of gold,
> The gate of Heaven, the ever-virgin rose.

The Faber Book of Twentieth Century Verse, ed. J. Heath-Stubbs and D. Wright (London: Faber, 1953), pp. 276–77.
27. See Petroff, *op. cit.*

Psychology and Hermeneutics: Jung's Contribution

Theological studies are today, to employ one of theology's own more banal euphemisms, in a state of flux. While it may not be entirely correct to state that the high and grand theologies of neoorthodoxy have run their course, their influence is hardly as pervasive and compelling as it once was. In the face of their decline, a variety of minor emphases or approaches have appeared: death-of-God theology, religionless Christianity, theology of the secular, and, more recently, the theology of hope. Each has made the claim of freshness and renewal; yet each too, it seems, has already largely spent much of whatever energy it had.

Alongside these shifts still another motif, somewhat stronger for the present at least, has appeared. It takes curricular form in an emphasis upon "religious" rather than "theological" studies. I am referring to a fundamental shift from a methodological orientation dominated by dogmatic and systematic theological considerations to one which places primary emphasis upon hermeneutics, upon theory of interpretation. This motif appears in two different but related movements. The first is theological hermeneutics, which insists that dogmatic and systematic concerns are less central to the nature of theological work than are interpretive concerns. A dogmatic statement implies something more fundamental; it implies something about the nature of interpretation itself. But the term "hermeneutics" has also become current in a second sense, that of the phenomenology of religion. Here it refers to the task of extracting cosmological and ontological meaning from the phenomenological explication of religious forms.

Characteristic of the high, neo-Reformation theologies has been an ambiguous stance toward the human sciences generally, and toward the psychological sciences in particular. These theologies have shown some interest in particular aspects of psychology, most notably dynamic-therapeutic psychology. They have, however, been primarily concerned with establishing the limits of psychology and only secondarily have they attempted to make use of its constructive possibilities. The various movements replacing these theologies, especially the death-of-God theology, have been more generous in their attitude toward psychology, allowing it a more substantial place in their constructive theological work.

In the writings of theological hermeneutics—that is, the so-called new hermeneutic—no intrinsic connection can be found to exist between the activity of interpretation and psychological meaning. In fact, the dogmatic and systematic orientation was, in its own limited way, more open to psychology than is the new hermeneutic. On the other hand, the phenomenology of religion is at least implicitly open to certain types of psychological thinking, especially insofar as such thinking has already been incorporated into anthropological studies.

But neither of these approaches has given explicit attention to the place of psychology in the work of interpretation. In this paper I first explore the possibility of relating psychological meaning and psychological processes to hermeneutics. Second, I take the psychology of C.G. Jung as the basis for specific inquiry into this issue. Jung's psychology is especially helpful in this regard for three reasons. First, his work began as an attempt to go beyond the methods and assumptions of Freudian psychology and behaviorism, the two psychologies which the neoorthodox theologies also address; second, Jung turned to Protestant theology itself for assistance in formulating the higher human processes which he felt Freud and experimental psychology had rejected; and third, Jung's psychology moved beyond both theological orthodoxy and Freud's psychology by developing a psychology of religious structures—that is, he was forced to develop what I call a psychological hermeneutic.

In this paper, then, there are two circles of emphasis. On the one hand, there is the wide circle of hermeneutics, understood in two senses, first, as it is used in theology, and second, as it is used in the phenomenology of religion. And there is a narrower circle of emphasis, consisting of psychological self-understanding, represented by Jung's psychology. I wish to argue that psychological understanding does have some bearing upon hermeneutics. In order to do so, I must also "interpret" the relation between psychology and hermeneutics, if the circles are to move closer and finally to intersect at important points. So there is interpretation of different types of thought, as well as interpretation in the theological and religious sense.

Interpretation in this second sense accomplishes its task, that of drawing the two circles closer together, by the introduction of a third circle, the nature of the religious image, which will be the unifying factor in the following discussion. The religious image is central to Jung's psychology and to the phenomenological study of religious structures, and it is also important to theological hermeneutics, although not nearly so central as in the first two cases. Jung's psychology is fundamentally dynamic and subjective, and the religious image has a dynamic function in the process of individuation. In the case of the phenomenology of religion, the religious image is endowed with a good deal more structural and objective significance, although dynamic considerations are also important. The religious image receives less discussion in theological hermeneutics. But when it is considered important, it is conceived of as disclosing to the believer aspects of the nature of God which lie beyond objective and subjective modes of comprehension. Here the religious image is closely related to the theological meaning of transcendence and faith.

The phenomenon of the religious image therefore makes it possible to explore psychological understanding in relation to these two different views of hermeneutics, while keeping in view the more orthodox theologies. This paper argues that Jung's psychology supports a movement away from dogmatic and systematic theology and toward hermeneutics; but it also argues that the deepest intentions of his psychology support the second use of hermeneutics rather than the first. In so arguing, it concludes that there is a psychological dimension to the religious image and to one's understanding of it. The religious image opens human consciousness not only to cosmological meaning but to psychological-developmental self-understanding as well. That is, this subjective dimension, which is generally unattended in theological hermeneutics, lies implicit in phenomenological approaches to religion. If this is the case, then it may be possible for psychology and hermeneutics eventually to enter into sustained conversation.

THE STYLE OF NEO-REFORMATION THEOLOGICAL THOUGHT

By way of initiating this exploration of hermeneutics and Jung's psychology, let us recapitulate the current theological situation in more detail, by annotating several of the more recognizable characteristics of Protestant theology. This is our starting point for our movement from a dogmatic-systematic approach to a hermeneutical and psychological approach. Neoorthodox theology addresses itself to two fundamental problems, those of methodology and anthropology, and in each case the problem of transcendence is central.[1] Methodologically the problem is, How is one to think about God's transcendence? Anthropologically the problem is, What is the nature of self-transcendence? The answers which this theology supplies with regard to psychology are clear: theological method transcends the methods of psychology, and the objective reality of which theology speaks transcends psychological processes.

This generalized stance toward psychology is expressive of a particular style, which I would characterize as a "style of the gaps," especially with regard to the problem of psychological self-understanding. Theology reads psychology in a manner which supports a split or dissociation between the developmental and existential dimensions of life. This splitting can be visualized as a gap between lower psychological processes and higher spiritual and religious aspects of the total life of the self.

For example, the early experiences of the self in family life are not considered to be of a theological order, but the self's relations to others at the level of society and history are considered central. There is a split or gap between the order of experiencing described by psychological constructs, often referred to as "merely subjective," and the objective reality to which theological understanding is directed. Put in the language of the demythologizing discussions, there is a split between the developmental process and myth, such that the structure of myth and the dynamics of personality are considered to be quite discontinuous. In each case transcendence is viewed as referring to a dimension of life which lies beyond psychological processes. While there is a strong emphasis upon a dialectic between transcendence and immanence in Protestant thought, the force of its work clearly emphasizes transcendence. Psychological processes are associated with the immanental side of life and are therefore neglected. Also associated with immanence is religious experience, at least the sort described by William James and his co-workers. Because of its focus upon transcendence, neoorthodox theology has been unable—perhaps it is more correct to say, unwilling—to assimilate religious experience into its understanding of faith and transcendence.

Since the decline of the neoorthodox systems, theological discussion has shifted over into a number of different, minor emphases, as already noted: death-of-God theology, religionless Christianity and theology of the secular. These movements have been accompanied by various individual inquiries into the vicissitudes of belief. The drift of all these discussions seems to be in the direction of rethinking the positive value of immanence and the resources of the human sciences. While these discussions provide no sense of unified approach or school, they can be viewed as a generalized effort to close the gaps—especially the gap between immanence and transcendence—so characteristic of a "high" theological tradition. As might be expected, most of these attempts combine traditionalistic perspectives and idiosyncratic innovation.

Out of this pluralism in theological reformulation more unified efforts are emerging, such as the "new hermeneutics," in which the dogmatic-systematic task is not abandoned but is rather brought under the control of the problems of the nature of interpretation and of language.[2] The activity of interpretation takes priority over dogmatic formulation and in fact makes such formulation possible. This approach is characterized by an intensive concern with the future, eschatology, and the ethical and political implications of hope. On the other hand, the phenomenology of religion, pursuing the problem of interpretation in a different way, presents us, quite interestingly I think, with what amounts to a reverse emphasis: primitive religions and the primordial are emphasized, rather than the futuric; beginnings are sought, rather than ends; in other words, nostalgia, rather than hope, seems to be the concern.[3]

The new hermeneutic carries forward the high theological tradition in its conviction that psychology is too concerned with personal experience, with the hero or great person, or with human personality, to assist either in determining the objective meaning of the text. Nor can psychology clarify the subjective conditions which characterize the situation of the interpreter. The second approach is more open to psychology at the point of interpreting texts or religious structures, but, like theological hermeneutics, it, too, is loath to admit any substantive influence of a developmental sort upon even the subjectivity of the interpreter. Both approaches fail to integrate into their theories of interpretation concrete analysis of the contemporary forms of individual and personal experiencing. Psychology is one discipline given over to such analysis.

What contribution can or should Jung's psychology make to this situation? That psychology, we now begin to argue, forces an abandonment of the first view of hermeneutics, creating a transition to the second. Jung moves us from dogmatics to hermeneutics of the second kind. In so doing, however, his work also opens this second view to developmental and psychological-cultural considerations. Such considerations raise what I call the question of a psychological hermeneutic.

The movement of the argument can be clarified in still another way by introducing the following distinction between two levels of analysis. There is, first, the level of methodological thinking, and here the movement is from dogmatics to hermeneutics, albeit of the second type, via Jung's psychology. Second, there is the level of the experiential or psychological process itself, and here the movement is from doctrine to religious image. Jung's psychology draws these two levels of analysis closer together, through his use of the triad of fantasy, image, and archetype.

The aim of our argument, then, is to arrive at the contribution which psychology can make to the activity of interpretation, for we cannot split psychological processes from the objects of interpretation; nor need we, for that matter, identify the two, as theologians, be they of a dogmatic or hermeneutic sort, fear. But we must not begin with the problem of the relation between interpretation and its object; we must begin with psychology. We begin with the problem of understanding Jung.

DIFFERENT VIEWS OF JUNG'S PSYCHOLOGY

How is one to read Jung's psychology? Here we can learn much from the directions taken by criticism of Freud. Until recently Freud's work has been understood either as a theory of personality

—as a metapsychology, to use his own term—or else as a clinical theory at a low level of generalization. According to these two views, Freud's work on fantasy and symbol, and on myth and culture, is always considered of secondary importance—it is one of the "applications" of his psychology. Only recently has this third or cultural emphasis been given serious attention, alongside the metapsychological and clinical, as a fundamental force of his psychology as a whole.[4] Dogmatic-theological discussions of Freud have worked primarily with the metapsychological and clinical views in mind to the neglect of the cultural point of view.

A similar situation exists with regard to views of Jung's psychology. Like Freud, Jung has been "read" in strikingly different ways. There are three general types of commentary on or understanding of Jung's work. First of all, there has been some theological interest in Jung's work.[5] Different scholars have found, oriented as they were by their respective theological traditions, special value in Jung's work. All have sought some kind of psychological enrichment of their own theological thinking. All have emphasized Jung's contribution to the psychology of doctrine, understood as a psychological exemplification of the Christian experience of faith. As such Jung's thought has been seen as supplementary to a particular theological tradition, and the interpretive power of his psychology has therefore remained in the service of doctrinal statement. An important element of this view has been the theologian's need to reject Freud's view of religion while at the same time maintaining that a more generous psychological view of religion is still scientifically possible. Jung's psychology provides both aspects and has thereby allowed these theologians to make use of psychology in doctrinal thinking while maintaining a clear separation between psychological science and theology.

This approach to Jung's work contains a double error: it says too much and too little. Our theologians rightly see the centrality of the archetype as an imaginative structure which organizes religious experience, and they recognize that the archetype has some relation to the processes of human development which psychology describes. But they do not, in their appropriation of Jung's thought, recognize the priority over even doctrine itself which he assigned to the appearance of the archetype and its interpretation. The interpretation of an archetype has the effect of releasing the self from the past—including the Christian past—and opening it to the not-so-Christian future. But in the minds of these theologians, the interpretation of religious structures simply has the purpose of clarifying the past and of transforming the present on the basis of the past. Yet Jung's psychology has a more subtle purpose. As we shall show, he interpreted doctrine—that is, he saw in doctrine more than doctrine sees in itself—rather than simply explicating it psychologically.

A second group of commentators in effect reverse this view of Jung.[6] Their interest is in the therapeutic process, understood as a "way," a quest for fulfillment and wholeness, and they consider this process to be religious in form if not in content. However, Jung's characterization of the therapeutic process resembles mystical and conversion experience more than it does the paradigms of faith found in Protestant thought. Furthermore, this view greatly emphasizes the use of historical-universal religious structures to clarify subjective developmental processes. There is in it very little desire to understand as an objective reality the transcendence of God and of faith as a response to God's transcendence. Jung's portrayal of the individuation process is taken as a secularized religious experience.

These theological and psychological frameworks tend to split Jung's psychology into either a supportive subdiscipline for the clarification of Christian faith, on the one hand, or a secularized religious experience appearing in the form of a "high" view of the psychotherapeutic process, on the other. Both the theological and psychological views ignore the problem of interpretation. For this reason we ask: Is there a third view, in addition to the above two? To what extent is Jung's psychology a theory of interpretation which locates and clarifies religious structures, such that they open self-understanding to both cosmological and ontological, as well as to developmental and psychological, meaning? In what sense does Jung's psychology have a fundamentally hermeneutical intent?

The key to Jung's psychology lies in his attempt to locate the archetypal dimensions of theological doctrine, religious myth, and the individuation process, and then to create interplay between these otherwise diverse and seemingly unrelated phenomena. The means for executing this task—to which he returned again and again—was the religious image.

THE CENTRALITY OF FANTASY AND ARCHETYPE IN JUNG'S PSYCHOLOGY

The meaning of Jung's psychology lies as much in its style as in its content. His work is incredibly rich, often difficult and obscure, and his appeal lies largely in the fact that he is a "bridge" figure. Jung is constantly crossing over from problems, issues, and resources of one discipline to those of another. When we approach Jung with a particular question in mind, we find ourselves drawn into thinking about things we did not expect, perhaps even about things we did not wish to entertain. The difficulty with such a style is, of course, the question of whether there is a center, a focus, a fundamental emphasis which draws things together.

In asking what Jung can contribute to psychological self-understanding, I now propose that his work is fundamentally concerned with the psychological process of fantasy and with the interpretation of fantasy. However, as one instance of psychological activity, fantasy cannot be separated from other psychological processes, and in the case of Jung's thought fantasy and archetype are closely related. Nor can fantasy be understood apart from the problem of subject and object. In Jung's view, fantasy, like thought, has an object; it is intentional. It is the intentional character of fantasy which distinguishes Jung from Freud and which also allies Jung with students of religion concerned with myth.

How can we best enter the Jungian psychology, quickly and incisively, in order to demonstrate this point? Erik Erikson has given us, as is his habit, an Eriksonian analysis of the origins of psychoanalysis.[7] He speaks of three dimensions which make up the total meaning of psychological discovery, each related closely to the others. The first is conceptual, the second is personal or developmental, and the third is a dimension of work techniques (or, in the older language, a dimension of vocation, or calling). So Erikson argues that Freud's discovery of psychoanalysis really consisted in three discoveries—a discovery in terms of the technique of doing therapy, a discovery in the conceptual formulation of that process, and a discovery in his own personal development. We refer to these three dimensions more simply as the interrelation of *thought, person,* and *work* in the process of psychological discovery, and we take them as means of interrogating Jung with regard to what is central in his psychology. Considerations of thought, person, and work intersect in Jung's psychology around the nature of the phenomenon of fantasy.

Let us begin at the easiest level, the level of thought, and, since we are reading Jung as a psychologist, this means his theory of personality. There is general precedent in speaking of the structure and dynamics of personality.[8] With regard to structural considerations, then, the most important concepts are the ego and the persona.[9] The ego is defined as an experienced inner sense of self-sameness and continuity. The persona is Jung's term for the psychological meaning of the social other, the social or collective expectations which the ego senses and to which it agrees to conform. The concepts of ego and persona are in many ways similar to Freud's concepts of ego and superego, and we may take them, at this point at least, to mean roughly the same thing. Jung, however, adduced a wider structural component of personality, which he called the self, which emerged, at least initially, as a result of certain dynamic changes in the relation between ego and persona.

The most comprehensive dynamic consideration in Jung's psychology is the process of individuation. While this process is difficult to define in summary fashion, it refers primarily to changes in the relation between ego and persona.[10] This process in turn presupposes the appearance and integration of the collective unconscious, which Jung considered to be the wider ground for the personal unconscious so central to Freud. The self, as a wider context for the ego and the persona, requires, for its development, integration of the collective unconscious. It is the collective unconscious, when taken into account, which permits an enlarging of the narrow sense of self characterized only by the ego and its matching of social expectations in the form of the persona. However, this collective dimension is accessible to the ego only through images, which Jung called archetypes. Archetypes mediate between the universal character of religious structures and the personal character of fantasy. They contain, therefore, a dimension of collective fantasy. Because the archetype does contain fantasy elements, and because its integration into the ego is central to the individuation process, we can conclude that fantasy is central to Jung's conceptual formulation of the structure and dynamics of human personality.

But the significance of fantasy for the process of individuation is best found in the therapeutic process itself—that is, in what we are calling Jung's *work,* as well as in his *thought.* Jung considered his rejection of Freud's psychology to be as necessary at the point of therapeutic technique as it was at the point of theory. While Freud retained a three-fold structure of personality (id, ego, and superego), Jung adduced the notion of the self as a wider structure that, in effect, contained both ego and superego, both ego and persona. What Jung considered to be characteristic of *his* therapy, however, was what he called the "breakdown of the persona"—a psychological crisis consisting of the failure of the ego and the persona together to continue to obscure the collective depths of psychic life, a crisis which resulted in the eruption into conscious experiencing of the archetypal images.[11] The distinctively Jungian moment in psychotherapy is the breakdown of the persona and the subsequent appearance—with what can unfortunately only be regarded as suspicious regularity—of archetypal images. Jung tells us that what distinguishes his therapy from Freud's is the final disposition of fantasy. The merely personal fantasies of the personal unconscious, fantasies which the superego opposes, weaken, but do not overthrow, the superego. But for Jung there is another level of imaginative activity continuous with the first, consisting of historical and cosmological images, embodying an archetypal dimension. So the appearance of fantasy is the crucial feature in Jung's therapy, and the disposition of fantasy is crucial to his theory of what is normative in the psychological functioning of the person.

What of the place of fantasy in that more elusive aspect of psychological discovery, Jung's personal experience?[12] Since the Jungian theory of personality and of therapy is a critical transformation of Freud's theory and therapy, it is interesting to note that Jung underwent a personal crisis which coincided with these changes in his theory and therapy, and that the crisis occurred in his personal relation to Freud. After the "break" in 1912 Jung reports in his autobiography that a sense of inner uncertainty settled over him, and he entitles the chapter which describes this uncertainty "Confrontation with the Unconscious"—as if, so to speak, the separation from Freud had a personal as well as professional and theoretical meaning.[13] Jung's break with Freud was in any case followed by an increased sensitivity on Jung's part to collective, archetypal images, and he considers this phase of his life crucial to what later became most unique and distinctive in his work. Interestingly enough, one of the important events leading to the break was an argument over the meaning of a dream, one of Jung's dreams. Jung outwardly accepted, but secretly rejected, Freud's interpretation of the dream. And Freud, eager, as he put it . . . to protect his authority, was willing to be put at ease.[14]

It seems clear that in Jung's thought (i.e., in his theory of personality), in his work (i.e., as a psychotherapist), and in his personal, inner life, what I have called the psychological activity of fantasy occupies a central position. Jung's psychology is intimately concerned with the therapeutic disposition of fantasy.

This concern, which I prefer to call the problem of the interpretation of fantasy, is not, however, the end point or goal of Jung's psychology but rather the starting point. It was the point of departure for all that is original in his investigations. Jung inherited the problem of the interpretation of fantasy from Freud, whose solution was to reduce fantasy to the reality principle.[15] Jung objected to this and attempted to expand the meaning of the phenomenon of fantasy into that of the archetype. This forced him out of the framework of classic psychoanalysis. It also forced him into an attitude of inquiry with regard to spiritual questions, and he turned to theology for assistance. He was again disappointed.[16] Although theology does address itself to an objective reality which lies beyond the lower developmental processes which Freud had documented, it does so by severing itself from the psychological realm entirely. However, Jung was loath to create any such final splitting between admittedly lower, psychological processes and higher, spiritual processes. He was forced, in other words, to reject both psychoanalysis *and* theology. This double rejection required, anthropologically, that he create the concept of archetype and, methodologically, that he create a theory of interpretation appropriate to archetypal structures. Let us explore Jung's objection to Freud in more detail. This objection forced Jung to create a higher psychological view of theology. That psychological view is precisely his contribution to hermeneutics.

JUNG'S CRITICISM OF FREUD'S PSYCHOLOGY

During the phases of their development, Jung's critical amendments to the psychoanalytic psychology appeared more radical and thoroughgoing than they in fact are. As already noted, recent discussions of Freud have shown that his psychology was far more oriented toward problems of myth and symbol, and toward a moral psychology of culture, than the earlier interpreters of Freud recognized. For this reason there may be less difference between Freud and Jung than the writings of each suggest. Nevertheless, Jung's objections to Freud remain finally substantive and are as well defined as they are thoroughgoing.

In a very general sense Jung felt that Freud had absolutized the oedipal myth, rather than having placed it in a wider context characterized by historical, collective, and universal features.[17] Jung was convinced that the oedipal situation was a "first mythology," opening out into other mythologies to which the self must relate itself in the process of individuation. In structural terms, for example, Freud spoke of the superego as the only form of social transcendence available to the ego. To insist that the superego was the final structure of limitation and possibility for the self unnecessarily limited growth to the forms of family life. Jung used the term "self" to designate a wide psychological structure which included additional objective referents beyond the acquisition of parental norms. Freud's phylogenetic view of the oedipal situation and his recognition of a collective unconscious mitigate only somewhat this criticism, for he also insisted that the individual and cultural superego are continuous.

With regard to the dynamics of the self, Jung also spoke of regression, but he assigned to this process therapeutic as well as pathological significance.[18] Characteristic of the regressive moment is the appearance of fantasy, and the interpretation of fantasy moves the developmental processes—individuation—forward. Again, Jung's dynamic revision of Freud's psychology considers transference to be first of all an active process involving change not only for the patient but also for the therapist. Jung considered Freud's notions of insight and working through to be excessively rational and constricting, and introduced the term "active imagination" to describe the process whereby the ego at once participates in archetypal forms and at the same time differentiates itself from them.[19]

With regard to methodology Jung adopted the phrase "phenomenological standpoint" to define the approach taken by the analytical psychologist toward the material requiring interpretation, whether it was the patient's productions or universal mythic structures.[20] The phenomenological standpoint is the methodological parallel to the therapeutic work of active imagination, permitting the differentiation of the interpreting ego from the contents of the collective unconscious.

There is no exact Freudian equivalent for these terms. Freud's vocabulary at this point remains clinical, restricted to describing the physician's attitude in such terms as "free-floating attention," what Theodore Reik has called "listening with the third ear."[21] However, this omission should not be allowed to exaggerate the differences between Freud and Jung, for Freud too "listened" to mythic structures in his religious writings. And these writings are much richer than his apparent adoption of a clinical model of interpretation suggests.

The major difference between these two psychologies, however, lies in the view of fantasy and its disposition, that is, its interpretation. In each case we must say that Jung expanded or dignified fantasy to include mythic structures. The phenomenological standpoint is addressed to both developmental and religious forms, such that both are accorded objective validity—neither can be reduced to the other. Freud's therapy presupposed two levels of psychic life: first, a surface reality characterized by clarity of self-awareness, self-control, and continuity between ego and perceptual environment; and, second, a deeper level of psychological functioning, the dominant characteristic of which is fantasy. The force of his psychology lies in an attempt to relate the second interpretively to the first, the reduction of fantasy to reality. Jung extended the formal aspect of this approach to mythic or archetypal forms and asserted that individuation was a double movement of the self between the appearance of archetypes and their subsequent interpretation. Jung therefore both affirmed and then criticized Freud's psychology. In attempting to go "beyond" Freud he found himself face to face with the question of religious experience and theological thought—and, from our own point of view, with the task of interpreting theological doctrine itself and, in particular, the doctrine of transcendence.

FROM DOGMATICS TO PSYCHOLOGY: THE COLLAPSE OF DISTANCE

The psychological activity of fantasy is central to Jung's psychology. At the center of his thought is a double movement characterized first by the appearance of fantasy elements and archetype and second by the activity of interpretation. Given this wider understanding of the nature of fantasy, such that it leads out into religious images or archetypes, this second movement is the point at which Jung attempted to formulate the meaning of transcendence. However, because this concept was so fraught with theological rather than psychological meaning, and because Jung found his work located "between" classic Freudian theory and theological statement, it is best to adopt a middle term, that of distance, one midway between insight or understanding in the psychological sense and the theological notion of self-transcendence.[22] Thus psychological insight may be understood as a form of distance from one's situation. In like fashion the theological view of self-transcendence implies the capacity to distance oneself from oneself in order to permit a deeper relation to oneself.

We can understand Jung's thought at this point through the notion of distance. The appearance of fantasy and archetype can be characterized as the collapse of distance, and the interpretation of the religious image, as the gaining or winning of distance. Methodologically one gains distance from the past through the interpretation of historical-universal religious structures, and experientially the self gains distance from itself through the differentiation of the ego from the contents of the collective unconscious. In both cases continuity between developmental and cosmological, religious structures is absolutely necessary. While Jung does not make explicit use of the notion of distance, it is, we argue, implicit in his thought. Therefore this is an "interpretation" of Jung the validity of which depends on how well it clarifies Jung's work in relation to Freud's thought, to theology, and to religion.

Jung took a distinctly psychological approach to theology. Like the early psychologists of religion, he spoke of such typical problems as conversion, mysticism, worship, and ritual. But unlike the psychologists of religion, Jung was far more interested in the psychological meaning of Christian doctrine—he approached it interpretively.[23] Doctrinal thought was founded psychologically upon what he called the rational attitude,[24] a characterization of modern, Western human beings closely associated with the extraverted attitude type and with a rather rigid relation between ego and persona. This kind of psychological organization prevents integration of the darker or "shadow" side of the self. Concern with the darker aspects of self-understanding led Jung ethically to the problem of evil, theologically to the doctrinal meaning of the demonic, and religiously to the image of Satan.

Jung's concern with the ethics of the irrational allies him with such religious existentialists as Berdyaev and Marcel. But it allies him even more intimately with Protestant theological existentialism. Jung's criticism of the extraverted attitude type, related as it is to the functions of sensation and thinking, resembles theological existentialism's criticism of the false objectivity of the subject–object dichotomy. But his psychological-interpretive approach to theology itself distinguishes his work from this type of theology. From the methodological point of view of this genre of theology, myth is the objective pole and the cultural situation is the subjective pole. The theologian's task lies in demonstrating the relevance of his myth for the cultural situation, which is nonmythic in character. For example, Reinhold Niebuhr's distinction between primitive and permanent myth allocates to such disciplines as psychology and anthropology the task of interpreting primitive myth.[25] But permanent myth, by which he means biblical myth, transcends primitive myth; therefore theological interpretation transcends psychological interpretation. Bultmann's demythologization program and Tillich's correlation of kerygma and situation exhibit a similar style. The theologian therefore moves from the givenness or priority of myth as a structure transcending natural and rational modes of knowing to the cultural situation.

Jung responded to this methodological style in two important ways. First, because he in effect had expanded Freud's psychological point of view, he was able to maintain a psychological approach to permanent myth without, however, being vulnerable to the criticism of reductionism. Consequently, he concluded that there was a psychological-archetypal structure not only to the highest forms of myth—that is, those of the Old and New Testaments—but also to doctrinal statement itself. The doctrine of the Trinity became extremely important in this phase of Jung's work; he found it closely related to the problem of evil and the image of Satan. Jung conceptualized this higher psychology of the darker, unconscious side of life in terms of the shadow archetype.[26] He concluded that the doctrine of the Trinity was excessively rational, that it was expressive of neglect of the darker, shadow side of life. However, it must be emphasized that Jung was also arguing for the mediating power and function of religious images, for what should be called an "archetypal a priori" in any doctrinal formulation of transcendence and faith.

Because this type of a priori is generally neglected in doctrinal thinking, Jung's psychology takes as its object not only religious experience but doctrinal statement as well. He seeks images which underlie doctrinal statement, for it is these images which make doctrine attractive to the believer. Gaston Bachelard, in referring to his own work of a psychoanalysis of objective or scientific knowledge, also described it as an indirect and secondary psychoanalysis which seeks "the subjective value under the objective evidence, the reverie beneath the experiment."[27] Transposing Bachelard's apt phrase, we say that Jung's psychology seeks the "reverie beneath the doctrine," and the particular reverie beneath the particular doctrine of transcendence. Analytical psychology is not, therefore, a different discipline which can be used to supplement theological statement, it is not an *ancilla fidei;* nor is it simply a secularized religious experience, transposed into the psychotherapeutic experience, as many Jungian commentators have suggested. Jung's psychology is an interpretation of doctrine, of the psychological, archetypal substructure of theological thinking. The immanental opposite to the doctrine of God's transcendence is the image of Satan, and this image in turn opens up the feminine, or anima, side of the divine life. Jung's psychology is an attempt to educe from doctrinal, dogmatic material such latent images.

Is this approach as reductive as it seems? Let us return to the phenomenon of distance. Jung argued that the doctrine of God's transcendence was closely related to a rational, extraverted psychological attitude. Transcendence in the Protestant tradition creates excessive distance between human consciousness and divine reality, whenever rational thinking is the only form of thinking permitted. Such distance is "false distance," and is collapsed by the emergence of latent archetypal structures. At this point Jung's work is a thoroughgoing criticism of the "high" theological tradition in the West, particularly its Protestant forms. Here Jung does in fact move from dogmatic theology to developmental processes. He collapses the transcendent, objective, divine reality into subjective, psychological processes.

At this point Jung's approach seems clearly reductive, for he forces doctrinal thinking to pass through its own archetypal infrastructure. Jung "humiliates" the dogmatic mode of thought by taking doctrine as his object of interpretation, reducing it to subjective psychological processes. But there is a second movement in Jung's work, one directed toward a recovery of transcendence, toward, in our terms, a recovery of distance. Jung's first movement seeks the religious image beneath the doctrine in order to make possible a second movement, one in which such images acquire the status of religious structures, which therefore in turn require interpretation. The psychological interpretation of dogma, and especially of the Protestant version of transcendence, is therefore only the first step of a twofold contribution. The second is a movement from psychological analysis to hermeneutics.

FROM PSYCHOLOGY TO HERMENEUTICS: THE RECOVERY OF DISTANCE

Jung opens dogmatic thinking to its own implicit, psychological meanings. In so adducing an archetypal infrastructure to doctrine, Jung takes the first step toward a psychology of religion. This first step is in some sense already interpretive, in that its view of dogmatics differs from dogmatics' view of itself. However, a second step assigns meaning to the archetypal infrastructure, rather than simply speaking in behalf of its phenomenal reality. At this point Jung's psychology openly becomes what we will call a psychological hermeneutic of religious images. We should keep in mind the very important fact that Jung's psychological work is methodologically situated midway between classic psychoanalysis and Protestant theology.

This second movement can be described at the points of method and the developmental process. In the case of method, Jung requires a movement from dogmatics, through the psychological criticism of dogmatic modes of thought, to the activity of interpretation. We have characterized the first movement as the collapse of distance, that is, of a false sense of distance closely related to the rational, psychological attitude and to its theological counterpart, a heightened sense of God's transcendence. The interpretation of the archetypal dimension of doctrine, the second movement, can therefore be characterized as the reverse, as the recovery or winning of distance. Such interpretation is related to developmental processes, for interpretation frees the ego from the effects of unconscious archetypal influence, by changing the relation of the ego to these contents. This freeing results in a new, more integrated relation between ego and collective unconscious, which is, of course, the essence of the individuation process. Interpretation therefore makes possible the process of individuation, and individuation requires interpretation.

By way of summary we note three fundamental principles which Jung's work requires of any view of hermeneutics. First, hermeneutics must be open to the possibility of a plurality of master myths, objectively and structurally. The interpreter may wish to emphasize the ascendancy of a single myth over others, its inherent capacity to transcend others, but this conclusion can be drawn only after the full range of myths has been recognized and then worked through. Second, hermeneutics must admit to a plurality of mythic structures subjectively as well. It must recognize that there are also mythologies of development and socialization. The interpreter may wish to designate these subjective structures as "lower" or more "immanental," but they still must be included in the total work of interpretation. Third, whatever correlations hermeneutics may wish to create—be they between the objective and the subjective, between kerygma and situation, between myth and modernity—must be made in the context of these two levels of myth.

Jung's work will, however, always be found largely incomplete and unsatisfying to those who are concerned with the full range of problems involved in a theory of interpretation of religious forms. His contribution is primarily at the point of dynamics and socialization. Only secondarily does he assist in structural and methodological considerations. Yet this dynamic emphasis is important, not only as one dimension of a religious anthropology but also because it makes possible fruitful interplay between structural and methodological considerations. This advantage is easily illustrated by drawing upon the work of Eliade and Ricoeur. Jung makes a permanent psychological contribution to Eliade's structural emphasis and to Ricoeur's methodological interests. Depth psychology makes possible a full return to the type of hermeneutics of which Ricoeur speaks, on the basis of a phenomenology of religion as Eliade has demonstrated it, without sacrificing—as they both tend to do—developmental considerations.

For years Eliade has been impatient with Freud's genetic reductionism of religion, an objection similar to Jung's.[28] However, Eliade has never closed the study of the history of religions to depth psychology, and he has even tentatively defined his own approach as a "metapsychoanalysis," the study of man "not only inasmuch as he is a historic being, but also as a living symbol," through the use of "a more spiritual technique applicable mainly to elucidating the theoretical content of the symbols and archetypes."[29] For Eliade the image alone reveals, the symbol is an autonomous mode of knowledge which possesses and evinces intrinsic cognitive value. Because of his predominantly dynamic emphasis, Jung often gives the impression of reducing the meaning of religious structures to a projection of internal, personal processes. However, Jung refused to identify his approach exclusively either with experimental science or with idealistic metaphysics and the theologies associated with it. What he called the phenomenological standpoint was an attempt to remain open to the structural status assigned to symbol, myth, and archetype by such writers as Eliade.

According to Eliade's distinction between historical and structural approaches to the phenomenon of religion,[30] structure refers to the images which embody a unity of wholeness which human beings in their historical life and thought lack. Because they lack such unity and wholeness, human beings know the difference between this possibility and their own actual condition, and the being for which they yearn is expressed to them through the medium of its mythic forms. Therefore, religious structures are "out there," existing neither as psychological projections nor as the hypostasized reality of dogmatic theological statement. The dynamic component of Eliade's phenomenology is nostalgia, the desire to participate in mythic structures and through them in unfallen being: "to be always, effortlessly, at the heart of the world."[31] Eliade's view is matched by Jung's psychological notion of the teleological significance of regression.

Paul Ricoeur employs the sort of phenomenological approach to religion developed by Eliade, but Ricoeur does so by moving through depth psychology. He therefore incorporates what we have called a psychological hermeneutic in order to arrive at the goal of his work, the concrete reflection upon symbols.

In his discussions of hermeneutics Ricoeur identifies three types of relation between consciousness and religious symbols.[32] This typology must be considered whenever one wishes to develop ways of thinking about religious symbols. There is first of all the original condition of primitive naïveté, of the immediacy of the symbol, a direct and immediate connection between the religious consciousness and symbols. This religious attitude is not, of course, available to modern people, who continually prefer to seek out the causes, function, and origins of myth, ritual, and belief. Modern people prefer awareness of myth as myth, the logos of the mythos. In so preferring, they dissolve myth into explanation and speak of truth without belief. This second relation between consciousness and symbols Ricoeur calls "truth at a distance." It calls for an interrogation of myth and symbol at the level of comparison rather than commitment; it runs from one symbol to another without regard for the existence and subjectivity of the interpreter.

The third attitude which can be taken toward symbols Ricoeur calls a second immediacy or second naïveté, a postcritical equivalent to a precritical hierophany, a return to the powerful immediacy of symbols—but all of this on the basis of distance, on the basis of demythologization.

This passage from truth at a distance to a second immediacy embodies a psychological step of fundamental importance. Ricoeur believes that Freud's psychology is primarily a hermeneutic, and it is Freud's hermeneutical style which fascinates Ricoeur. He uses Freud's psychology to move from phenomenology to hermeneutics. Phenomenology, used here in two senses, refers philosophically to the method of pure description and to a phenomenological approach to religious structures. Ricoeur likens the *cogito* of phenomenological description to Freud's description of the surface quality of the ego's relation to reality. Ricoeur describes this relation as the pretension of consciousness to rule the senses.[33] At this point Ricoeur and Freud, each in his own way, support Jung's objection to the rational extraverted attitude which, we have argued, so readily articulates with the Protestant sense of transcendence.

It is the thinking subject, the *cogito,* and not the object, the religious symbol, which must undergo deeper exploration, in order that it can become open to the meaning of symbols. Interpretation, Ricoeur argues, must pass through desire. The *cogito* must be "humiliated" it must "pass through" the experience of narcissism. Ricoeur therefore adduces psychoanalytic psychology as an antiphenomenology, the purpose of which is to conduct an archaeology of the subject, in preparation for philosophical reflection on symbols.

Narcissism is usually considered to be a metapsychological construct, referring to the quantitative distribution of libido among ego, id, and objective reality. However, Freud also gave it mythic exemplification in the oedipal narrative, which Ricoeur refers to as the fantasm.[34] It is the interpretation of this subjective, mythic structure that opens the way to hermeneutics proper, to reflection on objective structures.

Consequently Ricoeur is prepared to ask several questions, all turning on the nature of the fantasm and each quite recognizable in the light of Eliade's view of symbols and Jung's view of fantasy become archetype: "Is there, in the affective dynamism of religious belief, the wherewithal to rise above its own archaism?" Is the fantasm "only a vestige of a traumatic memory," or is it "a symbol, capable of providing the first stratum of meaning to an imaginative presentation of origins, more and more detached from its function of infantile and quasineurotic repetition, and more and more suited to an investigation of the fundamental meanings of human destiny?"[35]

Ricoeur's work is therefore an interpretation of Freud, a critical expanding of Freud's approach. As such, it too has a double movement, first educing fantasy and then interpreting it. In this regard Ricoeur's approach to the hermeneutical implications of Freud's work is similar to Jung's. Both see in Freud's work a first mythology that opens understanding to other mythologies. Ricoeur and Jung could agree that the *cogito* is possessed of an archetypal infrastructure and that a psychological hermeneutic must be employed in order that thought can be released for a return to mythic structures—not, however, for the purpose of demythologizing or for preaching, but for the purpose of thinking about symbols. This thinking creates new moral possibilities, as well as new possibilities for thought. Clearly for Jung, ethics, understood as the fruit of individuation, was the more important. Becoming takes precedence over thinking in his psychology.

THE SYMBOL GIVES RISE TO BECOMING

Ricoeur has been fascinated by the formula, "the symbol gives rise to thought." By this he means that once the *cogito* is freed from its own archaism, once the archaeology of the subject has been carried out, thought is capable of listening to symbols; it can be shaped by them. For Ricoeur the deepest levels of thought are engaged by symbols. However, we must not overlook the fact that Ricoeur, in developing his view of hermeneutics, has drawn substantively on Freud, and that Freud's psychology is essentially developmental. This is acknowledged, for example, in Ricoeur's proposal of an "epigenesis of the religious sentiment."[36] Therefore his adaptation of Freud's hermeneutical style implicitly authorizes a second formula, "the symbol gives rise to becoming." Our own argument regarding the fundamental thrust of Jung's psychology explicitly insists upon such a formulation. As we have noted, his psychological hermeneutic opens the deeper strands of the subject to its own concealments, in order that the ego can return to the objective religious structures. This means that the objective cannot be separated from the subjective or developmental. Once the strategy of adducing psychological hermeneutical considerations has been adopted, it becomes necessary to recognize that the activity of interpretation bears a reciprocal relation to the subject's personal history as well. Therefore, the symbol also gives rise to becoming, to individuation, to the metamorphosis of personality.

I have tried to show the inherent propriety of bringing together certain psychological and hermeneutical considerations, by way of Jung's work. The point of departure for that work was the separateness of developmental and existential factors in human life, so characteristic of the separateness advocated by theological and psychological approaches to self-understanding. Jung's work transforms the opposites of developmental and existential into a second polarity, that of objective religious symbols and the archaic structure of the interpreter's own subjective being. For this reason a recent discussion, although not addressed to psychological questions, nevertheless summarizes well for us the import of Jung's psychology for hermeneutics: "Reflection proceeding from religious symbolism has the merit of correlating the interpreter as he seeks to discover his being with a level of historical expression commensurate with this intention. The interpreter as he moves from symbolism to rationality will find that he must make another movement, back into the shadows of his ego and history, for he discovers that his being is mirrored in the reality of life and history and simultaneously created by him in the moment of comprehension."[37] It is that other movement, back into the shadows of the ego and its history, which Jung's psychology sought to document, and which constitutes that contribution to hermeneutics which we call psychological.

Notes

1. For review of the problem of transcendence in this style of theology, see John B. Cobb, Jr., *Living Options in Protestant Theology* (Philadelphia: Westminster Press, 1962); and Edward Farley, *The Transcendence of God* (Philadelphia: Westminster Press, 1960).

2. The works of Fuchs, Ebeling, and Otto are often cited in this regard. See especially Gerhard Ebeling, *The Nature of Faith*, trans. Ronald Gregor Smith (Philadelphia: Fortress Press, 1961); and *The New Hermeneutic*, ed. James M. Robinson and John B. Cobb, Jr., New Frontiers in Theology, vol. 2 (New York: Harper & Row, 1964). For a review discussion see Robert W. Funk, *Language, Hermeneutic, and Word of God* (New York: Harper & Row, 1966).

3. The works of R. Otto, Van der Leeuw, Wach, and Eliade are often cited in this regard.

4. See David Shakow and David Rapaport, *The Influence of Freud on American Psychology*, Psychological Issues, no. 13 (New York: International Universities Press, 1964); Herbert Marcuse, *Eros and Civilization* (New York: Vintage Books, 1965); Philip Rieff, *Freud: The Mind of the Moralist* (New York: Viking Press, 1959); Paul Ricoeur, *De l'interprétation: Essai sur Freud* (Paris: Editions du Seuil, 1965).

5. David Cox, *Jung and St. Paul* (New York: Association Press, 1959); Raymond Hostie, *Religion and the Psychology of C.G. Jung* (New York: Sheed & Ward, 1957); Hans Schaer, *Religion and the Cure of Souls in Jung's Psychology* (New York: Pantheon Books, 1950); Victor White, *God and the Unconscious* (Cleveland: Meridian Books, 1952); Thomas

J.J. Altizer, "A Critical Analysis of C.G. Jung's Understanding of Religion" (Ph.D. dissertation, University of Chicago, 1955).

6. For example, Gerhard Adler, *Studies in Analytical Psychology* (New York: G.P. Putnam's Sons, 1966); Jolande Jacobi, *The Psychology of C.G. Jung* (New Haven, Conn.: Yale University Press, 1962); Dieter Wyss, *Depth Psychology: A Critical History* (New York: W.W. Norton, 1966), pp. 321–61.

7. Erik Erikson, "The First Psychoanalyst," in *Freud and the Twentieth Century*, ed. Benjamin Nelson (New York: Meridian Books, 1957), p. 87.

8. Calvin S. Hall and Gardner Lindzey, *Theories of Personality* (New York: John Wiley & Sons, 1957).

9. See C.G. Jung, *Psychological Types*, trans. H.G. Baynes (New York: Pantheon Books, 1923), p. 540; and *Two Essays on Analytical Psychology*, trans. R.F.C. Hull (New York: Meridian Books, 1956), pp. 166–68.

10. Jung, *Two Essays on Analytical Psychology*, pt. 2, esp. pp. 182–83.

11. Ibid., p. 170, and "Fundamental Questions of Psychotherapy," in *The Practice of Psychotherapy*, trans. R.F.C. Hull, Bollingen Series 20 (New York: Pantheon Books, 1954).

12. C.G. Jung, *Memories, Dreams, Reflections*, trans. Richard and Clara Winston (New York: Vintage Books, 1961).

13. Ibid., p. 170.

14. Ibid., pp. 157–60.

15. Sigmund Freud, "Formulations Regarding the Two Principles of Mental Functioning," *Collected Papers*, trans. Joan Riviere (New York: Basic Books, 1959), vol. 4.

16. Consider, for example, the following well-known remark by Jung: "The Mystery of the Virgin Birth, or the homoiousia of the Son with the Father, or the Trinity which is nevertheless not a triad . . . have stiffened into mere objects of belief" ("The Archetypes and the Collective Unconscious," *The Archetypes and the Collective Unconscious*, Bollingen Series 20 [New York: Pantheon Books, 1959], p. 8).

17. See "Fundamental Questions of Psychotherapy."

18. C.G. Jung, *Freud and Psychoanalysis*, trans. R.F.C. Hull, Bollingen Series 20 (New York: Pantheon Books, 1961), pp. 179–80.

19. *Two Essays on Analytical Psychology*, pp. 224–38.

20. Jung, "Concerning the Archetypes with Special Reference to the Anima Concept," *The Archetypes and the Collective Unconscious*, esp. pp. 54–62.

21. Theodore Reik, *Listening with the Third Ear* (New York: Farrar, Strauss & Co., 1954), p. 157.

22. For a psychological discussion of distance, see Alfred Adler, "The Problem of Distance," *The Practice and Theory of Individual Psychology* (New Haven, Conn.: Harcourt, Brace & Co., 1924); and David Bakan, *Sigmund Freud and the Jewish Mystical Tradition* (Princeton, N.J.: D. Van Nostrand Co., 1958), chap. 30. For a phenomenological discussion of distance, see John Wild, *Existence and the World of Freedom* (Englewood Cliffs, N.J.: Prentice-Hall, Inc., 1963), pp. 108–13.

23. C.G. Jung, *Psychology and Religion* (New Haven, Conn.: Yale University Press, 1960), pp. 61–62, 73–74; and "A Psychological Approach to the Dogma of the Trinity," *Psychology and Religion: West and East,* Bollingen Series 20 (New York: Pantheon Books, 1958).

24. *Psychology and Religion,* pp. 73–77.

25. Reinhold Niebuhr, "The Truth in Myths," in *The Nature of Religious Experience: Essays in Honor of D.C. Macintosh* (New York: Harper & Bros., 1937).

26. In addition to the writings on religion already mentioned, see also Jung, "Answer to Job," in *Psychology and Religion: West and East.*

27. Gaston Bachelard, *The Psychoanalysis of Fire,* trans. Alan C.M. Ross (Boston: Beacon Press, 1938), pp. 21–22.

28. Mircea Eliade, *Images and Symbols,* trans. Philip Maret (New York: Sheed & Ward, 1961), pp. 9–32.

29. Ibid., p. 35.

30. For a discussion of this problem in Eliade's thought, see Robert Luyster, "The Study of Myth: Two Approaches," *Journal of Bible and Religion* 34 (1966): 235–43.

31. Mircea Eliade, *Patterns in Comparative Religion,* trans. Rosemary Sheed (Cleveland: World Publishing Co., 1963), p. 383.

32. Paul Ricoeur, *The Symbolism of Evil,* trans. Emerson Buchanan (New York: Harper & Row, 1967), pp. 347–57.

33. *De l'interprétation,* pp. 410–16.

34. Paul Ricoeur, "The Atheism of Freudian Psychoanalysis," *Concilium* 16 (1966): 59–72.

35. Ibid.

36. *De l'interprétation,* p. 515.

37. Charles H. Long, "Archaism and Hermeneutics," in *The History of Religions: Essays on the Problem of Understanding,* ed. Joseph M. Kitagawa (Chicago: University of Chicago Press, 1967), pp. 86–87.

Jung on Scripture and Hermeneutics: Retrospect and Prospect

In his preface to *Answer to Job,* Jung provides a key for understanding the role of scripture in his life and thought. Jung states: "I do not write as a biblical scholar (which I am not), but as a layman and a physician who has been privileged to see deeply into the psychic life of many people."[1] This statement corroborates Peter Homan's thesis in *Jung in Context: Modernity and the Making of a Psychology,*[2] that the analysis and appraisal of Jung's thought is best done by noting its place in the context of Jung's personal life, which should include not only his relationship with his family, his reaction to traditional Christianity, his break with Freud, and his view of the role of religion in our culture as a "counterbalance to mass-mindedness"—as Homans suggests, but also for our purposes, his personal agenda. Jung refers to this agenda in *Memories, Dreams, Reflections* as his "main business" and describes it thus: "My life has been permeated and held together by one idea and one goal: namely, to penetrate into the secret of the personality. Everything can be explained from this central point, and all my works relate to this one theme."[3]

Accepting these contextual factors as critical for interpreting Jung's *curriculum vitae,* our purpose here is to provide an overview of the role scripture plays in this *curriculum.* Jung shows keen interest in the contribution scripture makes to the life of the psyche, specifically among persons rooted in the west, both in its adverse as well as constructive effects.

We will comment on three aspects of the role of scripture in Jung's life and thought: (a) Jung's actual use of scripture, professionally and personally, and its ubiquity in his life and thought; (b) Jung's attitude toward the method and result of critical biblical scholarship; and (c) Jung's understanding of scripture as sacred text.

We will conclude with observations on some programmatic implications of the foregoing for a future hermeneutic.

JUNG'S USE OF SCRIPTURE, PROFESSIONALLY AND PERSONALLY

At first glance, the Jungian corpus provides little evidence of Jung's interest in scripture. *Answer to Job*, written in 1952, is the most conspicuous testimony to Jung's biblical interests and is the only work of Jung's devoted solely to the discussion of a biblical text.

However, as one ruminates through the *Collected Works* one uncovers a thesaurus of biblical passages, personages, phrases, images, and concepts. In the course of the twenty volumes Jung manages to refer to all but thirteen of the sixty-six books of the biblical canon. In addition he cites inter-testamental writings, e.g. Slavonic Enoch, II Esdras, and Tobit, along with works from the Apocryphal New Testament, e.g. the Gospel of Philip, the Acts of Peter and the Book of the Apostle Bartholomew. He even betrays a seasoned familiarity with the nuanced observations of the textual critic, remarking on the variant textual versions of the dominical sayings.

In addition one finds a glossary of biblical names, expressions, and terms. Adam and Abraham, Peter and Job, Elijah and Salome appear along with dozens from the cast of characters that populate the biblical narrative and symbolize biblical experience. The weighted biblical images of the "inner man," the Pharisee and the publican, and of the "spirit searching the deep things of God" (1 Cor 2:10) surface with remarkable naturalness in Jung's essays and letters. Repeatedly Jung makes clear his recognition of the power of these figures to touch the depths of the soul and to give voice to the depths of human experience with impressive and probing accuracy. Jung confesses familiarity with the wounding and binding up that Job experienced at the hand of God; he identifies with Abraham and Paul who went against the storm; and on his tombstone he chose to have inscribed not only the words of the Pythian oracle, "Vocatus atque non vocatus Deus aderit" ("Summoned or not summoned, God will be present"), but also words of the apostle Paul: "Primus homo terrenus de terra; secundus homo coelestis de coelo" ("the first man is of the earth, a man of dust; the second is of heaven") (1 Cor 15:47).

Beyond these explicit allusions to biblical expression, one should mention Jung's general approach to experience that reflects what might be labeled a biblical *Weltanschauung* (though certainly not a biblical *Weltbild*). Jung exhibits in his work an angle of vision that renders visible many of the biblical realities that have been rendered virtually invisible from a rationalistic perspective. The realities and experience that count most in Jung's internal biography are those that occupy primary attention in the writings of the biblical authors, e.g. an awareness of the numinous depth of life, a sense of *vocatio*, a responsiveness to the wisdom of dreams and visions, and a seasoned sense of the paradox that "where sin is great, grace abounds."

Scripture is a central reality for Jung, imaginally and thematically; and though it never emerges as a subject for concentrated critical comment from a psychological perspective aside from *Answer to Job*, it appears to be a fundamental factor in Jung's personal and professional vocabulary as he pursues his "main business."

JUNG'S ATTITUDE TOWARD THE METHOD AND RESULT OF CRITICAL BIBLICAL SCHOLARSHIP

In his Terry Lectures at Yale in 1937, Jung makes a passing observation that is probably his most explicit commentary on critical biblical scholarship. He writes:

> Nor has the scientific criticism of the New Testament been very helpful in enhancing the divine character of the holy writings. It is also a fact that under the influence of so-called scientific enlightenment great masses of educated people have either left the church or have become profoundly indifferent to it.

And he adds, "if they were all dull rationalists or neurotic intellectuals the loss would not be regrettable. But many of them are religious people, only incapable of agreeing with the actually existing forms of creed."[4]

One might gather from this that Jung is unsympathetic with the historical-literary-critical analysis of sacred texts. This is hardly the case. Reading in the Jungian corpus one is continually impressed not only with Jung's mastery of Greek and Latin texts ranging from the New Testament and apostolic fathers to the medieval church, but with his familiarity with literary-critical issues and with his native talent for what would be regarded by contemporary scholars as a serious and informed historical-critical approach.

An instance of this approach surfaces in a letter Jung wrote to the American writer, Upton Sinclair, who had solicited Jung's opinion on his new novel, *A Personal Jesus.* Jung begins with reference to the earlier attempts of Strauss, Renan and Schweitzer to write about the historical Jesus, as preamble to his comments on Sinclair's work. Acknowledging that *A Personal Jesus* might "be convincing to a modern American mind," Jung contends that

> ... seen from the standpoint of a European scientist, your *modus procedendi* seems to be a bit too selective; ... you exclude too many authentic statements for no other reason than that they do not fit in with your premises.

"They cannot be dismissed as mere interpolations," he writes.

> We can learn from your book what a modern American writer "thinks about Jesus". ... We can draw a portrait of Jesus that does not offend our rationalism, but it is done at the expense of our *loyalty* to the textual authority. As a matter of fact, *we can omit nothing* from the authentic text. We cannot create a true picture of Hermetic philosophy in the IVth century if we dismiss half of the *libelli* contained in the *Corpus Hermeticum.* The New Testament as it stands is the "Corpus Christianum," which is to be accepted as a whole or not at all. We can dismiss nothing that stands up to a reasonable philological critique.[5]

The point, however, that Jung makes to Sinclair in the end is that no satisfactory "rational" portrait of Jesus can ever be constructed from the text, not because of the complex historical problems, but because "the Gospels do not give, and do not even intend to give a biography of the Lord."[6] The gospel is less a biographical portrait of the historical Jesus than it is testimony to the Christological impact of Jesus within the lives of the gospel writers and their communities. Jung contends that "we cannot unravel a rational story" from the gospels unless we interfere with the texts, because the story the gospel tells is of "the life, fate, and effect of a God-man."[7] To gain insight into such a text it is necessary to go beyond the methods and assumptions of rational-historicism to develop a conceptual perspective and method equal to the task of grappling with the fundamentally arational effect of the historical Jesus upon the earliest Christians and with the congeries of stories, symbols, and images generated in that experience and eventually gathered as "gospel."

Thus although Jung endorses scientific criticism of scripture for its method and rigor, he faults it for the narrowness of its line of inquiry. Commenting in analogous fashion on popular response to the promulgation of the dogma of the assumption in 1950 (another "religious text"), Jung observes that the newspaper and professional journal articles assessing this event were "satisfied with learned considerations, dogmatic and historical, which," Jung contends, "have no bearing on the living religious process."[8] "Arguments based on historical criticism will never do justice to the new dogma," Jung maintains, because they are "out of touch with the tremendous archetypal happenings in the psyche of the individual and the masses" which provide what Jung calls the psychological "need" or occasion for such a dogma. *Mutatis mutandis,* an *exclusively* historical-critical approach to scripture is also out of touch with the "tremendous archetypal happenings" scripture has generated and continues to generate in the psyche of individuals and communities.[9]

Jung anticipates a breed of biblical critics who would not be content with studying scripture (or dogma) simply as part of an historical or literary process. They would be willing to reflect on it also as part of a psychic or psychological process, that is, as a constellation of laws and apocalypses, epistles and gospels, psalms and prophecy, etc., that appeared in written form because of their archetypal significance for the scriptural authors and their communities, and that continued to be preserved and read because of their archetypal significance for the readers and their communities. In both instances they follow rules of the psyche that are inaccessible to mere historical-critical assessment.[10]

JUNG'S UNDERSTANDING OF SCRIPTURE AS SACRED TEXT

At a time when biblical criticism was drawing attention to the Bible's rootedness in history, Jung was reflecting on the rootedness of scripture in the human psyche or soul. Commenting on a passage in Tertullian's *De testimonio animae,* in which he speaks of the soul as the "mistress" of God and "diviner for men," Jung states, "I would go a step further and say that the statements made in the Holy Scriptures are also utterances of the soul." What Jung intends is elaborated as follows:

> . . . religious statements are psychic confessions which in the last resort are based on unconscious, i.e., on transcendental processes. These processes are not accessible to physical perception but demonstrate their existence through the confessions of the psyche. . . . Whenever we speak of religious contents we move in a world of images that point to something ineffable. We do not know how clear or unclear these images, metaphors, and concepts are in respect of their transcendental object. . . . I am also too well aware of how limited are our powers of conception. . . . But, although our whole world of religious ideas consists of anthropomorphic images that could never stand up to rational criticism, we should never forget that they are based on numinous archetypes, i.e., on . . . [a] foundation which is unassailable by reason. We are dealing with psychic facts which logic can overlook but not eliminate.[11]

Thus, although as a professional psychologist Jung does not regard himself competent to speak of the sacrality of scripture as a metaphysical fact, he does speak of its quintessentially spiritual or soulful character as a psychological fact. In so doing, Jung reminds the critical scholarly community that the text is not to be examined primarily as a source of information on social, historical, cultic, or linguistic matters, but as a source of insight into the nature of the soul, its images, its visions, and its truths. The primary subject matter of scripture is *numinous;* its primary *raison d'être* resides in the realm of the psycho-spiritual; and its main business is "soul-making."[12] It is with these objective qualities of scripture in mind that Jung can speak to his scientific colleagues in psychology and biblical criticism of the "divine character of the holy writings," drawing their attention not only to the special psycho-spiritual genre scripture represents but also the special hermeneutical approach this reality recommends. The purpose of scripture in Jung's judgment is not primarily to inform the mind, but, to borrow a phrase from D.H. Lawrence, "to change the blood." Jung would hold that a biblical-critical strategy failing to recognize this fact is apt to miss the point.

IMPLICATIONS FOR A FUTURE HERMENEUTIC

Jung once commented that "to gain an understanding of religious matters, probably all that is left us today is the psychological approach."[13] Though the statement may appear shamelessly bold, it does reflect an insight gaining acceptance even within biblical-critical circles. In a 1968 *Festschrift* article honoring Erwin R. Goodenough, F.C. Grant, classicist and New Testament scholar, writes:

> Dr. Goodenough pointed out the value and importance, even the necessity, of the psychological interpretation of the Bible. This is a new kind of biblical criticism. The earlier disciplines, Textual Criticism, Historical Criticism, Source Criticism, and Form Criticism, are all parts of or stages in Literary Criticism, necessary and important and not to be ignored. But Psychological Criticism opens up a wholly new and vast, far-reaching scene where the creative function of tradition and writing is fully recognized but where the real incentive comes from a far deeper spring, viz. the immediate testimony of the religious consciousness. . . . In a word, beyond the historical and exegetical interpretation of the Bible lies the whole new field of depth psychology and psychoanalysis.[14]

Fifteen years earlier Henry Cadbury made a comparable observation, expressing the hunch that New Testament research may in time proceed from questions of origin, date, and authorship to questions of "culture and *Weltanschauung*." "To put it bluntly," Cadbury writes, "I find myself much more intrigued with curiosity about how the New Testament writers got that way than with knowing who they were." Suggesting that the key issues in biblical interpretation are often "psychological rather than literary," he writes, "it is regrettable that so little has been done and is being done to match the study of expression with a study of mind and experience."[15] And more recently, in 1975, Peter Stuhlmacher in *Historical Criticism and Theological Interpretation of Scripture* proposes that historical critics take the necessary steps to find a way of measuring

> to what degree we actually need additional psychological and sociological, even linguistic categories and methods of interpretation to broaden and give precision to our understanding of tradition.[16]

Traditionally, of course, biblical scholarship has regarded any attempt to apply psychological insight to biblical analysis with suspicion. What is often overlooked, however, is that the risk of applying psychological insight to scriptural interpretation is in principle no greater than that of applying historical or literary-critical insight. In all cases the risk is the same, namely of submitting to the temptation of reducing the biblical text to *nothing but* a psychological, or historical, or literary phenomenon. Jung himself warns against this possibility. In his essay "On the Relation of Analytical Psychology to Poetry" he writes that:

> in the realm of religion . . . a psychological approach is permissible only in regard to the emotions and symbols which constitute the phenomenology of religion, but which do not touch upon its essential nature. If the essence of religion and art could be explained, then both of them would become mere subdivisions of psychology. This is not to say that such violations of their nature have not been attempted. But those who are guilty of them obviously forget that a similar fate might easily befall psychology, since its intrinsic value and specific quality would be destroyed if it were regarded as a mere activity of the brain.

Applying this observation to the psychological analysis of art, Jung counsels,

> . . . Art by its very nature is not science, and science by its very nature is not art. . . . If a work of art is explained in the same way as a neurosis, then either the work of art is a neurosis or a neurosis is a work of art. . . .

In summary, Jung maintains,

> Psychology has only a modest contribution to make toward a
> deeper understanding of the phenomena of life and is no nearer
> than its sister sciences to absolute knowledge.[17]

But, he would insist, it nevertheless has a contribution to make.

What are some of the programmatic suggestions Jung's insight
into scripture might make for the ongoing work of biblical scholarship and hermeneutics?

First, the biblical scholar might consider the exegetical implications of regarding the text not only as a product of an historical,
theological, literary, and linguistic process, but also as the product of
a psychic process, pondering what the human psyche in its conscious
and unconscious dimensions is and how it functions, not only as a
factor in the life of the biblical author and his community, but also in
the life and work of the biblical reader and his community and in the
continuing history of the reception and interpretation of the text. As
Jung observes,

> No matter how low anyone's opinion of the unconscious may be,
> he must concede that it is worth investigation; the unconscious is
> at least on the level with the louse, which, after all, enjoys the
> honest interest of the entomologist.[18]

If there is reason to believe that unconscious factors play a role in the
emergence of scripture along with the habits of human consciousness into which psychology and psychoanalysis have given us insight, it behooves biblical scholarship to spend some time coming to
terms with these realities.

Second, the biblical scholar might consider the exegetical implications of regarding the text as a bearer of symbols, laden not only
with the meanings they have accrued in the writer's personal unconscious, but also with the meanings they negotiate in a broader, spe-
cies-wide, or collective sense. As Jung points out, "even the most
commonplace of images or objects can assume powerful psychic
significance." For the biblical critic to ignore this fact is to risk
insensitivity to the range of meanings a text inevitably conveys,
some of which are consciously intended by the author and con-

sciously registered by the reader, but others of which are conveyed apart from the conscious intention of author and reader alike, and in some instances may not surface for generations until a readership appears ready to receive them.[19]

Third, in an attempt to understand biblical symbols and images in their psychological depth, biblical scholars might consider undertaking the task of amplifying their already rich collection of comparative archaeological, historical, and linguistic data, by adding comparative mythological and symbolic data, in an attempt to enhance our understanding of the range of potential values a given biblical symbol might convey.

Fourth, biblical scholarship might examine Jung's psychology of archetypes with respect to coming to a clearer understanding of the phenomenon of the catalytic effect the biblical story can have on its readers. The angle of vision that archetypal psychology provides, with its proposal that humans in all times and places tend to voice their experience of fundamental life situations with a cast of stock-images that recur in the stories, fairy tales, myths, dreams, and legends around the world, suggests that new light might be cast for the biblical scholar on the riddle of the astonishingly rapid spread of the Christian kerygma in the first century of the Christian era. Biblical scholars in the past have sought to account for the phenomenon in everything but psychological terms. They have traced it to historical, economic, intellectual, and social causes, all the while ignoring the fact that the phenomenon of the kerygma and the kerygmatic event is above all, to use Jung's terminology, a psychic event or an event in the life of the soul, and should be examined from this perspective.[20]

Fifth, biblical hermeneutics might also consider Jung's proposal that one of the primary ways to interpret a text is to "dream the myth on." Applied to scriptural scholarship this would entail a renewed study of and a more empathetic approach to the rabbinic and medieval methods of allegory, anagogy, and tropology as modes of unpacking and amplifying the meaning of a text in a way consonant with the original intent of the biblical authors, a fact that contemporary form-critical scholarship is helping us to see in its insight into the fact that the text was originally intended not simply as a document of record, but as a sacred text to be used and amplified in the worshiping, teaching, and preaching life of the community.[21]

To return to the beginning, Jung does not pretend to write as a biblical scholar, "but as a layman and a physician who has been privileged to see deeply into the psychic life of many people." But the biblical scholar can benefit from his insight and as a result probe with greater consciousness into the soulful life of the text, the author, the community of interpreters past and present, and his or her own self.

Notes

1. C.G. Jung, *The Collected Works of C.G. Jung,* Vol. XI, ed. Gerhard Adler, Michael Fordham, Sir Herbert Read, and William McGuire; trans. R.F.C. Hull, Bollingen Series XX (Princeton: Princeton University Press, 1953–78), p. 363.
2. (Chicago: University of Chicago Press, 1979).
3. Ed. Aniela Jaffe; trans. Richard and Clara Winston (New York: Pantheon, 1963), p. 206.
4. "Psychology and Religion" in *Collected Works,* XI, pp. 21–22.
5. C.G. Jung, *C.G. Jung Letters,* I–II, ed. Gerhard Adler and Aniela Jaffe, Bollingen Series XCV (Princeton: Princeton University Press, 1973–75), II, p. 88.
6. *Ibid.,* p. 90.
7. *Ibid.,* p. 89.
8. "Answer to Job," *Collected Works,* XI, p. 461.
9. For an overview of the occurrences and functions of the term *psyche* in the New Testament corpus, cf. Wayne G. Rollins, *Jung and the Bible* (Atlanta: John Knox Press, 1983), pp. 45f.
10. It should be noted that structural criticism has addressed some of the issues Jung identifies. Approaching the text not only as an *informational entity,* but as a *meaning-bearing entity,* structural criticism explores the "system of deep values or convictions" implicit in a text that exercise a "meaning effect" on the reader. But as Daniel and Aline Patte observe in *Structural Exegesis: From Theory to Practice* (Philadelphia: Fortress Press, 1978), p. 12, structural exegesis "makes no pretense of being an objective description of the manner in which aspects of meaning are produced and apprehended by the human mind." To explore such phenomena will require critical methods and approaches other than those of the structural critic; cf. *infra,* "Implications for a Future Hermeneutic."
11. "Answer to Job," *Collected Works,* XI, pp. 360–62.
12. Cf. Rollins, *Jung and the Bible,* pp. 97f., commenting on 2 Tim 3:16–17.

13. "Psychology and Religion," *Collected Works*, XI, par. 148, cited in Edward F. Edinger, *Ego and Archetype* (Baltimore: Penguin Books, Inc., 1973), p. 131.

14. "Psychological Study of the Bible," in Jacob Neusner, ed., *Religions in Antiquity: Essays in Memory of Erwin Ramsdell Goodenough*, Numen, Spl. XIV (Leiden: Brill, 1969), pp. 112f.

15. "Current Issues in New Testament Study," Harvard Divinity School Bulletin, p. 54, cited in Howard C. Kee, *Christian Origins in Sociological Perspective* (Philadelphia: Westminster Press, 1980), p. 11.

16. (Philadelphia: Fortress Press, 1977), p. 86. Cf. also G.B. Caird, *The Language and Imagery of the Bible* (Philadelphia: Westminster Press, 1980), p. vii, who cites the need for psychological as well as linguistic, anthropological, philosophical and theological expertise in approaching the study of biblical language.

17. "On the Relation of Analytical Psychology to Poetry," in *The Portable Jung*, ed. Joseph Campbell (New York: Viking Press, 1971), pp. 302ff.

18. C.G. Jung, "Approaching the Unconscious," in C.G. Jung, *et al.*, *Man and His Symbols* (New York: Doubleday and Company, 1971), p. 32.

19. With respect to the latter point, cf. Hans Robert Jauss, "Literary History as a Challenge to Literary Theory," in Ralph Cohen, ed., *New Directions in Literary History* (Baltimore: Johns Hopkins Press, 1974), p. 31, who speaks of a "new phase of literary evaluation" that may "unexpectedly" illumine past works.

20. Cf., for example, Jung's statement that "Christ would never have made the impression he did on his followers if he had not expressed something that was alive and at work in their unconscious. Christianity itself would never have spread through the pagan world with such astonishing rapidity had its ideas not found an analogous psychic readiness to receive them," in "Answer to Job," *Collected Works*, XI, p. 441.

21. Cf. the observation of James Wiggins in *Religion as Story* (New York: Harper and Row, 1976), p. 9: "Origen, Clement, Jerome, and Augustine reflected their training in the rhetorical, satirical, and allegorical traditional forms of the Greeks, as well as an immersion in the stories preserved in the sacred writing. We have tended in historical studies to focus on the rationalistic theologizing through which the intelligentsia were wooed to Christianity. Correspondingly, we have been less sensitive to the quantitatively far greater tradition through which the masses encountered Christian communication—sermons, commentaries, romances, legends, lives of the saints, and histories. . . ."

Robert J. Loftus

Depth Psychology and Religious Vocations

Vocation has always been seen as a call and response, a call that comes from within and a call that comes from without. Different terminology has been used to explain the various aspects of the vocational call. Depth psychology has recently begun to apply its insights to the investigation of religious life. Such an investigation is worthwhile and productive because depth psychology deals in a particular way with the inner life of human beings. It gives a new perspective to the existential situation of one who responds to a call that sets him or her apart from the ordinarily accepted modes of life.

Great care must be taken in order that we don't attempt to put new wine in old wineskins. Depth psychology brings an awareness of a new wine, namely, the unconscious and the preconscious motivational factors in all our choices. Luigi Rulla, S.J., in his work, *Depth Psychology and Vocation,* performs an exploratory analysis of the influence of conscious and unconscious motivation in the choice of priesthood or religious life. Such exploration is essential in our day of transition and change, redefinition and reformulation of what it is to be priests or religious in a post-Vatican II community. Such an exploration has to be an ongoing process that touches both the external and internal life of the priest or religious. Simple answers are not appropriate for difficult and complex questions. A vocation calls one to lose one's life and to find it in the service of the Church. Such a paradox cannot be understood simply by psychology or sociology. It needs to consider and to reflect on the deeper meaning of the gospels as they call the individual to grasp the symbolic significance of life. The response to the call to priesthood or religious life is in itself a symbolic action. Only the human being can respond to and be influenced by the symbolic. In these times of redefinition and reformulation of the meaning of religious life and priestly vocation the symbolic may hold the key. The symbolic calls us to more than the sign value of religious life, for it touches the mystery inherent in the life given in service of the unseen God. Part of the present day confusion about religious vocations may be due to an attempt to make them relevant in a manner that excludes the essential mystery of a response to an inner call.

SIGN VERSUS SYMBOL

A sign communicates abstract objective meaning, whereas a symbol conveys living subjective meaning (Edinger, 1962). It is a representation which points to something essentially unknown—a mystery. A symbol has a subjective dynamism which exerts a powerful attraction and fascination on the individual. It is a living organic entity which acts as a releaser and transformer of psychic energy. The symbol transmits to the ego, either consciously or unconsciously, life energy which supports, guides, and motivates the individual. Symbols have valid and legitimate effects only when they serve to change our psychic state or conscious attitude (Edinger, 1962). An undeveloped awareness of the symbolic dimension of the priestly or religious vocation removes the possibility of seeing that life way as a numinous encounter between the ego and the transpersonal psyche. The symbolic life in some form is a prerequisite for psychic health. The symbol leads us to the missing part of the whole person. It relates us to our original totality. It heals our split, our alienation from life. It is the symbol that can activate those forces within the self that strengthen and clarify the union between the individual and God.

A symbol is a summons for integration and joining; it puts us in touch with our origins. The symbol is a summons to meet with the structure of one's past history and one's future possibility. The symbol expresses history and points to what transcends history (Ulanov, 1975).

The religious or priestly life has symbolic significance for the community in that it speaks of God's continuing love and concern for his people. The discovery of its symbolic dimension requires the giving up of Western people's investment in the security that comes from attempting to live all of life from a conscious ego standpoint.

Such a stance gives a sense of artificial control and security but it exacts a high price, for it denies a large part of the individual's being, since the conscious, rational ego is only one small part of who he or she truly is. The giving up of such a conscious, rational stance is both threatening and rewarding. It is threatening because it removes control long used to give security and stability to a life way. It is rewarding because it opens the individual to the discovery of the psyche, and in the discovering of the psyche there is the reclaiming of soul, and in the reclaiming of soul there is a new and richer understanding of the scriptural injunction: "What does it profit a man to gain the whole world and suffer the loss of his soul?" The ability to live the symbolic life is a prerequisite for psychic health. It is the means for reclaiming the soul of religious life. Here the symbol as summons to meet with the structure of one's past history and one's future possibility is especially relevant.

WITNESS TO THE WORD

The definition of priest given by Rahner is: "A priest is a herald of the word of God, united—at least potentially—to a certain community; he speaks because of the sending of the whole church and, therefore, officially, in such a way that to him are sacramentally conferred the highest degrees of intensity of this Word." This conferring of the Word to the highest degree means that the priest must be aware and conscious of what motivates him; otherwise, the word that he proclaims is colored by his unconscious and unmet needs and what he proclaims is not the Word but his word. He can become a wolf in sheep's clothing without being aware of it. The vocational calling lays a claim upon the total existence of the one called. Undiscovered and unrecognized needs can prevent the one called from truly making a total gift of himself or herself to the people of God. A symbolic awareness enables the one called to mediate the inner processes by which integration of the personality can take place. The challenge that faces the giving of one's self in a vocational response is an ongoing process so that the self can be more and more possessed and therefore more and more available as gift to God's people. This giving has to be a free giving. In the course of life, the vocational choice must become more and more a choice that could not be other.

This can take place only through the development of the personality of the one called. "Personality is a seed that can only develop by slow stages throughout life. There is no personality without definiteness, wholeness, and ripeness. The achievement of personality means nothing less than the optimum development of the whole individual human being. Personality is the supreme realization of the innate idiosyncrasy of a living being . . . the absolute affirmation of all that constitutes the individual, the most successful adaptation to the universal conditions of existence coupled with the greatest possible freedom for self-determination" (Jung, 1964). For this development to take place there needs to be a living connection between the conscious ego and the suprapersonal psyche bringing about a symbolic awareness and capacity to experience subjective meaning.

CONSCIOUS AND UNCONSCIOUS INTEGRATION

The conscious ego needs a definite sense of self that is congruent with developmental stages. If this is lacking, it is doubtful that the interaction between the conscious and unconscious elements of the personality can be mediated successfully by the symbolic. Unresolved conflicts or incomplete developmental tasks can hamper the process of personality integration. Three components of the conscious ego identity need to have obtained a firm and differentiated existence before there can be a healthy tension between the opposites that can facilitate the integration of unconscious material through interaction with the symbolic. These components are independence, psychosexual development, and role identity.

INDEPENDENCE VERSUS DEPENDENCE

Independence is a clear sense of who I am accompanied by adequate self-acceptance. The individual has a clear sense of where he or she ends and the other begins. If this is lacking, unconscious dependency needs can exist.

Dependency needs often come from a lack of a clear understanding of one's parental relationships. Often part of the motivation to accept priesthood or to embrace the religious life is founded in a need to win approval and acceptance from parental figures. The candidate can easily and unknowingly transfer this need for security and approval from parents to the institution of the Church or to a particular community. Here the Gospel injunction that unless one hates his or her father or mother, such a one is not worthy to be a disciple seems to be particularly true. Hate is understood not in the sense of a rejection of or a turning away from, but hate in the sense of finding one's own identity and being able to approve of one's self for who one is and not so much for what one does. This need for parental approval, which manifests itself in a deep dependency and a need for outer affirmation, can frequently inhibit an individual's full response to the vocational call to become one's self in the service of the kingdom. It can make it particularly difficult for priests or religious to deal with their anger or hostile feelings. They are inhibited in interpersonal relationships from saying who they are or what they stand for for fear that it will cost them the approval of the other person. They are, therefore, forever held in the bind of childhood and are prevented from finding their own individuality and independence. Their anger becomes a passive, aggressive behavior that locks them in an unending conflict between independence and dependence. They are unable truly to share in a loving way in the lives of others, and in spite of their conscious protestation of loving all people, they are unable truly to love themselves as individuals and they are forever hindered from entering into mutual, open, loving relationships.

This lack of independence makes it impossible for them truly to follow the Gospel injunction that they love their neighbor as they love themselves. The measuring rod of their ability to love their neighbor is their ability to love themselves. To love one's self requires the acceptance of not only the good that is present, but also the shadow, the sickness, and at times the inner darkness. Instead of the vocation being an opportunity to enter into mutually open and loving relationships, it may become simply a way of seeking approval from others. If not, it may become a means of controlling others through being of service to them. Guggenbuhl-Craig, in his book, *Power in the Helping Professions* (1976), clearly explains the occupational hazard that religious people face in being of service to another. Unconsciously the individual may be of service in order that he or she can have the approval of the one that is served. Unconsciously this undermines and weakens one of the most necessary conditions for a true and free vocational response. If one has not accepted one's self and approved of one's self, it is impossible to give that self in the service of others. To break the shadow of power, there needs to be a mutuality in loving. A priest or religious needs to be not only a loving person, but a person who is open to being loved by others. In the mutuality of loving and being loved the shadow of power is dispelled.

STAGES OF SEXUAL DEVELOPMENT

A sense of one's sexual identity and a comfortable owning of it is necessary before one can make the free gift of celibacy or chastity to the Church. Where this developmental task is incomplete the vow of chastity can be an unconscious means of avoiding the task of integrating one's sexual energy into the personality. The task of sexual integration is a task that goes on throughout the course of life. The sexual energy cannot be seen as simply a call to genital activity, but it must be seen in a symbolic sense as a call to be in relationship, particularly in relationship with the people of God. Analytic psychology divides the process of sexual maturation into three levels, the first level being the level of auto-erotic development, the second homo-erotic, and the third hetero-erotic.

The first stage calls the individual to begin to be able to take pleasure in his or in her own body. It is a stage that is most clearly manifest in adolescents, where the young people seek to accept themselves as sexual beings. It is a stage that calls for one to be at home in one's own body, to be able to accept, to integrate, and to control the sexual impulses and to channel the resulting sexual energy in a productive way. This at-homeness in one's physical body is an absolute necessity if there is to be a true and conscious integration of the spiritual and physical aspects of life. One who is ridden by a fear of being physically inadequate is never able comfortably to welcome the other into his presence or to commune truly with the spirit within. Guilt of unresolved masturbatory practices or auto-erotic behavior can make the body and its sexual impulses not a friend, but an enemy. The priest or religious has to come to terms with the physical impulses and needs of the body. This seems to be best accomplished by facing squarely the necessity of self-denial and asceticism in responding to the call to be a sign of the transcendent relationship with God.

The second developmental stage in the psycho-sexual evolution of the person is the homo-erotic stage. At this stage the person is called to become comfortable with and to be able to derive pleasure from the company of the same sexed person. At the first stage of sexual development, the individual becomes comfortable with him-self or herself. The second stage calls for the individual to be able to become comfortable with the same sex. In our Western culture, such a comfortableness can be threatening and can surface the fears that seem to be part of any analytical counseling process, and that is the fear of homosexuality. The inability to face squarely that fear and to work it through can cause many individuals to be very guarded in all of their relationships. They are unable to deal with strong affec-tive feelings for the same sexed person without being threatened by them. To be comfortable and secure with the same sexed person means that one has come to grips with his or her own masculinity or femininity and found it acceptable and rewarding. An unresolved fear of homosexuality can cause an individual to be defensive or overcautious in friendship. A fear of homosexuality can cause the priest or religious to deny and to repress the opposite or the contra-sexual side of the self. It makes it impossible for such a one to attain the fullness of personhood that would allow for a total gift of self to the kingdom and to God's people. The Gospels give clear and suffi-cient testimony that Christ was comfortable in close personal rela-tionships with men as well as women, thus enabling Him to give Himself as gift to people.

As the conscious ego completes the final stage of psycho-sexual development, the hetero-erotic, the individual is called to be com-fortable with the opposite sexed person. Authentic service to the people of God cannot be predicated on one sex being less than or a threat to the other. It is only through comfortable relationships with a male or female outside that one can hope to be comfortable with the masculine or feminine within. The heterosexual relationships in the life of a priest or religious need to be governed by self-discipline and asceticism. The tension of relating in a celibate manner to the opposite facilitates the acceptance of the inner feminine or masculine and brings about the union of the opposites. It is this inner union that makes the celibate life creative and fruitful for the Church. "For what the celibate is seeking is deeper than sex, that is to say a direct union with 'the other' which is God" (Layard, 1972). Embracing the celibate state is not an end but a beginning. Analytical psychology takes as axiomatic that every instinctive desire must ultimately be satisfied, and that what therefore cannot be satisfied in the flesh must be satisfied in the spirit. It is only by understanding celibacy in its symbolic meaning that its real purpose can be seen.

PERSONA

Finally, a clear sense of role identity is needed if the conscious ego is to be able to integrate the discovered contents of the unconscious. Part of the call to priesthood or religious life has certain definite characteristics that stamp it as such and that must be accepted by anyone who wishes to become a follower of Christ. However, as Rulla says, each follower must discover his or her own individual way and the form of following the way that is valid for him or her. That is, the community of the Church has a right to expect certain norms to be followed and easily identified in the lives of those who embrace the priestly or religious vocations. To use the terms of analytical psychology, the community of the Church has the right to expect people to develop the persona of the priestly or religious role. The persona is the mask or skin that allows for the mediation of inner needs and outer expectations. There are certain legitimate expectations that the Church has for those who embrace the priestly or religious life. Rahner groups those expectations in terms of priesthood under the cultic element and the prophetic element. The cultic element is exercised in the sacrifice and sacraments, and the prophetic element is seen in being an apostle, teacher, and ruler in the community. "It is the witness he has to give to the salvific word of God that claims and works his whole existence" (Rulla, 1971). The community can expect the priest to be one who finds the deepest meaning of his life in his witnessing to Christ. For the religious there is a legitimate expectation that he or she will give witness to the evangelical counsels of poverty, chastity, and obedience.

This role that one is called to fulfill through a free response to a vocational call is meant neither to inhibit nor to imprison the personality. Living the role is meant to be the means by which the vocation begins to move from an external to a more deeply internal response to a vocational choice. Thus it is perfectly acceptable and understandable that in a period of formation and in the early years of priestly or religious life there is a struggle to adapt to the demands of the role and the needs, both conscious and unconscious, of the personality. With the passage of time and life experience, it can be expected that the priest or religious, through the process of internalization, becomes more and more congruent with the ideals of priestly or religious life. The mediation between the role expectations of priest or religious and the psychological needs of the individual is a gradual process of growing more and more aware of what the vocational call is and how it corresponds to and channels the psychological needs of the individual.

The mediation between the needs of the outer work and the inner work of the individual demands that the individual be able to say "yes" to things that are difficult and even painful. The ascetical practice of the response to the vocation begins more and more to shape the personality of the individual in such a way that the inner response becomes the response of Christ who identifies himself as the way, the truth, and the life. His life was one of conforming himself to the will of the Father. The life of the priest or religious is also to be one of conformation to the will of the Father as it is expressed in the existential life situation of the person. The vocational response that allows the individual truly to answer the call of the inner self can never be pure individualism or simply a holy personalism. It must take into account the needs of the community in which the individual finds himself or herself called to work out his or her salvation and to be a sign of God's continuing love and concern for his people. This task of vocational mediation between the inner and the outer world begins to bring about a gradual awareness that self-actualization and self-fulfillment find their deepest realization in the response to the vocational call that is made manifest through the community and life experience.

UNION OF OPPOSITES

The Church in her official teaching places clear emphasis on growth in the spiritual life as a process. "All who are called by God to practice the evangelical counsels . . . devote themselves in a special way to the Lord" (Vatican Council II, Perfectae Caritatis No. 1). To the acquisition of this perfection priests are bound by a special claim, since they have been consecrated to God in a new way by the reception of orders . . . priests mortify in themselves the deeds of the flesh and devote themselves entirely to the service of men (Presbyterorum Ordinis No. 12). This process of spiritual development is aided by clearly facing and bearing the tension required to bring about the union of opposites.

The union of the opposites is a creative process that develops through the individual's ability to bear the tension of conflict in one's life. A vocational response is seen here as a fundamental option and that, according to Fransen (1957), is an orientation imposed on one's whole life. The vocational commitment, then, is seen as a fundamental option that determines our stance toward life. In this process two elements have to be considered: first, a permanent stance toward life, and secondly, the existential situation of the lived condition. A permanent stance toward life points or directs the individual in a particular way. It cannot, however, control either the inner development of the individual or the circumstances of life as it is lived out day by day. The fundamental option is the container wherein the elements of life are mixed to a certain consistency. This mixture cannot take place without the ability to bear the tension that comes with the process of living. A permanent commitment does not alter essentially the ebb and flow of life. It gives, rather, a certain direction to that ebb and flow. This direction is not imposed on the happenings of life without a certain suffering and an ability to take life as it comes and to weave it into a meaningful pattern.

The tension of the opposites is felt in all of the events of the priestly or religious life. There is the tension of being called to live in the light and at the same time being conscious of one's own shadow and of the shadow of the institutional Church. There is the tension of following obediently the will of God and at the same time the pressure to follow one's own will. There is the tension of availability for service and at the same time the need for privacy. There is the tension of following the celibate way and being conscious of a human need for deep personal relationships.

The tension of life is not resolved by denying the opposites but rather by clearly affirming the differences that exist and the necessity of free choice between them. This choice receives added impetus from the fundamental option, but the fundamental option does not remove the necessity of choosing again and again the fidelity to one's life's way. This fidelity is based on the ability to trust one's self and to trust the God who calls.

The symbolic value of the priestly or religious life is that it relates the community to the God who calls. "To the man in the street it has always seemed miraculous that anyone should turn aside from the beaten track with its known destinations and strike out on the steep and narrow path leading into the unknown" (Jung, 1964). The one who answers the call to religious or priestly life needs to trust his ability to be faithful to the call.

Secondly, there needs to be a trust in the provident care of God. We are told quite rightly that the beginning of wisdom is the fear of the Lord. A confident respect and awe for the God who calls allow the committed person to struggle with the conflicts and difficulty present in the living out of his or her vocational response. Priests and religious have to be able to acknowledge how deeply their vocational commitment touches the very depths of their soul and at the same time how the grace of God can lead them along in the process of living out their fundamental option.

SYMBOLIC DIALOGUE

The etymology of the word symbol derives from the Greek word *symbolom* which combines two root words, sym, meaning together or with, and bolon, meaning that which has been thrown. The basic meaning is, thus, that which has been thrown together (Edinger, 1962). Symbols, in Greek usage, referred to the two halves of an object such as a stick or coin which two parties broke between them as a pledge and to prove later the identity of the presenter of one part to the holder of the other.

The vocational response is to place oneself in a continuing dialogue with God. The elements of this dialogue, according to Rulla, are fivefold: Scripture, liturgy, institutions, people, and the deep meaning of reality. These are the symbols of the dialogue between God and the priest or religious.

A prayerful reflection on the Scriptures presents a never ending sequence of people who have been faithful to the call of God. This prayerful Scriptural orientation constantly renews the strength necessary to bear the tension of the inner struggle that draws the religious toward a more congruent life way.

The liturgy with yearly cycle and rich symbolic movement touches the conscious and unconscious processes of the individual and helps to orient and re-orient him or her to his or her vocational response. The Sunday liturgy is the time of symbolic interpretation of the changing conditions of life. It introduces into the unpredictable movement of existence the continuity that comes from the belief in the saving actions of Christ. The liturgical use of the symbolic stirs the deep waters of the unconscious like the angel stirring the waters of the pool of Bethesda. From this inner stirring, healing and renewal result. "For in experiencing the profound symbolic contents of his psyche, the believer will encounter the eternal principles which confirm the workings of God within him and reinforces his belief that God created man in his own image" (Jacobi, 1973). The liturgy allowed to speak its language draws forth from the psyche those energies that unite God and humanity.

The institution of the Church with its rules, moral teachings, and doctrine acts as the guide to the journey. The community over time has developed ways and guidelines for helping those called to its service to persevere in their resolve. While certain adaptations are required in modern time, the basic truths of past experience remain the same. It is the community that nourishes and sustains the individual on the way.

People who touch the life of the priest or religious are symbols who renew and invigorate the energies necessary for the continuing process of development. For life to be truly human, it has to contain eros or relatedness. "Eros is that which binds together, unites, synthesizes, and heals. Eros is the cement of human relationships, the font of inspiration, . . . the bond between a man's consciousness and his inner meaning, and the door through which a person walks to spiritual insight" (Sanford, 1970). The activity of the soul is characterized by eros. The God who calls is made incarnate in the love the priest or religious experiences from other persons on the journey. They help mediate the inner dynamics that call the individual more and more to his or her own inner relatedness.

The constant confrontation with reality as it is and not as the individual might like it to be illuminates the meaning of the vocational response. Reality continually calls the person to meet the structures of his or her own past history and future possibility. It is in the interaction with reality that the priest or religious more and more has the sense of being seized by God, and that being seized is not a constraining grasp; rather, it is a gentle, sensitive urging toward the discovery of and the owning of the priest or religious within. The paradox of the priestly or religious life is that, in the end, the vocational response leads the individual most deeply to be who he or she is. It is the realization that the life that has been lost is found, and it is a deeper and clearer awareness of the call that is in a most profound way a saying "yes" to God and is a saying "yes" to one's deepest self.

Depth psychology is no threat to religious life or priestly vocation; rather, it provides many helpful avenues to the discovery of the soul and to the discovery of those elements most constructive to a deepening relationship with the God who calls.

References

Edinger, Edward F. "Symbols: The Meaning of Life," *Spring Publications*. New York: Spring Publications, 1962.

Fransen, P. *Lumen Vitae*, 12, 1957, pp. 209–240, as cited in Rulla, Luigi M., S.J. *Depth Psychology and Vocation: A Psycho-social Perspective*. Chicago: Loyola University Press, 1971.

Guggenbuhl-Craig, Adolf. *Power in the Helping Professions*, 1976.

Hull, R.F.C., tr. "The Development of Personality." *Collected Works of C.G. Jung*, Vol. 17. New York: Bollingen Foundation, 1964.

Jacobi, Jolande. *The Psychology of C.G. Jung*, Eighth Edition. New Haven: Yale University Press, 1973.

Layard, John. *The Virgin Archetype*. Switzerland: Spring Publications, 1972.

Rahner, K., S.J. R.W. Gleason, ed. *Contemporary Spirituality*. New York: The Macmillan Company, 1968, pp. 123–140, as cited in Rulla, Luigi M., S.J. *Depth Psychology and Vocation: A Psycho-social Perspective*. Chicago: Loyola University Press, 1971.

Rulla, Luigi M., S.J. *Depth Psychology and Vocation: A Psycho-social Perspective*. Chicago: Loyola University Press, 1971.

Sanford, John. *The Kingdom Within: A Study of the Inner Meaning of Jesus' Sayings*. J.B. Lippincott Company, 1970.

Ulanov, Ann Belford. *Religion and Unconscious*. Westminster, 1975.

James A. Hall

Jungian Concepts in
Religious Counseling

Carl Jung was one of the few physicians to pursue psychiatry beyond its usual boundary posts, making a significant impact on the modern world. Freud was another, and one thinks also of Jaspers and Binswanger. The impact of Jung, like that of Freud, has been tied to the importance of psychoanalysis in western culture. But within that wave of psychoanalytic interest there are crestings and undertows. It may be fair to say that classical psychoanalysis has crested and is receding, leaving in its wake an expanded number of studies about its essential nature and structure. Most of these studies have focused on Freud, but an increasing number are concerned with Jung: is he an alternative to Freud or a minor branch of the psychoanalytic movement? If he is an alternative to Freud, as I believe, it is highly possible that we have not yet seen a cultural digestion of Jung's ideas, although he has been a great (but largely uncredited) source of the humanistic psychology movement.

In this discussion I hope to address both the importance of Jungian analytical psychology and the importance of what has been called religious counseling (in distinction to pastoral counseling). Basic structural concepts of Jungian psychology will be briefly defined. I also intend to mention the importance of Jung's work for the scientific study of religious experience.

For a number of years I have been involved as a consultant with the intern program of Perkins School of Theology, Southern Methodist University, and have also participated in teaching several courses on the psychology of religion. The work as a consultant to a field unit, comprising approximately six pastoral interns and their minister field instructors, has included various forms of group therapy. This has permitted me to observe at very close range the reflections of interns upon their own religious experience, which would form at least part of the basis from which they function in their later careers.

While I have been deeply impressed by the seriousness and integrity of the students, I have been deeply disturbed by the difficulties of what is called "theological integration." Theological integration is meant to be a practical integration of theological knowledge with the complexities of actual experiences. This was attempted at times through discussion of hypothetical cases, often largely an intellectual exercise. It did seem possible, at times, to accomplish a useful discussion of theological concepts in the group therapy sessions, by asking persons to reflect, in theological terms, upon what they had just experienced in intensely affective interaction.

I have also been concerned in treating a number of pastoral counselors and dealing with many others in various contexts, such as the Dallas Group Psychotherapy Society. My concern has been that many pastoral counselors are either (a) assimilating the clinical problems to a dogmatic religious position (rare in the counselors I have seen), or (b) treating the problems of their clients with whatever secular therapy style was in vogue at the time of their training. Older ministers would often use Freudian approaches, while the younger pastoral counselors traded largely in Transactional Analysis and Gestalt Theory. This appropriation of the changing secular styles of psychotherapy is evidence again of the fundamental lack of integration between theological concepts and the clinical practice of pastoral counseling.

The term *religious counseling* arose in discussions with pastoral friends, particularly Harville Hendrix, director of the Center for Psychotherapy and Religious Counseling, and James Gwaltney, formerly Executive Director of the Intern Program at Perkins. In those discussions we have come to use the term *religious counseling* as indicating a separate concern from pastoral counseling. The presence of "religious counseling" in the name of Dr. Hendrix's counseling center comes from such discussions.

The basic concept of religious counseling is that it would identify and respond to religious problems in whatever form they are presented, relying both upon a developed clinical sense of theological integration and upon a more psychological understanding of religious experiences, an understanding not limited to a specific denominational stance nor, in fact, to the Christian tradition. It is in this enterprise that the framework of Jung's analytical psychology has been most important, there being no other source in the history of depth psychology with such a clear concern with religious experience and with such a developed system of clinical practice.

Jung's mature thought spanned more than six decades, and his most creative work, after the break with Freud, more than half a century of that time. The collected works now comprise twenty volumes and there are many other sources, such as letters, that are under active scholarly investigation. Wider interest in Jung and Jungian thought is in its preliminary stages and rapidly expanding. In addition there are areas of special interest within Jungian psychology, producing sub-schools of varying emphasis, all considering themselves Jungian. The person approaching the field from outside may be confused by the particular form in which Jung is presented, especially if secondary sources are used. A direct approach to Jung's writings, however, may also be confusing to someone with no actual experience of Jungian analysis. Many readers find Jung's style of writing difficult in its accretion of images and willingness to follow subtle nuances in the material, returning later to the main theme as if from an underground source.

I cannot hope to convey the entire complexity of Jung's basic concepts in this paper, but I shall attempt to indicate the major outlines of those most relevant to religious counseling.

EGO

In Jungian terminology the ego is conceived of as the center of subjectivity in the conscious mind, the "center of consciousness." Complexes that become associated with the ego acquire the quality of consciousness. Complexes are groupings of images held together by a common emotional tone, and the ego is also a complex, specifically that complex whose quality is consciousness. Each complex is based upon an archetypal core, the core of the ego being the archetype of the Self (intentionally capitalized), which has also been referred to as the "central archetype."

SELF

The Self in Jungian terminology refers to the actual center of the psyche, while the ego is the center only of consciousness. Much confusion arises if the Self as central archetype is mistaken for the usual sense of self as in *self-aware* or *self-assured*, which would in Jungian terms be *ego-aware* or *ego-assured*. Self is used with three different senses: (1) the actual organizing center of the psyche, (2) the totality of the psyche, and (3) the archetype of the ego. When the Self as the center of the psyche is perceived by the ego as an *archetypal image* (archetypes in themselves being beyond conscious apprehension) the imagery tends to be that of other centers of systems: the sun in the solar system, the nucleus in the atom, the King in a political system, or in religious terms, God.

THE EGO-SELF AXIS

The term ego-Self axis was introduced by Neumann (Edinger, 1960) to refer to the important relationship of these two entities. An extended discussion of the ego-Self axis in terms of Christian imagery has been presented by Edinger (1972). On the basis of this model, for example, the ego's experience of its own innermost structure would likely appear as the image of the Self, that is, in the imagery that has traditionally been associated with deity. This is observable, for example, in many of the psychic inflations that have occurred with psychedelic drugs, where it was not uncommon for the ego to feel that it had transcended its ordinary limitations, even to the point of identifying with God. It is also a useful model for understanding some eastern cults, now established in this country, in which practitioners are encouraged to experience their actions as God acting through them. I must mention in passing the psychiatric observation that this would also be the structure underlying a psychotic delusion of identity with God.

In the Jungian literature there is active interest in the ego-Self axis, not all supportive. One major writer has declared to me in conversation that "The ego is a concept and the Self is always present, so we don't need to talk about them." I disagree, as you might guess. I am currently supervising theses for two analytic candidates of the Inter-Regional Society of Jungian Analysts, both dealing with the ego-Self axis in creative ways, one drawing clear parallels to eastern traditions and the other relating the concept to the current interest in narcissism. There is some dissatisfaction with the term *axis*, which is felt by some Jungians to be too rigid an image. My own preferred term for the activity of the ego-Self axis is *spiration*, indicating the mutual dependence and ceaseless interaction of the ego and the Self and, I feel, giving more the sense of this interaction as experienced from our only point of observation, the ego.

EGO-IMAGE

In my own thinking, I have found it useful to introduce the term *ego-image* (Hall, 1977) to refer to various images the ego may entertain of itself. Among these, there is at any given time a dominant ego-image. A dominant ego-image that persists over time is essentially equivalent to character structure, but it is still only one possible organizing image among others. My concept of ego-image is closely related to *persona*, and can be thought of as an organized system of self-other relationship (note uncapitalized *self* in the sense of ego-other relationship).

PERSONA

The *persona* is a term for the outer personality, adaptation to the collective world in which one lives. It is a role that is a compromise between the individual's wishes and the structure of society, a role that inevitably takes a toll upon the narcissistic desires of the ego. It is possible for the ego to over-identify with the persona, to have an inappropriate persona, or to have an inadequate persona—all of these are pathologies of the persona. When the persona is well-adapted it is simply a vehicle for the ego in the world of collective consciousness.

SHADOW

The term shadow has no necessarily negative connotation, but stands for an alter-ego image, arising in childhood, containing those qualities of the personality that have been judged unacceptable and therefore dissociated from the ego-image and repressed (or more gently suppressed) into the shadow. The return of the shadow qualities for re-decision by a more mature ego structure is the essential work of most psychotherapy. It is likely that the shadow is equivalent to much of what Freud called the Id, but without the bedrock biological implications of Id.

ANIMA-ANIMUS (THE SYZYGY)

Phenomenologically, these are concepts that refer to a contrasexual image in the mind. A man would have a female image, the *anima,* and a woman would have a masculine image, the *animus.* These figures can be projected onto actual persons in the outer world, leading to irrational attraction (falling in love?) or repulsion. Their functional purpose is to enlarge the sphere of the ego's world, and they are therefore frequently involved in a revision of the dominant ego-image. They are often called "soul images" in reference to the primitive sense of "loss of soul" upon separation from a loved person. There is no necessary theological implication in this use of "soul image." The anima and animus may be referred to jointly as the syzygy, a co-ordinated pair of opposites, but that is rarely done in the literature.

OBJECTIVE PSYCHE

Becoming displeased with faulty understanding of his term *collective unconscious,* to which some attributed racial overtones, Jung introduced the term *objective psyche* to refer to the underlying basic psychological structure in humankind. It is a reminder that there is an inner psychological reality that is just as objective as outer physical and social reality. In the language introduced by Popper (Popper and Eccles, 1977) this is equivalent to saying that World 2 (mental states) is as objective as World 1 (physical reality) and World 3 (the cultural world of human productions). The contents of the objective psyche are archetypes. It is well-appreciated that it is impossible in practice to separate the objective psyche (collective unconscious) from the personal unconscious, which contains complexes that involve more personal imagery (Williams, 1963).

ARCHETYPES

Archetypes represent the basic underlying structure of the psyche, possibly parallel to the basic underlying structure of the nervous system. They are not inherited images, but are rather the innate tendency to structure experience in certain ways. There is not an inherited image of the mother, for example, although there is an innate tendency to structure early experience around the image of a mother. The similarity to animal studies of imprinting or innate releasing mechanisms is apparent. Archetypes are considered to have perhaps a developmental history, but they are such a slow variable that their development, if present, cannot be observed within historical time. The archetype is an organizing form that may perhaps influence both the psyche and the material world, a very interesting but difficult area of study. Evidence for this underlying unity of the world may possibly be found in what Jung called *synchronicity*, a group of phenomena that includes but is not limited to parapsychological events.

INDIVIDUATION

Individuation is the term that Jung used for the basic process of development of the individual psyche. It is considered innate to the human organism and will take place with or without the ego's participation. The work of Jungian analysis is largely to facilitate, as an obstetrician of the psyche might, this natural birth process of the personality. When individuation takes place with conscious participation of the ego, it is possible for the ego to reflect upon the process but the process unfolds in any case. Attempts of the ego to avoid necessary steps of individuation lead to neurosis and symptoms that fixate development at the stage where growth is needed. In a strict sense, individuation is a directional and vectored tendency rather than a goal that is achieved, although the goal of the process may be indicated symbolically. A frequent historical symbol of the individuation process is the path of the sun, the cycle of the "night-sea journey." Ancient rituals of kingship and renewal may symbolically represent the individuation process (Perry, 1966). Ideal cultural types, such as Buddha or Jesus, represent individuation.

TOWARD RELIGIOUS COUNSELING

The ego's perception of an archetypal content of the psyche, whether in an introverted fashion or projected onto an outer form, is a numinous and awe-inspiring experience. Such experiences may be a significant part of the individuation process, particularly if the ego is sufficiently strong to contain and integrate them. They may be, however, destructive and disintegrative, either because a weak ego is overwhelmed by the numinosity of the archetypal experience or because the archetypal experience is taken only in projected form and not as part of the individuation process. There is also the danger, as in some cases of schizophrenia, that the archetypal content that exercises fascination over the ego is not sufficiently integrated itself into the individuation process by the Self or central archetype, a situation that is rare in my experience.

Perhaps it would be useful to consider that all religious experiences that are affectively active involve the perception by the ego of something which transcends its current dominant image in a meaningful fashion. There is thus what might be called a religious vector moving from a current dominant ego-image toward a more inclusive image, one that may symbolically unify paired opposites (such as ambivalence in a primary relationship). The image of a vectored force correctly represents the dynamic quality of the process as well as its being innately directional rather than toward a static end-stage. The direction may prove to have been mistaken, which is simply to say that it is an actual process that may actually miscarry. If such a miscarriage occurs, however, there will inevitably arise another religious vector leading in an also numinous direction. In Jungian terms, this is an individuation process that moves along the pathway of realizing innate potentialities, a process which may pass through many mistaken ego-images (false gods?) in the search toward (or, as Jung might say, the circumambulation of) a numinous center of meaning that is ultimately unknowable, except symbolically.

A particularly appropriate representation of the religious vector is the well-known form of the Tibetan wheel of existence, in which various worlds are shown (the gods, mankind, the hungry ghosts, hell, etc.), none of which is considered permanent. In each world there is a figure of Buddha, varying in accordance with the nature and needs of the inhabitants of that world. In each world, therefore, there is a representation of the religious vector, a direction of appropriate religious movement, but none of the worlds is permanent —there is no stopping place, but there is process and meaningful movement toward (or away from) the religious direction.

You will notice that I have just attempted a translation into the terms of analytical psychology of what might also be called a religious quest. I have spoken of process rather than achievement and have allowed for mistaken directions and false starts.

Religious counseling, as I conceive of it, would accomplish much this same translation, offering persons a means of finding a religious process in what has appeared to be simply secular concerns. Of course, the opposite translation is also possible: everything crying "religion, religion" is not necessarily so—it may be a religious persona over a simple power game or avoidance of the personal shadow. A friend of mine remembers that as a little girl she attended a tent revival meeting where a woman of the town confessed that she had sinned three times in her life, then, pointing to a married man sitting with his wife and children, shouted "And so has he!" It is questionable that the woman was experiencing true religious fervor.

Religious counseling differs from pastoral counseling or psychotherapy in that it intentionally leaves open such metaphysical questions as the existence of a divine agency, personal survival of death, the existence of transcendental or spiritual realities, etc. These possibilities are not closed by dogmatic assertion but are considered open questions, for which serious speculation is appropriate and for which evidence may be possible (Eccles, 1979a, 1979b). Attention is closely directed to the personal religious vector, which *is* discernible, whatever the conclusions on matters of wider religious meaning.

The concepts of Jung's analytical psychology allow the identification of a religious vector in the close examination of the conscious and unconscious products of the individual mind, including dreams (Hall, 1979). It is asserted that this is a natural and unavoidable process of being human and is the prototypical form of religious experience. The existence of metaphysical realities are allowed for, but not asserted, in Jung's thought, permitting further scientific exploration.

JUNG AND THE SCIENTIFIC STUDY OF RELIGION

It is clear that a major interest of Jung's was religion, particularly the Christian tradition. His essay *Answer to Job* (CW 11*) is a major undertaking in the study of Christianity as a living and developing mythology. His rehabilitation of the study of mediaeval alchemy as a harbinger of depth psychology re-established the history of alchemy as worthy of serious inquiry (CW 12). His studies in the phenomenology of the Self (CW 9, part 2) rely heavily upon an analysis of Christian imagery. There are also seminars (as yet unpublished) on kundalini yoga, interest in the Taoist *Secret of the Golden Flower* (CW 13) and the *I Ching* (CW 11), as well as discussion of transformation symbolism in the mass (CW 11).

Jung's approach to religion did not consist simply in historical analysis and studies of symbolism. His interest in parapsychology, the attempt to study supposedly paranormal events in a scientific manner, is evidenced by an active correspondence with J.B. Rhine (Jung, 1976), founder of the parapsychology laboratory at Duke University, and in an essay originally published together with a paper by physicist Wolfgang Pauli (CW 8). In a recent symposium, Rhine (1978) himself raised the question of possible religious significance of his scientific work.

There seem to me three ways in which Jung's thought is relevant to the scientific study of religion.

1. His understanding of the individuation process, and its reflection in religious symbolism, permits an actual field of practice, religious counseling, that can identify and work with religious

problems presenting in secular form. This is the work of psychiatrists, pastoral counselors, psychologists, and other mental health professionals.

2. Jung's historical understanding of religious traditions as living mythologies permits an historical study in depth of religious movements of cultural significance. This is the work of historians, sociologists, and theologians.

3. Jung's concepts of the objective psyche, archetypes, and synchronicity open a field of experimental inquiry into the relation of the religious structure of the mind and measurable paranormal events. This is the work of parapsychologists in particular, but also opens, however slightly, the rusty hinge upon which mankind's two greatest concerns, religion and science, yet may be jointly articulated.

* Note: Reference to Jung's Collected Works are indicated by the letters CW followed by the volume number.

References

Edinger, E. "The Ego-Self Paradox." *J Analytical Psychology* 5(1):3–18, 1960.

Edinger E. *Ego and Archetype*. New York: Putnam's, 1972.

Eccles, J. *The Human Mystery*. Berlin, Heidelberg, New York: Springer International, 1979a.

Eccles, J. "The Human Mystery: The Self-conscious Mind and its Brain." Symposium (unpublished) sponsored by the Foundation for the Study of Theology and the Human Sciences and the Department of Psychiatry, Southwestern Medical School, University of Texas Health Science Center, Dallas, Texas, 27 November 1979b.

Hall, J. *Clinical Uses of Dreams: Jungian Interpretations and Enactments*. New York, San Francisco, London: Grune & Stratton, 1977.

Hall, J. "Religious Images in Dreams." *J Religion and Health* 18(4):327–335, 1979.

Jung, C.G. *Collected Works* (Read H., Fordham M., and Adler G., eds.). London: Routledge & Kegan Paul, in process.

Jung, C.G. *Letters*, in two volumes. Selected and edited by Gerhard Adler with Aniela Jaffe; translated by R.F.C. Hull. Princeton, N.J.: Princeton University Press, 1976.

Perry, J. "Reflections on the Nature of the Kingship Archetype." *J Analytical Psychology* 11(2):147–162, 1966.

Popper, K. and Eccles, J. *The Self and Its Brain: An Argument for Interactionism.* Berlin, Heidelberg, London, New York: Springer International, 1977.

Rhine, J.B. "The Parapsychology of Religion: A New Branch of Inquiry." *J Texas and Oklahoma Societies of Physical Research,* 1977–1978, pp. 1–23.

Williams, M. "The Indivisibility of the Personal and Collective Unconscious." *J Analytical Psychology* 8(1):45–50, 1963.

Swanee Hunt

The Anthropology of
Carl Jung: Implications
for Pastoral Care

The purpose of this article is to sort through some of the later writings of Carl Gustav Jung and compile a profile of his anthropology, that is, his answer to the question, "What does it mean to be a person?" This will include his understanding of the structure of the psyche, or the inner workings of a person, the relationship of the person and other individuals, the relationship of the person and society, and the place of religion in personhood. After completing that sketch, I will examine problems in both his content and his method, especially as they relate to the Judeo-Christian tradition. Then I will draw from his work contributions to the field of pastoral care and counseling.

This article has several major limitations. First, it draws very heavily from two essays written by Jung toward the end of his career. These works, "On the Psychology of the Unconscious" and "The Relations Between the Ego and the Unconscious," cover a wide range of his thought. They were edited several times by Jung, and they evolved with his own theories. Thus, they are probably a more solid source than are earlier works that may deal with the same subjects. Nevertheless, notes in these essays refer the reader on to other works which I have not included in my research. There are, no doubt, misunderstandings in my summarizing of Jung that could be cleared up by study of other works.

A second limitation is my grounding in Western thought, which Jung says is unable to grasp certain of his concepts. The Tao, the Middle Way, he uses as a symbol of the coincidence of opposites. This "most legitimate fulfilment of the meaning of the individual's life" is not expressed in Western culture at all, but one must look to the East for understanding.[1] My logic in this article, however, relates to the concept of opposites from a Westerner's point of view, and I am aware that Jung would probably shake his head at my attempts and say that I am a case in point for his argument.

Finally, the work of Jung is dotted with disclaimers as to his certainty, his evidence, and his authority. He describes his theorizing as "experimental incursions" into unknown territory, and he hopes that someone will come along after him who will have more insight and clarity.[2] These disclaimers, however, are not fully appreciated by the students of Jung as we accept, reject, or evaluate his work. When he writes theology, asserting that he will not attempt to write theology, we must criticize him as a theologian. When he writes philosophy, though claiming to be an empirical psychologist, we must evaluate him as a philosopher. This article, then, will look at what he actually does in his writings, not what he says he intends to do (or not do). Some may think that I am being unfair to the author in doing this. But his disclaimers, while endearing, do not exempt his thought from careful analysis.

JUNG'S ANTHROPOLOGY

The person divided. Jung developed his theory of the psyche from work with persons whom we would call "sick" mentally. Therefore, let us enter that theory through his definition of the most common mental sickness, neurosis.

"Neurosis," says Jung, "is self-division."[3] Within the same work, he calls it "unbalanced psyche" in that part of the split psyche has been brought into awareness and is being dealt with, and the other part is not.[4] Thus, one person has parts which are not unified, not working together in a complementary way, divided in more than their essential differentness, and creating maladaptive behavior in their disunion. Unless the structural divisions within the psyche are acknowledged and dealt with appropriately, they are the root of most of the problems that afflict individuals, relationships, and society as a whole. Jung describes the division within a person through two models: types and intrapsychic structure.

The concept of types is based simply on the fact that we characterize ourselves and others with certain attributes, to the exclusion of other attributes.[5] But since we all actually have all attributes, our characteristic description is the result of our splitting off from our awareness certain parts of ourselves. For example, "with the introvert extroversion lies dormant and undeveloped somewhere in the background, and that introversion leads a similar shadowy existence in the extrovert."[6] Maturity, health, and balance require that we bring into awareness the parts of ourselves that we have relegated to the shadow side of ourselves.

In Jung's second model, he describes the total psyche as divided into three sections: the collective unconscious, out of which emerges the ego, which represses material into the personal unconscious.

It is in the realm of the collective (or racial, impersonal, or transpersonal) unconscious that we encounter archetypal themes and symbols, bringing us the wisdom of all experience of all the ages past.[7] This part of the psyche is autonomous and can be perceived only through intuition, fantasies, projections, word associations, the arts, folklore, and dreams.[8] But its inaccessibility belies the importance of its function, for it is through the wisdom of the collective unconscious that we learn of our dividedness and imbalance; and, likewise, it is through the power of the collective unconscious, unharnessed, that we may destroy ourselves and our world.

The second division of the psyche, the conscious ego, emerges out of the collective unconscious in the form of a mask, the persona.[9] The task of maturity is to develop a conscious ego that is distinct from the unconscious persona, no longer feigning individuality, but rather meeting and accepting into consciousness all parts of oneself. As the ego develops strength, it can more and more criticize material from the unconscious, interpreting the images that rise continuously through dreams and fantasies and projections.

The material that the ego is not strong enough to accept is repressed into the third part of the psyche, the personal unconscious. These historical data include

> lost memories, painful ideas that are repressed (i.e., forgotten on purpose), subliminal perceptions, by which are meant sense-perceptions that are not strong enough to reach consciousness, and finally, contents that are not yet ripe for consciousness. It corresponds to the figure of the shadow so frequently met with in dreams.[10]

The exclusion of this material from consciousness results in a lack of wholeness and a sense of inferiority in the person, and from its hiding place in the personal unconscious the repressed material has great power over the individual. As with the collective unconscious, the material from the personal unconscious must be accepted into consciousness in order to overcome imbalance and neurosis. Until these personal, historical data are integrated back into the person's ego, the material from the collective unconscious cannot be heeded, accepted, and integrated.

The person in relationships. Jung orients his discussion of the person in relationship with others around the inner dynamics of the individual, and so it is in the context of his words about inner division and projection that we hear him address the difficulties that emerge in relationships. For example, when he talks about types, he describes the disharmony that develops between two persons of different types when they begin to act according to their shadow sides, their uncharacteristic behavior. Each person becomes extra sensitive, which is "a sure sign of the presence of inferiority."[11] This inferiority is the inferior function, which has been repressed but which autonomously exercises itself, causing confusion and disharmony between people.

But the most salient difficulty in relationships stems from the projection of parts of ourselves that we have repressed.

> If people can be educated to see the shadow-side of their nature clearly, it may be hoped that they will also learn to understand and love their fellow-men better. A little less hypocrisy and a little more self-knowledge can only have good results in respect for our neighbor; for we are all too prone to transfer to our fellows the injustice and violence we inflict upon our own natures.[12]

Thus, our ability to deal with the dark sides of ourselves bears directly on our ability to have healthy relationships with others. At our worst, we make others scapegoats to compensate for our own inadequacies and destructiveness.

Jung speaks of the parents as the child's closest and most important relations. But the parents' influence diminishes, and they are replaced by women in a man's life and, we may assume, by men in a woman's life. (Jung's discussion is heavily weighted toward the male experience.) Now a most remarkable thing occurs between the adults of different sexes. Within each man there is a feminine part of the soul-complex, a combination of both the man's feminine side, that is, his feminine traits, and the deposit of all man's historical experiences of woman. This complex, this archetype, is called the anima, and she is characterized by moodiness and irrationality. A man who has not made conscious his anima will, when he marries, transfer the anima to his wife in the form of the mother-image. He, in turn, will become "childish, subservient, or else truculent, tyrannical, hypersensitive, always thinking about the prestige of his superior masculinity."[13] In a woman, the animus is marked by strong views that have little rational base to them. The woman acts overbearing, with opinions based on irrational feelings. The animus is the deposit of all of woman's historic experiences of man. When the animus is in control of a woman (because it is still unconscious), she irritates a man terribly, often eliciting a response from his anima. Here we see the seeds of much disharmony between men and women.

From the point of view of typology, marriages between opposite types may not turn out as ideal as they seem at first. Once the symbiosis, the fitting together of opposites to form one whole, has accomplished its purpose, the two people often turn to each other for understanding, only to find that they are so different that they have too little in common to have a meaningful relationship. It is not enough simply to turn to another to act out the parts of oneself that one is repressing. There is no substitution for wholeness within the individual. Again, inner dividedness, repression, and projection reappear to cause major problems in relationships with others.

The person in society. Society makes certain demands upon the individual, and by practical necessity the person must construct an artificial personality, the persona, which will satisfy the demands of decorum. But there are grave dangers if one comes to identify oneself with the persona completely. The process of separating out one's true self from the many images of the collective unconscious is the vital process of the maturing individual.

The struggle between the individual and society threatens the achievement of differentiation in the individual. The society automatically stresses all the collective qualities in its individual representatives, and a value of mediocrity results. "The morality of society as a whole is in inverse ratio to its size; for the greater the aggregation of individuals, the more the individual factors are blotted out. . . ."[14] True morality is discouraged, for morality requires freedom. Instead, civilization and culture stress the domestication of the animal in a person and encourage disunity within.

But the causality is mutual, for the individual affects society again through projection of the unconscious. And this projection takes on collective force within the culture. Thus, the evil that has been denied within the individuals of a culture breaks forth in acts of warfare, genocide, and other atrocities committed by a civilized, proper people. It is not enough simply to blame the culture for contributing to one's own lack of freedom. The individual must also take the responsibility of becoming whole within, so that he or she is not contributing to the world's ills through projection of the shadow.

Involvement in bettering the world is the sign of the person who is becoming whole. After one works one's way through the material of the personal unconscious, one begins to have dreams of collective significance, of solutions to the problems of the world. It is impossible to induce this collective unconscious force artificially. The only route to becoming a person who is able to answer some of society's needs is by way of one's own inner individuation. Then one will face collective concerns brought forth from the unconscious, concerns such as moral, philosophical, and religious problems. The individual destiny that is stressed in the growth process does not mean alienation from the world. But meaningful contact with the world is dependent on the inner growth of the individual.

The process of individuation. This process of inner growth toward wholeness Jung calls "individuation," the process of differentiation, "having for its goal the development of the individual personality."[15] Individuation is a process of separating one's conscious self from the unconscious images that lead to blind illusions. The task is unending, but it is absolutely necessary for the fulfillment of the individual and the betterment of the world.

The process making this separation Jung calls the "transcendent function," and he says that it is synonymous with "progressive development toward a new attitude."[16] Attitude is the hallmark of the progress, attitude toward one's self, one's fellows, and one's world. This new attitude, this new revelation of the essence of being human, is accomplished not by repressing the unconscious but by consciously putting the unconscious material before oneself as that which one is not.[17] This transcendent function is purely natural, yet it may be blocked for a number of reasons. It is the task of psychotherapy to help a person come face to face with the content of the unconscious, moving first, as I have said, through the personal unconscious, through the analysis of dreams and other evidences of the unconscious. As the individual actively meets the unconscious contents such as animus and anima with reflection, they will begin to disappear from the dreams. They will be replaced with new contents to be processed, contents that guide the person toward a more integrated wholeness.

Once the symbols of the unconscious are broken down, they must be synthesized and amplified. They are shown by this means to represent critical events and decisions in the individual's life, and the symbols may have several levels of meaning. The goal toward which the symbols ultimately point is wholeness, the symbol for which is the archetypal circle, the mandala. Often the circle is divided into four sections, representing quaternity. In this symbol all poles are united. Everything that is related, part of one whole.

The Self must be distinguished from the ego-self in that it is superordinate to consciousness and cannot be fully grasped by the conscious ego.[18] Since it is beyond rationality, it is sensed only indirectly. But persons who are moving toward individuation do have a sense that their awareness is only one part of a larger whole.

Jung conceptualizes a midpoint of the personality which is the center of the Self. It is in the center because it is between the conscious and unconscious, as a meeting point where unconscious material is brought into consciousness and unconsciousness is accordingly expanded. This is "a point of new equilibrium, a new centering of the total personality, a virtual center which, on account of its focal position between conscious and unconscious, ensures for the personality a new and more solid foundation."[19] Jung draws from several cultures in finding evidence for this midpoint, including the Tao of Lao-Tzu, and the Christ within. Opposites are held in polar tension with neither side of any opposite truncated or inflated.

This is true individuality, as opposed to the false identifications with the archetypes of the unconscious. With all contents available to consciousness, repression and projection no longer control the person.

Individuation as described here must be distinguished from the imbalance of individualism. In the former, a whole is embraced. In the latter, a person is singled out on the basis of one particular quality. Naturally, if this is the basis of recognition, the opposite of that quality will be repressed and denied. Individualism, then, works against wholeness. It separates a person out from the rest of society. But individuation recognizes the differences among us as interesting variations of groupings of our common (collective) traits. The emphasis is on common, as opposed to distinct.

Individualism is a dangerous state both for the individual and for society, but there are also many dangers on the way to individuation. The first is a matter of timing. If the unconscious material is not interpreted early enough, it arranges often damaging or even lethal symptoms and situations to thwart the conscious, creating a ruckus to get attention, as it were. The archetypes "must not be suppressed out of hand, but must be very carefully weighed and considered, if only because of the danger of psychic infection they carry with them."[20] It is very difficult to keep the psyche in equilibrium as the process develops. In the face of seemingly insurmountable difficulties, for example, the person will regress into the pre-infantile realm, that is, the collective unconscious. There may be a regressive restoration of the persona, even though the ego had already been differentiated in the past. Or the individual may, instead of really differentiating from the collective, imitate persons she or he admires, and thus have to learn the hard way that the unconscious cannot be fooled. As another example, if the conscious is not able to assimilate the unconscious and the unconscious completely dominates the conscious, the result is psychosis. Still another danger is inherent in the therapeutic process. As a person moves along, separating the ego from the persona, then from the anima/animus, an arrogance, an "almighty self-conceit" is likely to develop.[21] There is a sense of personal prestige at having gotten so far, a sense of identity with the gods. With the anima/animus out of the way, a same-sex identification occurs on the symbolic level, leading to the assumption of a mana-personality, or delusions of great power. This is not, however, the sign of a truly differentiated person. With the process of individuation comes a modesty that reflects one's awareness of weakness as well as strength, and the commonness of all traits.

Central to his anthropology, Jung posits an "automatic and instinctive activity of the unconscious, which is aiming all the time at the creation of a new balance. . . ."[22] This is the part of the collective unconscious which is more than compensatory, but actually guides the individual toward the goal of self-realization. It is this urge that leads one to modesty and a full understanding of humanness, through widened horizons and deeper self-knowledge. Though the urge toward self-realization is universal, it is not effective in some lives, in lives where persons are simply not able to carry out the urge to assimilate new materials from the conscious into the unconscious.

THE MEANING OF GOD AND RELIGION

Jung's depth psychology breaks radically from most contemporary psychological theories by affirming the universal presence of the idea of God, and by regarding this phenomenon as healthy rather than pathological. Quite apart from the question of whether or not God exists, which Jung is willing to hand over to the philosophers and theologians, Jung asserts that God is an archetype that cannot be ignored or denied, as is true of any archetype. And, as with any archetype, one is much better off recognizing overtly one's God, rather than letting one's worship be unconscious and, therefore, uncontrolled.[23]

As an archetype, God is beyond our rational grasp. Rather, God is sensed, intuited, felt. God is both beyond our ken and deep within us, a psychic reality. God is our center, the point at which the beginning of our whole psychic life seems to be rooted. But this is the description of the Self, and, in fact, Jung asserts that the Self is "God within us."[24] The Self and God are indistinguishable, though Jung cannot say if they are definitely one and the same.

Now, one of the most important characteristics of the Self is the tension of polar opposites, the concurrence or coincidence of opposites. And likewise, this is a very important part of the nature of God. Granted, ". . . the conception of God as an autonomous psychic content makes God into a moral problem—and that, admittedly, is very uncomfortable. But if this problem does not exist, God is not real, for nowhere can he touch our lives. He is then either an historical and intellectual bogey or a philosophical sentimentality."[25] We cannot simply cut away from the totality of God, including only those parts that we find acceptable and denying those parts that are hard for us to look at. To remove the shadow from God is to leave God two-dimensioned, "a more or less well brought-up child."[26] We repress acknowledging that evil is part of God in the same way that we repress the shadow, or the evil that is within ourselves. Our temptation is to make God only good, the *summum bonum*, and in doing so, to make God other than us. We fail to realize that God is within us, and this is the only sense in which God can be known. It will not do for us simply to project the mana-personality, the great and wonderful fantasy that we have about ourselves, onto some extraterrestrial being. The goal of our lives, and this is a religious goal, is union, wholeness, completeness.[27]

What, then, are the advantages and disadvantages of the religion that organizes worship of God? First, religion makes overt our worship. We, therefore, do not delude ourselves with a professed atheism but a practiced worship of some secularized god. Second, religion provides symbols, and it is through symbols that we move toward union of our individuality and our collective psyche.[28]

There are, however, major problems with the God professed in modern religion. God is made absolute, that is, cut off from the people. God is wholly other, a truncated personality who is quite unlike humankind. The parts of ourselves from which we hide, the shadow and the anima/animus, are also missing from God. Theologians, notoriously male in both body and spirit, have created a male God in their image, and this God corresponds to their fantasies about themselves, to the exclusion of the feminine anima. Religion, then, concretizes a Father-God in the heavens. Thus, "theology . . . proclaims doctrines which nobody understands, and demands a faith which nobody can manufacture."[29]

When God is made the good, then a balancing personality must be created, that is, the devil. This construction, of course, denies the wholeness of God and posits a power that is outside of God. Religion is living and valid only as long as it creates symbols which include the totality of experience as part of God. It is all too possible for the *mysterium magnum* to become hidden in the forms of the mother church, and thus to be lost as a guiding force in our religious quest.

PROBLEMS WITH JUNG'S THOUGHT

Part of my motivation for writing this article has been the enormous popularity of Jungian thought I have observed in several circles where I travel.[30] One of these has been the church, including persons trained as pastoral counselors, and the clergy. This section will address seven difficulties, the first three found in Jung's method and his logic, the last four having to do specifically with the Judeo-Christian tradition. Jung does not easily adapt to this religious tradition, and, in some of the areas that I discuss below, he may be simply incompatible.

Unclear boundaries. Brilliant as he was, Jung sometimes lapses into unclear, even sloppy thinking. The reader may go over and over his writings about God, for example, and remain hopelessly confused as to whether he is describing archetypes in general, an archetype called God which is totally within the individual, or a God which may be outside the individual but is experienced through psychic realities. As if aware of such problems in his theorizing, Jung apologizes for the lack of clear rational logic in his statements, saying that he is, after all, dealing with the irrational contents of the unconscious. But such an apology is not adequate defense for contradictions and inconsistencies.[31]

Perhaps the most flagrant disregard for rational limits is found in Jung's disregard for the boundaries of his discipline. At times, such as in his *Answer to Job*, he disclaims any attempt at theologizing, and then he enters into a theological exposition and argument. At other times, he begs to be excused for his philosophizing, saying that "whether we will or no, philosophy keeps breaking through, because the psyche seeks an expression that will embrace its total nature."[32] Certainly, a sign of differentiation is concern for religious and philosophical questions, and the disciplines are not so distinct as we might often like to make them. Nevertheless, Jung does not approach his philosophizing with the rigor of a philosopher. Nor does he bring to his theologizing the methodological care of a theologian. The reader may ask on what basis Jung equates the characteristics of the archetype of the Self and the archetype of God. And how does he decide that the God represented in the Judeo-Christian tradition is not evidence of the collective unconscious but rather is evidence of repression of the shadow? His prior assumptions seem to determine how he will arrange and interpret the data he collects.

For example, in doing theology, he ignores the value of traditions, a source that at other times he uses to support his views, and he asserts that God must include evil. The strength of his claim rests on the concept of the shadow-side within each person. And the argument is that if one does not affirm evil as part of God, it is because one is as afraid of God's shadow as one is of one's own shadow. To deny is to affirm. That is, to disclaim this premise is to have evidence of how true it is, else why would we need to repress it so thoroughly? It is easy to get caught up in the circular motion of this argument, especially since we recognize so much truth in Jung's understanding of the psyche. But his sharpness as a psychological theoretician does not give him license to make theological claims out of the blue, such as his assertion that Paul's statement, "Christ lives in me," is actually a reference to the concept of the Middle Way, or the archetype of the Self!

Jung throughout his work seems to be aware of the need to defend himself on this point of unclear boundaries. On the one hand, he draws marked lines of distinction: "Here faith or philosophy alone can decide, neither of which has anything to do with the empiricism of the scientist."[33] On the other hand, he defends all of his statements as within his proper domain, whether they appear so or not: "Everything about this psychology is, in the deepest sense, experience; the entire theory, even where it puts on the most abstract airs, is the direct outcome of something experienced."[34] I am not convinced.

Reductionism. It is ironic that Jung should be open to the criticism of reducing reality to a single mode, since one of the trademarks of his depth psychology is its wide openness to varieties of sources of experience. But though he is careful to include everything from conscious thought to fleeting fantasies in his data, though he expresses great respect for the element of mystery in his theorizing, and though he is explicitly critical of reductionism in the theories of others, Jung falls into the trap himself, interpreting all phenomena in terms of psychology. The psyche, according to Jung, is a micro-cosmos, in which the universal struggle between fragmentation and wholeness rages. And so we need only look inside ourselves to discover the scheme of the universe.

Jung does not trust reason. He argues against being confined to "the narrowly intellectual, scientific standpoint," but he, in turn, is willing to confine his operational definition of reality to the realm of the psyche.[35] Even the culture, upon which Jung relies for examples of the work of archetypes, is discounted by his psychologizing. The culture is also not to be trusted, for it squelches the individuation process, domesticating the spirit, producing mediocrity in both our behavior and our understanding. Only psychoanalysis can unlock the truth of our existence.

Jung's curiosity about psychic phenomena is inexhaustible. But his method does not probe into other sources of understanding. For example, psychosis and neurosis and depression are all seen as stem-ming from the same problem, the forces of the unconscious breaking through to consciousness. He pays little or no attention to somatic causal factors or environmental influences. All the actions from within; all the understanding is by means of psychology.

On the subject of reductionism, Jung is critical of Freud and Adler.[36] He makes a helpful observation that reductionism can only destroy, it cannot build. Certainly there are many misunderstandings that need to be destroyed, and to that extent reductionism is benefi-cial. But one cannot build an adequate understanding by reducing, he says. Compared to Freud, Jung is much broader in his method and his interpretation. But he still confines his anthropology and therapy to the boundaries of psychology. By doing so, he limits himself in terms of what he can build. That is, Jung can build a much broader psychology than can Freud, but his psychological world view is too limited to build an adequate anthropology.

Lack of awareness of contemporary influences. Jung describes the archetypes as blueprints upon which the best and greatest thoughts of persons shape themselves.[37] Thus, we find in our culture themes around which our everyday experiences are clustered. Our daily events take on special meanings because of the underlying archetypes of the collective unconscious. Now the question must be raised, to what extent do cultural influences, biases, prejudices, shape views? This is a question that must be put to any theoretician; but in Jung's case, it quickly becomes answered with a circular argument. To ask about cultural influences is, within his system, to ask about archetypal molds that are preserved in the collective unconscious. He might agree that the images are not always desirable. But he would insist that they are, nonetheless, natural and inevitable; to deny them is only to empower them.

The most obvious example of probable influences from Jung's contemporary society is in his treatment of masculinity and femininity.[38] In the first place, Jung's theorizing is heavily weighted toward the psychological experiences of men, although we must assume that he knew many women as patients. For example, he devotes six times the space to discussion of the anima, the archetype in men's psyche as he does to the animus, the archetype in women's. When he talks about the insufficiency of the trinity symbol, he says that the symbol leaves out femininity and evil and it would be better replaced with quaternity. How are evil and the feminine united in the missing part? His logic here is not clear until one realizes that he is talking about the omission of the shadow (evil) and the anima (femininity) which is relevant only to the psyche of men. And so his discussion turns out to be another example of male exclusiveness, rather than a refreshing inclusion of the female experience, as it first appears.

The anima is marked by moodiness and unreasonableness. The animus is marked by opinions held fiercely but without cause. The feminine word is linked to emotions, and the masculine word is linked to cognition. More stereotyping is found in his description of parenting roles, for "the father acts as a protection against the dangers of the external world and thus serves his son as a model persona . . . the mother protects him against the dangers that threaten from the darkness of his psyche."[39] (We have no discussion, by the way, of a parallel in the life of a daughter.) And, finally, we have samples of his views in phrases like "an effeminate weakness"[40] and in statements describing women's psyches: "Personal relations are as a rule more important and interesting to her than objective facts and their interconnections."[41] This attempt to describe the female psyche makes no mention of the influences of tradition, economic systems, and social injustice in shaping a woman's field of interest. It is one more example of Jung's reducing all to psychology and ignoring the influences of the society.

Limited hope. "Nature is aristocratic . . . only those individuals can attain to a higher degree of consciousness who are destined to it and called to it from the beginning, i.e., who have a capacity and an urge for higher differentiation."[42] In several places, Jung expresses reservations about the universal applicability of his hope for wholeness in persons. Some are simply not capable of integrating the unconscious and the conscious. To do so would be so threatening to them that they would fall apart, become psychotic, etc., in the effort. The best they can do is simply to limp along as they are now, at the mercy of the unconscious dominants that keep their lives in upheaval. It is a hopeless task to try to help such people, except maybe to help them "keep up the show, for the truth would be unendurable or useless."[43]

Here Jung touches a chord of realism inside us, for we all have known the sadness of having to give up on another. We have known persons so defended that we wonder if they are beyond change. We have known persons so limited by their past, their environment, or their cognitive constructs that we doubt if they can ever break out of a syndrome of failure and defeat.

So how shall we deal with this position theologically? Certainly, it is reminiscent of scriptural passages describing persons who have hardened their hearts or are willfully blind or perhaps predestined to salvation or damnation. But there is another strain throughout the scriptures, an emphasis on value recognized where it was least expected. Salvation and health are intermingled in Judeo-Christian tradition, and mental wholeness is certainly not divorced from the salvific work of God.[44] Judgment is not reserved for a few. We all stand under the judgment of God. And that means that we are all accountable to God. No one is dismissed as hopeless. Likewise, no one is beyond redemption. Nature may be aristocratic, but the God of the Judeo-Christian tradition is not. God's love reaches each one of us, calling us to redemption. Some may not respond to that call, but that is not for us as brothers and sisters to determine. There is no power that is stronger than the love of God, no assessment of differentiation that replaces the relationship between creator and creation. Jung's elitism is not adequate for the Christian understanding of the saving love that is available to all.

Inwardness is all. As I discussed in light of his method, Jung's attention is turned inward upon the psyche, to the practical exclusion of external considerations. In the Christian and Jewish traditions, such an emphasis would parallel the mystics and the pietists, and it would run counter to the prophetic and social gospel emphases. These latter focus on the events in the world, and they call believers to a way of life that both expresses their inner faith and shapes it. The starting point in these traditions is not limited to the soul, but rather outward actions both signify and develop the inner state.

This dialectic between inner and outer worlds has been a common theme in Christian history, and we find Jesus, Paul, and the writer of the Epistle of James struggling with it in the New Testament. Jesus upset the pious folk of his society with his boldness in alleviating pain and misery where he found it, but at the same time he preached an inner state of peace and love. Paul gave lengthy instructions about the practical functioning of the church, but at the same time he preached a life of inner freedom rooted in the acceptance of God's grace. And the writer of James stressed the importance of works, without which the concept of faith is empty.

The Christian ideal has been a path lined with pitfalls on either side. On the one side is a preoccupation with external signs which somehow would validate one's existence. This has led to an effort to buy grace through works, and Luther's reformation message on the true meaning of grace must be continually reinforced to save us from this trap. But on the other side of the path is the trap of focusing on our inner states and defining the external world in terms of that inner world.

It is in this inner world that we find Jung's thought firmly rooted. Social change is seen as a natural by-product of inner wholeness, but it is not important enough to be a possible starting point in and of itself. Liberation theologians of this century have called us to accountability for the extent to which our concern with our individual well-being has failed to challenge the oppressive systems of our world.[45] This failure has led to criticism from the secular world as, for example, B.F. Skinner has challenged the whole notion of the psyche or soul, saying that this concept has been a distraction and an excuse for not taking responsibility for the great problems of society.[46]

Jung's preoccupation with the inner state of the individual as the sole starting point of efforts in the alleviation of pain and injustice in the world offers an elegant solution to extremely complicated and troubling problems. It allows us the luxury of an answer where, perhaps, we would otherwise feel despair. Therein lies its attractiveness. If Jung is right, then we have answers to all the problems of the world contained within the neat circle of our psyche. We know exactly where to look.

Unfortunately, the solution Jung proposes is too simple. As much as we may wish he were right, the problems around us do not answer to an elegant, comprehensible therapeutic process. Jung's focus on the inner world does not answer the serious critiques from such sources as modern psychology and theology, and it ignores a very important emphasis of the Judeo-Christian tradition.

Confusion between God and the Self. A very important problem in Jung's thought is his linking of what he defines as two archetypes, God and the Self. It is extremely hard to pin down Jung's thought on God as he slips between theological and psychological methods and systems of thought. He is also unclear as he moves between remarks about his personal faith and his theoretical position. Nevertheless, it is not surprising to read from a Jungian thinker that

> concern with the inside of life as expressed in the collective unconscious is a fair description of the human search for God, not as a father or big brother out there. . . . When the outer world goes astray, pay attention to the inside of life. The answer is there.[47]

For Jung, we must look inside to find God. But that is not all. We look inside to find God because God is what we find inside. God is "wholly ourselves," says Jung.[48] In attempting to avoid idolatry, he has fallen into idolatry. He claims rightly that God must not be identified with our projections, and then he announces that God is identified with the archetype of the Self, which is the coincidence of all opposites. How has he separated one projection from another?

He has not done it by carefully weighing the evidence of tradition in which the archetypes should be expressed. The Hebrew God could never be identified with the psyche of a person, but rather was over against, other than, and in covenant with. God was expressed in Christian tradition as related to and redeeming the world, but not identified with the world. This is very different from Jung's God who is Self. In fairness, there are many places where Jung says that his psychological interpretation is concerned with the workings of the psyche and should not be taken as final or complete theological statements. His understanding of God as within should "bring him closer to the possibility of being experienced."[49] (No notice is given to the masculine gender.) Nevertheless, the confusion between God and the inner being of the individual is not the biblical meaning of *imago dei*. To hold such a position is to depart from the biblical and church traditions of the Judeo-Christian faith.

The moral problem of God. The old ethic of the Judeo-Christian tradition is rejected by Jung as a product of the repression of the shadow. In Jungian theology,

> . . . the creator of light and darkness, of the good and of the evil instinct, of health and of sickness, confronts modern man in the unity of his numinous ambivalence with an unfathomable power, in comparison with which the orientation of the old ethic is clearly exposed as an excessively self-assured and infantile standpoint.[50]

"Numinous ambivalence" is the attribute of God, in contrast to justice or righteousness or love or goodness. Any of these latter are balanced by their opposites and included within the Godhead.

There are two major problems with this assumption. The first has to do with the source of values. There is no external standard against which to measure our values, since the ultimate goal toward which we strive is an internal archetype. Jung describes this archetype as whole, inclusive, poles rounded into a circle. All opposites are included. Now the problem is this: Shall we say that the whole is good? Or shall we say simply that it includes good? Or shall we say that wholeness is a good thing? And if wholeness includes all opposites, does it also include fragmentation? Jung does not say why he values wholeness, but we may assume that he sees it as an aesthetic good, and he clearly includes moral evil within this aesthetic good. That may unravel one tangle, but we find we are left with others, for there is not internal consistency in the concept of the coincidence of all opposites. Wholeness has an opposite that is not included in wholeness. One can only speak of the coincidence of opposites within one category, such as ethics, and see that whole from the point of view of another category, such as aesthetics. The claim must be put within limits, and this Jung fails to do.

Assuming that Jung has simply not carefully enough qualified his statements about wholeness to include only moral categories of good and evil and not aesthetics, we must now look at his theology. God, for Jung, is not identified with moral good over against moral evil. Instead, in God, evil and good coexist. Good and evil are seen as relative to the mature believer, for in the most evil times are the seeds of good, and the greatest good can lead to terrible evil. Maturity means accepting good and evil as part of life and part of God, living with them, not denying them, facing them, and dealing with them.

Where is the moral imperative that is at the heart of both Jewish and Christian traditions? It is replaced with an acceptance that ironically minimizes the significance of sin. Jung is afraid that strict codes of morality only lead to denial of evil in our actual lives. He has much evidence for this point, as Christian ethicist Stanley Hauerwas makes clear in his brilliant essay on self-deception.[51] But the two men lead to very different conclusions. Hauerwas says that we can accept the limits on our claims to righteousness and thus avoid self-deception. Jung does not seem to think that this is possible within the Christian ethic. He builds his argument around the idea that morality automatically leads to denial of evil.

The Christian church, however, has written its history with a strong emphasis on the universality of sin and the presence of evil in the lives of believers. Though there are cases where evil has been projected onto others because it was considered so antithetical to the goal of goodness, the doctrine of sin has certainly been a balance to such projections. The Christian doctrine of the person has held in tension both sinfulness and *imago dei,* not, as Jung would have it, with the former being included within the latter, but rather with the two in contrast. Jung's description of God as not clearly lined up on the side of good is contrary to major themes in both Old and New Testaments, and it cuts at the heart of Christian ethics. In place of this strong ethical tradition, Jung offers a value system that is unclearly defined and basically relative, and he identifies this system as being descriptive of God. This is incompatible with the revelation of God that the Jewish and Christian faiths claim.[52]

CONTRIBUTIONS OF PASTORAL CARE

On the basis of the problems outlined above, some would say that Jung cannot be a resource for Christian ministry. But we find in his work extremely valuable correctives and guidance in the work of pastoral care. My earlier discussion of the ways in which he is incompatible with Judeo-Christian theology is meant to set limits within which we may learn from Jung, and not to discredit him as an important contributor to this field. This final section will examine many of the ways in which he illuminates pastoral care, focusing on the areas of methodology, and the doctrines of persons, healing, and God.

Methodology. As I have mentioned earlier, we find in Jung a refreshing openness to the varieties of human experience, including nonrational experience. Jung has a tremendous appreciation for mystery and is willing to set limits on reason. "Reason and will that is grounded in reason are valid only up to a point. The further we go in the direction selected by reason, the surer we may be that we are excluding the irrational possibilities of life which have just as much right to be lived."[53] This openness is able to learn new things, and it implies a certain humility in the face of the vastness of reality.

Symbols are an important part of Jung's method, and he regards them as the method of uniting the dissociation between the collective and the individual. This is true also in religious worship, for symbols carry with them religious themes that have been passed down for generations, bringing a depth into the experience that would not be there without the sense of continuity. Pastoral care has often been poor in symbolism. Now Jung directs us back to reexamine symbols of religious imagery such as creation, cross, and resurrection, as well as to look for ways to maintain rituals such as eucharist and baptism in our caring.

And, third, Jung comments that the patient is really the one to confirm if a dream interpretation is correct. After all, the patient knows him- or herself much better than the therapist does. What a refreshing contrast to the self-aggrandizement of many professionals! We cannot minister from a position above our parishioners. Only as we stand beside them and are willing to learn from them can we serve with integrity, exemplifying in our very method of ministry the value of every person in the love of God.

Doctrine of persons. We find in Jung a balanced assessment of what it means to be a person. On the one hand, there are major problems that are inherent in the human condition. We are divided and, therefore, prone to illness of mind and spirit and body. Even when we seem to be making some good progress in the maturing process, we fall into the trap of pride and inflation of our self-opinions. And there are some of us who will not get much better at living fulfilling and meaningful lives. This is the down side of human experience, and it is an essential component of any doctrine of personhood.

This realism in seeing the ways in which we fail others and ourselves is not contrary to the Christian faith. Pastoral care must never neglect the side of ourselves that knows ourselves as sinners, as failing to live by the values we say we hold. Paul certainly was aware of his own inner-dividedness when he wrote that he does things that he does not intend to do and does not do the things that he intends. We must be able to see the splits within persons, helping them know themselves as vulnerable to both evil and pride. The temptation is to confuse our egos with the archetype of God and to think that we in our limited awareness have somehow been elevated to the place of God.

But Jung also talks about many positive characteristics of the person. He can be hopeful, because there is within us an urge toward self-realization, an urge toward God. Granted, for some the urge is not strong enough to counter their dividedness, but it is nonetheless present in all. We can hope as well in the ever-changing nature of life. Unlike Freud, Jung does not see persons as fixated at certain levels of development. Nor are we indelibly damaged because of some childhood event. The process of integrating the collective unconscious into our awareness is continual. And as long as it continues, we can hope.

The person is seen by Jung as tremendously influenced by forces from the unconscious, much more so than we realize. We rarely control and order our lives, as we would like to think. This idea is very pertinent to our pastoral care, as we minister to persons who are in the midst of grief and trauma. Jung calls on us to face the happenings of our lives with openness, to look for meaning within ourselves. For many, this would be looking for the Spirit of God in what happens in life, taking time to search out the meanings sometimes only thinly hidden in otherwise oblique situations. "God must have a reason for this," is an attempt to do just that. We, as ministers, can lead persons to more serious reflection than that statement, and away from either a stoic acceptance or an insecure denial.

Finally, for all his emphasis on the individual, Jung does stress the individuated person as related to all and acknowledging commonness with all. Pastoral care needs to keep the aspect of humanness always in the forefront. Persons who come to the minister for help often feel alienated from the rest of the world and, specifically, from the church community. These persons are part of the family of God, in a position both to give and receive from their sisters and brothers. This "sense of solidarity with the world"[54] is essential to the Christian view of the person as co-creator with God, working to bring about the reign of God.

Doctrine of healing. As we set about our work, Jung would have us first remember that persons we are helping have different needs at different times. The adolescent who needs to separate from parents will be helped by something quite different from the older person who needs to examine the meaning of his or her life. Life's morning and afternoon both have their meanings, says Jung. It is critical that we be able to meet our parishioners with a willingness to know them as they are right now in their lives. That means an awareness of developmental issues that change throughout a lifetime, and a flexibility in our own agendas of subjects that we will be concerned about.

Second, we must learn to heal by helping others face the realities in their lives. For Jung, this means facing the unconscious, looking within, staring at the evil, and accepting it as part of oneself. It does not mean renouncing evil once and for all and being done with it in some sort of dramatic and final conversion. Healing happens one moment at a time. We must help our parishioners learn the process of bringing about their own healing. This means time alone. It means time to reflect, to be quiet, to be in prayer. It means facing up to who we are, giving up on distortions and idolatries. It means knowing ourselves as sinners and confessing that knowledge. As pastoral practitioners, we can be midwives to confession, helping persons integrate their new understanding of themselves into constructive, healthy lives.

Another of Jung's emphases is that we must constantly be reevaluating our symbols, our beliefs, and our objects of worship. It is not enough simply to rest on the work of others or on our work of the past. Since we are constantly having new material to process from the collective unconscious, we are always in need of new assimilation and integration. The need for healing is not a one-time occurrence. Our lives are regularly disrupted in small and big ways, and we will either experience healing and learning at those times or we will deny the pain and repress the content of the disruption. Pastoral care works to help persons open up their faith to the constant changing of their experience. Faith must be dynamic and always related to every part of the person's experience. And this, Jung would remind us, means both rational and nonrational.

In his discussion of trauma theory, Jung asserts that crises in our lives actually serve the function of bringing to our awareness underlying issues. Charles Gerkin has developed a very important theology and theory of pastoral care based upon this idea.[55] It includes facing the shadow parts of ourselves, experiencing shame and disappointment and confusion, and in those times breaking open our former limited understanding of both ourselves and the world so that we can build a new, more inclusive understanding. Crises, then, become actual occasions of hope, for they can lead to new understanding that we would not otherwise have. For Jung, the forces of the collective unconscious, when they are being ignored, may demand attention through accidents and psychological trauma. These times must be seen as opportunities for new learning, with reliance on the presence of what Jung would call the urge toward self-realization, what Gerkin would call providence, what I would call the Spirit of God.

Finally, healing means helping a person live out relatedness with the world. After neurotic conflicts are cleared away, says Jung, the person experiences "a consciousness which is no longer imprisoned in the petty, oversensitive, personal world of the ego, but participates freely in the wider world of objective interests ... bringing the individual into absolute, binding, and indissoluble communion with the world at large."[56] In pastoral care this may mean introducing the person to happenings in the community and to others who are involved in bettering the world, positively reinforcing new efforts to reach out, and interpreting that reaching out in the language of faith.

Doctrine of God. A major contribution of Jung to pastoral care is his description of God as mystery. God is bigger than our understanding and cannot be grasped by reason. Thus his pastoral care must always leave room for the numinous experience of the Spirit of God. It is not enough simply to find Bible texts to answer the questions of meaning and values and interpersonal relationships in our lives. Nor can pastoral care be dedicated to finding psychological explanations that make experience more compatible with the technology of our scientific society. Religious experience must always have an element of the holy.

In addition to God as mystery, Jung's theology emphasizes God as identified with evil. Edward Edinger, a foremost interpreter of Jung, writes,

> One of the essential features of the Christian myth and the teaching of Jesus is the attitude taken toward weakness and suffering. A real transvaluation of ordinary values is brought about. Strength, power, fullness, and success, the usual conscious values are denied. Instead, weakness, suffering, poverty, and failure are given special dignity.[57]

I have already criticized Jung's formulation of evil as a part of the nature of God, saying that Jung is not compatible with the Christian doctrine of God. But here we see how Edinger draws out the elements of what we call evil and shows their relevance to the Christian story. The christology of Jürgen Moltmann emphasizes the link between the Christ story, suffering, and God.[58] God, for Moltmann, suffered with Christ, died with Christ, identified with the suffering of humankind. And God continues to suffer with humankind; hence, we have a mandate to identify with human suffering in order to relieve suffering for God's sake. In pastoral care, this means helping persons in pain know that God is with them in pain. It means bridging the gulf that some experience between themselves in times of troubles and a powerful "God who must be doing this to them." Jung is right in saying that we have separated God apart and absolute (cut-off). We must be willing to integrate our lives of faith with our lives of everyday experience. Only then can our faith be relevant to our being. And only then can the real potency of the Christian story, that the crucified is to be worshipped, transform our individual and our social lives, turning our values upside down, and opening up our awareness of the crucified among us every day.

Finally, for Jung, God is not only mystery. God is near and accessible to us, and related to us. The fact that God is a built-in part of our psyche meant for Jung that God could not be denied. It meant that God is not some faraway being that may or may not show Godself. This is a theme of pastoral care which seeks to help persons know the comfort of an immanent God. The love of God is available to our apprehension in every moment of our lives. Jung struggled with the problem of theodicy and relatedness. How could God have all power and be all-loving and be related to the world? To be able to change the way things are, and to be all-loving, would result in changes in this world that we do not see. Therefore, God must not be related to the world. Not so, says Jung. God is related, but God is not all-loving. Not so, says process theologian David Griffin. God is related and God is all-loving, but God is not all-powerful.[59] The minister must choose a position, even if it is uncertain, or if it simply rests on mystery. It is, nonetheless, vital to pastoral care for persons to have a faith in a God who is related to the world. Jung is right to address the theodicy question as crucial. I do not agree with his conclusion, for he sacrifices the Christian God of love on the altar of his psychology. But we must learn from him the importance of this question, and we must learn to minister in situations where the choice among the power and love and relatedness of God is a major issue.

CONCLUSION

This article has attempted to appreciate both the contributions and the limitations of the work of Jung for the Christian minister. In the face of a frequent lack of respect felt by ministers from their psychological colleagues, Jung appears as a welcome bridge. He takes seriously the issues of theology, wrestles with them, and shows himself to be a man of faith. In relief, many persons of the Christian faith have turned to Jung as a sort of new messiah, who accepts and validates the often difficult position of the twentieth-century believer.

May we not fall into the very trap of which Jung warned, becoming rigid and dogmatic in our adherence to beliefs and ideas (even those found in Jung's writings). Contrary to Jung's theology, the ongoing experience of the Judeo-Christian tradition calls us into faith in the ultimate love and grace of God. The work of pastoral care is not charged with melding or merging psychology and theology, but rather with maintaining a dynamic dialogue between the two disciplines which will lead us closer to understanding ourselves, each other, and God.

Notes

1. C.G. Jung, *Two Essays on Analytical Psychology*, Vol. 7, *The Collected Works of C.G. Jung*. Princeton, Princeton University Press, 1966, par. 327.
2. C.G. Jung, *Memories, Dreams, Reflections*, revised ed., recorded and edited by Aniela Jaffe, trans. Richard and Clara Winston. New York, Vintage Books, 1965, pp. 318–319.
3. *Two Essays, op. cit.*, par. 18.
4. *Ibid.*, par. 92.
5. For full treatment of Jung's typology, see his *Psychological Types. The Collected Works*, Vol. 6, *op. cit.*
6. C.G. Jung, *Two Essays, op. cit.*, par. 81.
7. Jung describes many of these archetypes and their significance in

analysis. Among the themes are the Self (which must be distinguished from the self of which we are fully conscious) or God; the magician or wise old man or hero, and the great mother (found in conjunction with "inflation"); the trickster; the persona (mask of the collective unconscious); the shadow (which includes instincts); the anima and animus (parts of men and women, respectively, which are usually underdeveloped); and animals (which point to the extrahuman, the transpersonal).

8. Unlike Freudian psychoanalytic theory, the projection onto the therapist is considered to be tolerable if it happens, grist for the mill of treatment, certainly not essential to the course of treatment. It often clouds the process and is more of a barrier than a help.

9. The persona is collective unconscious data, felt and claimed to be personal. It meets the expectations of society in terms of behavior that is socially acceptable, identities which are socially intelligible, attitudes and life goals which are predictable and therefore comfortable for the rest of society. The persona is a collection of ways of being which are arbitrarily chosen from the repertoire of the collective unconscious. Yet the individual has the sense that the persona is in reality the totality of who she or he is.

10. Jung, *Two Essays, op. cit.*, par. 103.

11. *Ibid.*, par. 85.

12. *Ibid.*, par. 28.

13. *Ibid.*, par. 316.

14. *Ibid.*, par. 240.

15. *Ibid.*, note on p. 15. Elsewhere in the same essay he translates individuation as "coming to selfhood or 'self-realization,'" par. 266.

16. *Ibid.*, par. 159.

17. For example, the persona is unconscious material. As a part of the individuation process, the individual faces clearly the persona and sees the limitations of the archetype, choosing not to be limited by what society expects of him or her. Or the person recognizes the anima or animus within, knows it as an archetype and not total reality, and thus does not need to be either controlled by it directly or project it onto someone else.

18. Jungian translators often capitalize the archetypal Self to distinguish it from the usual meaning of the word "self." I will maintain that form in this article for the sake of clarity.

19. Jung, *Two Essays, op. cit.*, par. 365.

20. *Ibid.*, par. 152.

21. *Ibid.*, note on p. 156.

22. *Ibid.*, par. 253.

23. One must be very careful with Jung on this point, for he also uses the

word "gods" to describe the power of the archetypes in general. Here, however, we are talking about one specific archetype, God.

24. Jung, *Two Essays, op. cit.*, par. 399.
25. *Ibid.*, par. 402.
26. *Ibid.*, par. 400.
27. C.G. Jung, *Psychology and Religion: West and East*, Vol. 11, *The Collected Works of C.G. Jung*. Princeton, Princeton University Press, 1969, par. 659. As with any archetype, there are many symbols we can find in cultures which are projections of the inner psychic reality. One is God; one is the Self; another is Christ; another is Tao. In the symbol of the crucifixion, complete with two thieves, one damned and the other saved, we have a symbol of the coming together of opposites. The evil of the murders is included as part of the story of God; the father allowed his son to be killed. There is nothing that is beyond God. There is nothing that is not of God. "All opposites are of God, therefore man must bend to this burden."
28. This union is essential if we are eventually to differentiate ourselves from the collective. That is, we can only differentiate ourselves from that of which we are conscious. And so the rituals and symbols of religion provide focal points for our integration of the primitive and the civilized within us.
29. Jung, *Psychology and Religion, op. cit.*, par. 285.
30. I feel great empathy with Naomi Goldenberg's charge "to question the veneration of Jung himself. He is regarded as a 'prophet' by the vast majority of Jungians, whose self-assigned role is to teach and explicate the Jungian opus." Goldenberg, "A Feminist Critique of Jung," *Signs*, 1976, *2*, 2,444.
31. For example, in speaking of the concepts of animus and anima, Goldenberg notes that they "are never clearly defined and are often used with different connotations, a slippery quality common to most Jungian concepts that serves to insulate them from much questioning." *Ibid.*, p. 446.
32. Jung, *Two Essays, op. cit.*, par. 201.
33. Jung, *Psychology and Religion, op. cit.*, par. 281.
34. Jung, *Two Essays, op. cit.*, par. 199.
35. *Ibid.*, par. 201.
36. *Ibid.*, par. 67ff.
37. *Ibid.*, par. 109.
38. For a related discussion of sexism in Jung's writings, but one which cites references different from those in this article, see Goldenberg, *op. cit.*, pp. 443–449.
39. Jung, *Two Essays, op. cit.*, par. 315.

40. *Ibid.*, par. 308.

41. *Ibid.*, par. 330.

42. *Ibid.*, par. 198.

43. *Ibid.*, par. 188.

44. J. Lapsley, *Salvation and Health.* Philadelphia, Westminster Press, 1972, pp. 31–45.

45. "Attempting to be *more* human, individualistically, leads to *having more*, egotistically: a form of dehumanization." P. Friere, *Pedagogy of the Oppressed.* New York, Seabury, 1968, p. 73.

46. B.F. Skinner, *Beyond Freedom and Dignity.* New York, Bantam/Vintage, 1971.

47. H.C. Meserve, "The Inside of Life," *J. Religion and Health,* 1981, *20*, 3, 171–175.

48. Jung, *Two Essays, op. cit.,* par. 398.

49. Jung, *Memories, op. cit.,* p. 348.

50. E. Neumann, *Depth Psychology and a New Ethic.* English trans., Eugene Rolfe. New York, Harper & Row, 1969, p. 133.

51. S. Hauerwas, "Self-Deception and Autobiography: Reflections on Speer's *Inside the Third Reich*," In *Truthfulness and Tragedy.* Notre Dame, Indiana, University of Notre Dame Press, 1977, pp. 82–98.

52. For a more extensive discussion of this discrepancy between Jung's thought and Judeo-Christian theology, see W. Clift, *Jung and Christianity.* New York, Crossroad Press, 1982, Part III.

53. Jung, *Two Essays, op. cit.,* par. 72.

54. *Ibid.*, par. 236.

55. C.V. Gerkin, *Crisis Experience in Modern Life.* Nashville, Abingdon, 1979.

56. Jung, *Two Essays, op. cit.,* par. 275.

57. E.F. Edinger, *Ego and Archetype.* Baltimore, Maryland, Penguin Books Inc., 1973, pp. 152–153.

58. J. Moltmann, *The Crucified God.* New York, Harper & Row, 1973.

59. D.R. Griffin, *God, Power and Evil.* Philadelphia, The Westminster Press, 1976.

Notes on the Contributors

MURRAY STEIN is a Jungian analyst in private practice in the Chicago area and a training analyst in the C.G. Jung Institute of Chicago. He holds a Ph.D. from the University of Chicago and is author of *In Midlife* (Spring, 1983), *Jung's Treatment of Christianity* (Chiron, 1985) and the editor of *Jungian Analysis, Jung's Challenge to Contemporary Religion* (Chiron, 1987) with Robert L. Moore, and the *Chiron Clinical Series* with Nathan Schwartz-Salant.

PETER HOMANS is Professor of Religion and Psychological Studies and Member of the Committee on the History of Culture at the University of Chicago. He is also Professor of Social Sciences in the College of the University of Chicago. He holds an A.B. from Princeton and a Ph.D. from the University of Chicago. His works include *Theology After Freud: An Interpretive Inquiry* (Irvington, 1970), *Jung in Context: Modernity and the Making of a Psychology* (University of Chicago Press, 1979), also available in Italian translation, *Jung: La Construzione di una Psicologia* (Casa Editrice Astrolabio, 1982) and in Japanese translation (Jinbun Shoin, 1986). His most recent work is *The Ability to Mourn: Disillusionment and the Social Origins of Psychoanalysis* (University of Chicago Press, 1989).

FRANK M. BOCKUS is a marriage and family therapist in private practice in Denver, Colorado. He holds a Ph.D. in Religion and Personality from the University of Chicago and has held faculty positions in two university graduate programs in the area of marriage and family therapy. Professor Bockus is the author of *Couple Therapy* and other works.

JOHN P. DOURLEY is Professor of Religion in the Department of Religion at Carleton University in Ottawa, and a practicing Jungian analyst. A Catholic priest, he is a member of the Oblates of

263

Mary Immaculate. Professor Dourley holds a Ph.D. from Fordham University in New York, an M.A. from St. Michael's College, Toronto, and an S.T.L. and an L.Ph. from St. Paul's University in Ottawa. He is also a Diplomate Analyst from the C.G. Jung Institute of Zurich-Kusnacht. Among his works are *The Psyche as Sacrament* (Inner City, 1981), *The Illness That We Are* (Inner City, 1984) and *Love, Celibacy and the Inner Marriage* (Inner City, 1987).

NAOMI R. GOLDENBERG is Associate Professor of the Psychology of Religion and Coordinator of Women's Studies at the University of Ottawa. Professor Goldenberg attended the Jung Institute in Zurich, Switzerland, during her graduate studies and received her doctorate in Religious Studies from Yale University in 1976. Her works include *Changing of the Gods–Feminism and the End of Traditional Religions* (Beacon Press, 1979) and *The End of God—Important Directions for a Feminist Critique of Religion in the Works of Sigmund Freud and Carl Jung* (University of Ottawa Press, 1982). At present she is working on a book titled *Returning Words to Flesh: Feminism, Psychoanalysis and the Resurrection of the Body*, to be published by Beacon Press.

DEMARIS S. WEHR is Professor of Pastoral Theology and a Pastoral Counselor at the Episcopal Divinity School in Cambridge, Massachusetts. She holds a Ph.D. in Religion and Psychology from Temple University and is the author of *Jung and Feminism* (Boston: Beacon, 1987) and numerous articles on the intersection of Jungian psychology and women's issues.

ANN BELFORD ULANOV is Professor of Psychiatry and Religion at Union Theological Seminary in New York City, and a Jungian Analyst in private practice. She received her M.Div. from Union Theological Seminary, her Ph.D. also from Union, and an L.H.D. from Virginia Theological Seminary. Professor Ulanov is the author of *Picturing God* (Cowley, 1986), *Receiving Woman: Studies in the Psychology and Theology of the Feminine* (Westminster Press), *The Wisdom of the Psyche* (Cowley, 1988), *Primary Speech: A Psychology of Prayer* with Barry Ulanov (John Knox Press; British edition, SCM Press), and *The Witch and the Clown: Two Archetypes of Human Sexuality* with Barry Ulanov (Chiron, 1987).

WAYNE G. ROLLINS is Director of the Ecumenical Institute and the Graduate Program of Religious Studies at Assumption College, where he is also Professor of Religious Studies. He received his B.D., M.A., and Ph.D. from Yale. Professor Rollins' works include *Jung and the Bible* (John Knox Press, 1983), and *The Gospels: Portraits of Christ* (Westminster, 1974).

ROBERT J. LOFTUS is pastor of St. Raymond's in Mt. Prospect, Illinois. He is a practicing psychologist, and conducts retreats on topics of spirituality and psychology. Dr. Loftus holds a Ph.D. from Notre Dame in Psychology.

JAMES A. HALL, M.D. is Clinical Associate Professor of Psychiatry at Southwestern Medical School. He is founding president of the Interregional Society of Jungian Analysts, and the C.G. Jung Institute of Dallas. Dr. Hall's works include *Clinical Uses of Dreams* (Grune & Stratton, 1977), *Jungian Dream Interpretation* (Inner City, 1983), *The Jungian Experience* (Inner City, 1986) and *Hypnosis: A Jungian Perspective* (Guilford, 1989).

SWANEE HUNT is Chairperson of the Hunt Alternatives Fund and President of the Women's Foundation of Colorado. A community leader and activist in Denver, Colorado, she holds a Th.D. from Iliff School of Theology. She has published several articles on pastoral care.

THE EDITORS

ROBERT L. MOORE, Ph.D. is a Jungian psychoanalyst in private practice. He has studied at both the Alfred Adler Institute and the C.G. Jung Institute in Chicago, where he also teaches. Professor of Psychology and Religion at the Chicago Theological Seminary, his works include *John Wesley and Authority: A Psychological Perspective*, and *The Cult Experience: Responding to the New Religious Pluralism* (with Gordon Melton). He edited *Carl Jung and Christian Spirituality*, and co-edited *Anthropology and the Study of Religion*, and *Self and Liberation: The Jungian–Buddhist Dialogue*. Dr. Moore is Series Editor of the Paulist Press series *Jung and Spirituality*, and President of the Institute for World Spirituality, which sponsors the series.

DANIEL J. MECKEL, M.A. is currently completing a doctorate in Religion and Psychological Studies at the University of Chicago Divinity School. Specializing in the cross-cultural study of psychology and religious healing, Mr. Meckel is also a student of South Asian Language and culture. He is co-editor of *Self and Liberation: The Jungian-Buddhist Dialogue*, and Managing Editor of the *Jung and Spirituality* series.